The Breath of Angels

THE
BREATH
OF
ANGELS

JOHN BEATTIE

MAINSTREAM
PUBLISHING
EDINBURGH AND LONDON

Copyright © John Beattie, 1995
Maps © Neil Smith, 1995

The moral right of the author has been asserted

First published in Great Britain in 1995 by
MAINSTREAM PUBLISHING COMPANY (EDINBURGH) LTD
7 Albany Street
Edinburgh
EH1 3UG

Reprinted 1995

ISBN 1 85158 697 0

A catalogue record for this book is available from the British Library

Typeset in 11.5/13 Perpetua by Saxon Graphics Ltd, Derby
Printed and bound in Great Britain by
Butler & Tanner Ltd, Frome and London

To Jessica, Emma and Maria

Contents

Part Three   TROPICAL WATERS

Acknowledgments

No man is an island, not even when he is alone at sea, and I am indebted to many for their help and support.

In addition to those mentioned in the text, I would particularly like to thank Dave Simpson, who first taught me to sail. I am also especially grateful to Pete Ganarelli, Paul Lambert, Dave Bateson and Alan Deakin, who all helped with the preparation of the boat before my departure.

Jim Mayer, Scott Davidson and Cathy Gibson encouraged me to write this book and without the assistance of Richard Kinsey I might never have found a publisher. Many friends took the trouble to read it and contribute invaluable criticism. Richard Jeffs, David Eadson, Magda Phillips, Ged McElwee, Lawrence Tasker, Eric Walton and Susan Bunting all helped me chart a course through the sea of words. Peter Frances, my editor, should not be omitted. His professionalism and thoroughness was much appreciated.

I would like to thank my employers, the University of Teesside, for buying a new suit of sails for the boat and granting me leave of absence. Without the support of Nick Hodge and Oliver Coulthard this would not have been possible. Gerry Burton and Kevin Whittle, who also work at the university, made and modified bits of gear for the boat in the engineering workshops and I am very grateful to them also.

I have a special debt to Peter Hansen, who helped me sail the boat through some very heavy weather on the way home from Antigua to the Azores. He, along with everyone else who sailed aboard the *Warrior Queen*, needs to be commended for having the patience and tolerance to put up with me.

Finally, I am indebted, as are many others, to the Royal National Lifeboat Institution. My personal gratitude is to the Baltimore lifeboat crew in Ireland, who put out to sea at three o'clock in the morning to pull me into port on the last leg of my homeward journey. May they long continue to save the souls of those at sea.

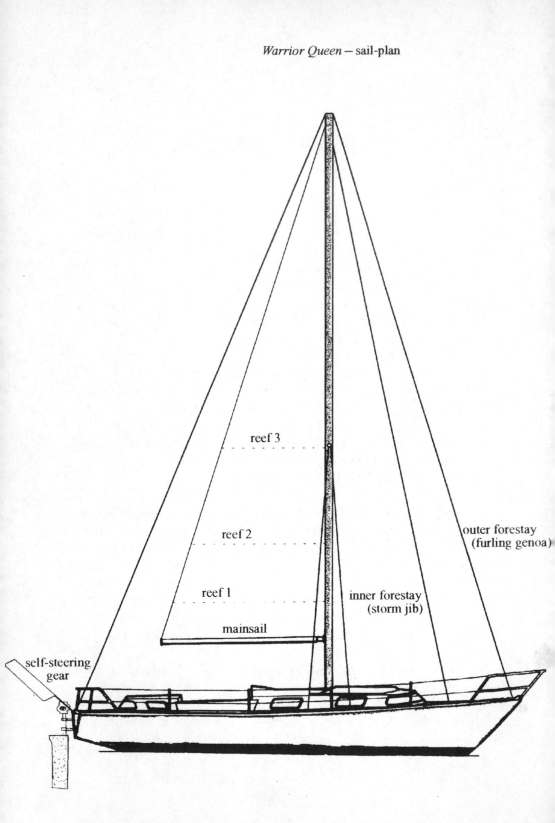

Warrior Queen — sail-plan

ENGINE

FUEL

FUEL FUEL

FRESH WATER

BALLAST

0 1 2 3 4 5 6 7 8 9 10 ft

AFT CABIN

COCKPIT

CHART TABLE

COMPANIONWAY STEPS

GALLEY

DINNETTE/ DOUBLE BERTH

THE HEAD

FOREPEAK

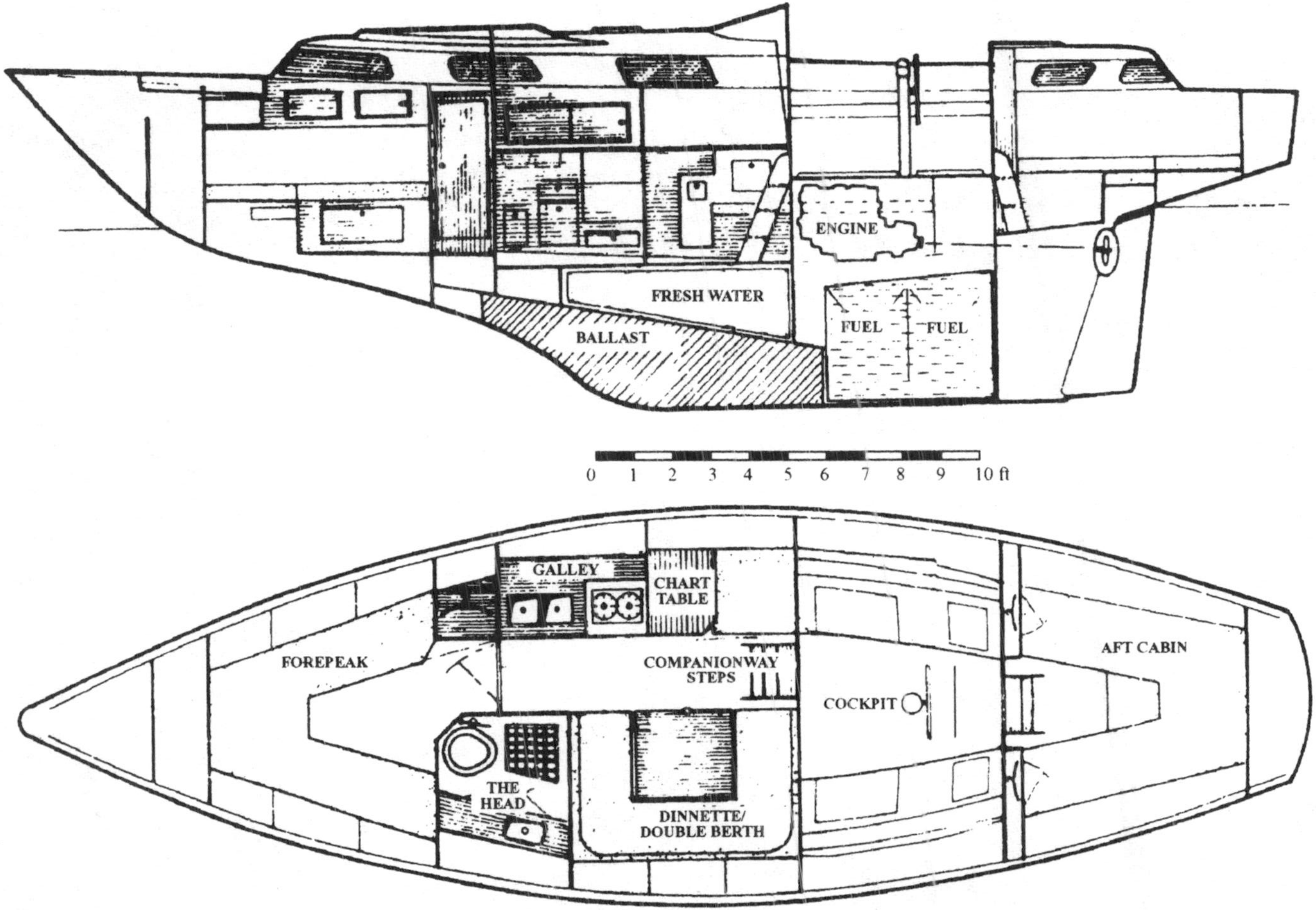

PART ONE

Home Waters

There is a tide in the affairs of men,
Which, taken at the flood, leads on to fortune;
Omitted, all the voyages of their life
Is bound in shallows and in misery.

WILLIAM SHAKESPEARE

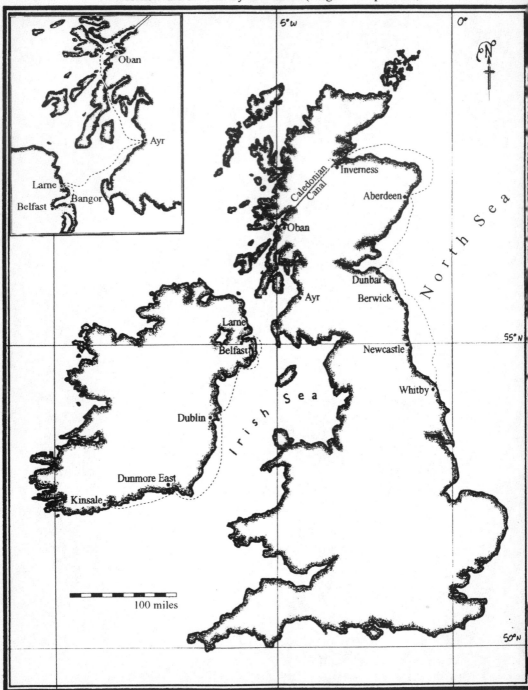

1. *Going Back*

I KEEP MARTIN'S LETTER IN MY INSIDE POCKET – CLOSE TO my heart. It is the most extraordinary letter I have ever received: he says that he owes me his life. There is an exotic stamp on the envelope, and the letter itself is written on unusual writing paper. Some letters are special and have their own unique intimacy: the handwriting, the words, the phrases, the thoughts and the feelings committed forever to the page. This one is very special. In one way it all seems like a dream; in another it has the compelling immediacy of the present – a present that is always with me, as if I am living it each day, over and over again.

I am now going back to see Martin. There isn't much time left to catch the plane but I manage a quick visit to the airport shop and find a few little gifts for him and his three young daughters. Laura has also visited the shop, and I suspect that she has something for me. The last call for the flight to Grenada is announced, and all remaining passengers are told to make their way to gate 17. There is some confusion when we get there: everybody is about to be marched off to another gate. Laura and I, as usual, are the last to turn up and have missed the earlier excitement. It looks like we have a problem with the flight but the ground staff are doing their best to placate the passengers. There is lots of whispered talk into closely held walkie-talkies and knowing glances exchanged between the smartly dressed young men and women holding them. Some of the passengers are giving the ground staff a hard time, and one of them declares, 'Look, we've been hanging about here for a long time and you've taken us from one gate to another, this is disgusting.'

The harassed young woman with the walkie-talkie is about to reply when someone else butts in, 'This is an absolute disgrace, we are being treated like cattle, it's appalling.' I can't see what the fuss is about. The flight is not as yet delayed, and the ground crew are doing their best to sort out whatever the problem is.

It turns out that we have no pilot. He has taken sick at the last minute, and they are looking for a replacement – a tall order at short notice for a long-haul flight two days before Christmas Eve. They manage

15

to find one in Oxford Street in central London doing his Christmas shopping. He is now on his way to Gatwick Airport. The flight will be delayed by about an hour, and in the meantime we can all go and get a cup of freshly made cappuccino.

When the plane is about to take off, a short time later, the breathless pilot comes on the radio and tells us of his little adventure. He doesn't seem to be quite sure, or bothered, about where he is going. There are intermittent silences as he is no doubt prompted by the co-pilot about the flight plan. Once airborne, the cabin crew distribute complimentary drinks which help soothe away any remaining frustration. I settle back in the seat to watch the overhead video.

It is showing one of those progress maps with a little plane depicted heading towards its destination. Before the first drink is finished, we are already out to sea, making for the Bay of Biscay. The contours of the seabed are shown in deepening shades of blue – it isn't long before we are crossing the continental shelf and the Atlantic Ocean lies beneath us. The last time I had made this journey it had taken me several months to get to where the plane is now. That was over a year ago and I was travelling on a small sailboat.

The aircraft is now up to its full cruising speed of about 600 miles an hour, which is a good 100 times faster than I had travelled then, and the pilot and crew are doing all the work. I have read Martin's letter many times and take it out of my inside pocket to read once more.

Dear John

I received your letter with greatest pleasure. I am happy to know that you reached home safely. I do owe you my life and I am forever in your debt.

Well, when I got back home it was pretty rough for me. I was, as soon as I landed, arrested and detained for one-and-a-half days where I was questioned intensively for hours at a time. Then I was released. I was glad to go home to my long-awaited family.

I tried getting close to the other guy's family but it was not easy because they were filled with anger, bitterness, remorse and suspicion. It was very difficult for me to deal with that for they said it was foul play. Well, I was convinced that my life was spared so I gave my life to Christ. I will tell you all about it when we meet. Since then my life has been ups and downs but I'm hanging in there.

I have no plans of travelling for Christmas. I was bitten by a barracuda and was hospitalised for nearly two months. I have a lovely girlfriend. We fell in love when she constantly visited me. I have plans to get married but will need to find work to execute them.

Anyhow, I can hardly wait to see you again. You will tell me what date you're coming so that I can meet you at the airport.

Yours faithfully

Martin

It's a rare privilege to receive such a letter. I fold it neatly and place it back in my inside pocket. The plane is flying a great-circle route almost directly over the path I had taken on the way home after saying goodbye to Martin in the hospital. My mind goes back. Every detail of my time aboard the boat is vivid – I suppose because it was all so different. I was on my own for part of that homeward voyage and the engine had broken down. The boat at one stage was becalmed for three days and rolled from side to side in the swell like a great pendulum. I had been motoring through the calm, trailing a heavy fishing line. There were small objects in the water, so I went over to have a closer look – turtle heads! I rigged up a turtle-catching net with a sailbag and a boat-hook and tried to catch one, just to have a closer look at it, but it kept swimming away at the last minute. When I backed up to have another go, the fishing line, which was now hanging down in the water, got entangled in the propeller and burned out the clutch in the gearbox – no wind, no engine and no turtle!

There had been no wind for what seemed like forever, and the surface of the sea was so smooth, apart from the long, rolling ocean swell, that it had an oily appearance to it. In one 24-hour period I logged a distance of half a mile – backwards! When the whales appeared, a few days after the engine packed up, the first one I saw almost made my heart stop. I heard it before I saw it. It was a low, loud noise, similar to a foghorn, and was followed by a big blow. The water soaked me. I looked over the starboard side and there it was – all 80 feet of it. The stench was unbelievable. My knees buckled. I held on to one of the grab-rails in case it struck the keel and turned the boat upside-down. It was even more frightening when it submerged. There was nothing, nothing except silence, but I knew that the monster was under the boat. I waited, frozen with fear, for the impact with the keel. The noise came again. This time it was on the port side, and I caught sight of its back as it surfaced once more before diving. Silence and yet more silence . . . Two then appeared on the starboard side. The one closest to the boat lifted its whole head right out of the water and eyeballed me. I was alone at sea, looking straight into the eye of the largest creature that has ever existed on the face of the earth. At the time, I remembered that one way of getting rid of whales is to pour a bottle of bleach over the side – bleach is to whales what tear-gas is to humans – but there was none aboard. I wasn't sure how many there were and had thought they had gone, when one surfaced directly in front of the boat. It was as if land had appeared from nowhere. The ocean parted. The water rolled off the whale's mighty back, and I looked down into the great blowhole on the top of its head. It was an awesome sight. The whales stayed with me for two more days but they never came as close again. That part of the trip from the Azores to Ireland took 16 days, and the lifeboat had to pull me into port.

It takes the plane less than three hours to cover the same distance.

As the plane approaches the Caribbean, the overhead video map with the little aircraft is displayed once more. I can see everywhere I have been to – St Lucia, with its high mountains, and the rest of the chain of Windward Islands that stretch down to Grenada. Trinidad is much bigger than these small islands, and the capital city of Port of Spain is marked. The Orinoco delta is also clearly shown, as is Caracas in Venezuela. Laura studies the map. I point out the route that I sailed from Caracas to Antigua to the north. She shakes her head, saying, 'It's incredible'.

It certainly was, but we are nearly there, and I take Martin's letter out to read again. Parts of it make me very angry. The suspicion of foul play and the rejection by the other man's family seems a terrible injustice. Maybe I will be able to do something about that when I arrive. I can't help feeling a little apprehensive, though, about going back. I don't know how I will find Martin or how he will find me. We had met in highly unusual circumstances, becoming very close in the days we spent together, but it might all be different now. If I hadn't been where I was that particular day, eight months ago, he would have died – one man already had – but he didn't really owe me his life. I had only done what anybody would do. And I owed him something. He had given my voyage a purpose.

2. *Brown Sauce and Dreams*

IT ALL BEGAN IN 1965 AND WAS STARTED BY A BOOK. I WAS then a young boy. A school teacher had taken me under his wing and was trying to introduce me to the finer things in life. His first attempt failed miserably. On Christmas Eve, he drove round to my house and picked me up. He had come to take me to church. The service didn't do anything for me but he wasn't the kind of man to give up easily, so when school started again in the new year, he decided to introduce me to literature. He must have been a member of a book club, because he was always bringing in plain-coloured, hard-backed books in gaudy shades of pink and yellow and blue, with the titles etched in gold in an oval frame on the spine. One day he said he had a book for me, handing over a yellow volume with a purple oval on the spine. Printed in gold was the title *Sheila in the Wind*!

I ambled home from school that day with the book in my canvas bag, and later that night, while sitting in front of the TV eating my dinner, felt obliged to have a look at it. Before it was opened, I spilled some HP brown sauce on the yellow cover. All attempts to clean it off only made it worse. Worried and guilt-ridden, I decided that the best thing to do was to read the damn thing — at least that would delay me having to return it.

From the first page I was hooked. It was a true story about a man called Adrian Hayter who bought a small wooden boat on the south coast of England and taught himself to sail and navigate before sailing the boat home to New Zealand. On the way there, he had a string of mishaps and adventures. The idea of sailing off in a boat took hold of me. From the day I finished the book I knew what I wanted to do when I grew up. My teacher's sauce-stained book was eventually returned. He graciously passed no comment about the state it was in but he never lent me another one.

It was 20 years after reading *Sheila in the Wind* before I got the opportunity to go sailing and a further five years before I managed to get a boat of my own. During that time, the idea formed and reformed in my mind. In school holidays, I visited public libraries and studied the largest-scale maps I could find. I became intimately familiar with all the islands of the North Atlantic and South Pacific and knew the main navigational passages between them. Many of my compatriots had been forced by economic necessity to seek work overseas, and after leaving school I joined their ranks from time to time. I took great pleasure in standing on the open deck of the ferry boats in bad weather, and great pride in never getting seasick. The fact that I never got seasick on any of these passages reinforced my inner conviction that I could sail a small boat in heavy weather. The dream, because it had long since ceased to be an idea, sustained me through a bleak marriage and at other times depressed me when it looked unattainable.

I knew the whole scheme had the stamp of a childish preoccupation and only confided it to my closest friends, who seemed slightly embarrassed. By the time I was in my mid-thirties and had as yet never sailed a boat of any kind, the project was beginning to look rather foolish.

It was just as I was about to give the whole idea up for lost that I had my first real break. I was settled into a steady academic job, and one of my colleagues and drinking companions was an experienced sailor. He didn't have a boat of his own but he suggested a bareboat holiday charter. This was just what I needed – to learn about sailing through the tutelage of a good friend. We picked the boat up in a remote part of West Cork, Ireland, and had a glorious week. She was a 35-foot fibreglass yacht built by Trident Marine – the type known as a Warrior.

Four years later, with a few more week-long charters behind me, my name came to the top of a long waiting-list for the allocation of a mooring in Whitby, where I was now living. The harbour master contacted me by telephone, asking what length of boat I had. I didn't even have a toy boat in the bath but I told him 36 feet. The berth was allocated, the bill was dispatched, and somehow or other I had to find a boat to put on the mooring.

By remortgaging my small cottage, I was able to raise some money and went looking for a yacht. I had figured that for a boat that could make long passages in reasonable comfort and carry enough food, water and gear, 36 feet was the minimum requirement. A quick look at the advertisements in the yachting press was demoralising because most of the boats I was interested in were outside my price range. Like all prospective first-time buyers, I was torn between wishful thinking and economic reality.

A circular letter to the main yacht brokers kept the postman busy. I was inundated with details of boats that were either too small or too expensive. The classified columns for private sales looked a bit more promising, and eventually I got the details of a 35-foot, long-keeled fibre-glass sloop called *Warrior Queen*. She was the same type as the first boat I ever sailed on, and I liked the name – it had a certain ring to it. When the owner rowed me out to where she was lying at anchor, just off the Thames estuary, my excitement mounted with each pull on the oars. When I stepped aboard and stood at the wheel in the cockpit, looking forward to the bow and up into the sky at the tall mast, it was a good feeling. It's easy for people to be overly sentimental about boats but something about her felt right. I had been on bigger and better yachts but she was strongly built and a good sea boat. With a little work, I could have her sorted out for long sea passages. But perhaps the most important consideration was that I could afford her. The deal was done on the day I first saw her. A week later, along with a crew of four, we were slipping the moorings and heading out to sea to deliver her to her new home port of Whitby.

My plan was to sail her round the world. If I was serious about it, I knew that the summer should be spent testing the boat, its gear and myself. Norway is about 350 miles across the North Sea, so I decided to sail there and back to see if this dream had any substance to it. If all went well, that would allow me the following winter and spring to prepare for a two-year circumnavigation. After installing a few bits of extra gear, five of us set sail from Whitby in mid-July. Every trip at sea on a small boat is eventful and teaches you something new about your boat, your crew, and yourself. I learned that the boat needed a lot of work. I also found out that a happy crew makes for a happy ship, that an unhappy crew makes a hell out of a heaven, and that it is very easy for people to become frightened at sea on a black stormy night. For myself, I learned that I lacked essential engineering skills and didn't have a clue about 12-volt electrics, but I also discovered that I loved the rhythm of life at sea. The trip to Norway and back lasted six weeks. At the end of it I knew that within a year I would set sail on the voyage I had been dreaming about for so long.

When the boat was lifted out later that year, I began to make serious preparations for the forthcoming voyage. The first thing to consider was where was I going to go? Many people have sailed round the world on all kinds of routes and on all sorts of ships. The fastest way to go is on an eastabout route via the southern capes of Good Hope and Horn. This takes you down to the Southern Ocean, where the prevailing westerlies are picked up in the roaring forties. By all accounts, it is cold, wet and miserable, and very hard on the most seasoned crews and well-found ships. The alternative is to go westabout via the Panama Canal. This route takes advantage of the tradewinds that blow in the tropics and is warm and relatively free from severe weather, apart from occasional hurricanes, which are seasonal in their occurrence and can be avoided by not being in certain places at certain times.

I was in no particular hurry and didn't feel the need to prove anything to myself or anyone else. Knowing my own limitations and those of my boat, I decided on the warm, tropical, tradewind route. The plan was to take two years' leave of absence from work and set sail in July 1992. I had decided to sail north to Scotland, through the Caledonian Canal, down the Irish Sea, and be across Biscay before the end of August. The Bay of Biscay lies in fairly high northerly latitudes and is prone to severe equinoctial gales in September and October, so it was important to stick to the plan. Once across Biscay, I would sail along the coast of Spain and Portugal before heading out to the island of Madeira. From Madeira, it's only a few days' sail to the Canary Islands, where I would wait for the tradewinds to carry me across the Atlantic. A landfall in the West Indies and a few weeks lying beneath a palm tree would follow before heading on to Panama, where I would spend Christmas on the Atlantic side of the canal and New Year's Eve on the Pacific side. When the New Year's Day hangover cleared up, I would sail west to the Galapagos Islands and cross the Equator. A long trip across the Pacific to the Marquesas, then on to Tahiti for a garland of flowers. Once Tahiti was left behind, I would island-hop all the way to Australia, where I had already reserved tickets for a night at the opera in Sydney Opera House for 31 August 1993. I thought it imprudent to plan beyond a year and would work out the return route home as I approached Australia.

Crew arrangements were equally straightforward. I had decided that the best number aboard was three (including myself), and I would pick up and drop off crew along the way in accordance with the above schedule. Some crew would be friends with whom I had sailed before, and if there weren't enough takers to sail the boat all the way, I would advertise in the yachting press. Finances were not going to be a problem either. Everyone joining me would share the cost of food and drink, and provided we caught plenty of fish, drank the local brew, and avoided expensive marinas, the day-to-day expenses would be very small. I had worked out an elaborate system, whereby I had costed the new safety gear and charts and set this against the resale value of all these items at the end of the trip. The cost per person per week worked out at about £30.

All that was left for me to do was overhaul the boat, install the new gear, find the crew, and buy the charts. I knew that it would take a lot of time to fit the boat out and was hoping that everyone taking part in the trip would get involved. The first stage in the master plan, therefore, was crew. I sent a circular letter to all my friends and set a deadline for replies. The deadline came and went but I only had one firm commitment for a three-month stint. It seemed that everyone was tied into work and family commitments, or was unemployed and couldn't afford the air fares and share of expenses. No doubt many thought, quite rightly, that I didn't have sufficient experience. The idea was a great one to enthuse about after a late night's session in a bar in Whitby, but when it came to a definite yes, or no, it was always a maybe. Somewhat set back but still undaunted, I drafted an advertisement for the yachting press.

The perfect crew member for a small sailboat on a long passage needs a range of skills. The most obvious of which are sailing skills. Engineering skills are also very important, as are domestic ones. Important as these are, they count for nothing if you are not able to get along with someone. Stories abound about crews falling out and people spending weeks on end without speaking a word. This makes life a misery for everyone. Just what makes different people get on well with one another aboard a small boat is difficult to say, but when things work out, personal shortcomings and foibles are tolerated. When people don't get on well, they become preoccupied with each other's faults, and a word or phrase spoken by one can be turned over in another person's mind for days on end. The confined living quarters – no bigger than a small tent and with nowhere to go to escape – and the difficult situations in which people aboard a small boat sometimes find themselves create a highly charged atmosphere of social intensity quite unlike anything on dry land. There is rarely a middle way. People aboard a boat either get on well or badly. If you don't get on with someone, it gnaws at you day and night, causing more discomfort than the worst gale. Anyone of sound body and mind can learn to sail, navigate and cook, but the best sailor in the world is a liability if he or she doesn't get on with other people.

I had drawn up an outline of the planned trip with details of the route, the schedule, the boat, the safety equipment, the cost, my responsibilities, and the responsibilities of prospective crew. To help me sort out the responses to the advertisement, I designed a questionnaire which asked a series of routine questions, the answers to which didn't interest me in the slightest, such as 'How much night sailing have you done?' But slotted in between the routine questions were the ones that mattered, such as 'What newspaper, if any, do you regularly read?' or 'Who is your favourite author?'

My little questionnaire was a first-stage screening device. I didn't want to take a chance with someone who read a newspaper that was only fit for wrapping fish in. I knew this was a somewhat crude way to go about selecting crew but it was better than nothing. The responses to the advertisement poured in – retired civil servants, unemployed businessmen, divorced women who invariably enclosed photographs, backpacking antipodeans looking for a ride home, peripatetic semi-professional crew seeking work, and quite a few who defied description. Most wrote a letter saying why they were interested, and I replied to each one. I wrote to about half informing them that all berths were taken and thanked them for their interest. The others received the detailed outline of the trip and the questionnaire. About half of these wrote back to me. When I got the replies, no matter how hard I tried, I couldn't see it working out with most of them. One person read the *Sun*, liked easy-listening music, and didn't like reading books; somehow I couldn't see myself sharing a night-watch in the tropics with him and enjoying it. By the time the correspondence had bounced back and forth and the filters at both ends had done their work, there were two people I was interested in, and who were interested in me. I asked both of them to visit me in Whitby to have a look at the boat and get acquainted.

The first snags in the plan were beginning to emerge and the boat wasn't even in the water. Not only did I not have crew but, by extension, I had less help than expected in preparing the boat and less funds to cover essential safety equipment. It had all seemed so simple when I outlined the sailing schedule: two people plus myself; a minimum commitment of three months; a nominal sum to cover the net cost of charts and essential safety equipment; and a willingness to get involved in preparing the boat. The reality was a boat needing a lot of work, a rapidly depleting bank balance, and not enough crew to get me to Spain, let alone Australia. For the first but not the last time, I realised that if the whole scheme was going to get anywhere, I would just have to keep plugging away and rely on what all sailors have at some time or other relied on in the past – hope.

By July '92 the boat was ready to be launched and most of the big jobs had been done. The engine had been lifted out and rebuilt, the standing rigging had been renewed, new sails had been made, an electronic autopilot had been fitted, a wind-operated self-steering system was installed, a wind generator to charge the batteries had been rigged up, the boat was rewired, and I was given a new life raft after a friend had read a true story about a family adrift in a clapped-out one. There were still many jobs to attend to, and, given the amount of work done, it was essential to sea-trial the boat before departure. I was already well behind schedule and was concerned about getting across the Bay of Biscay before the equinoctial gales set in.

Last-minute problems arose every hour of every day. The engine wouldn't start, a persistent leak through the rudder gland, which I thought I had cured, was worse than ever, the new sails didn't fit, and a close relative of a friend died suddenly in Ireland the day before I was due to leave. I sent the sails to the loft for modification and the engine bits to a workshop for repair and travelled to Ireland to attend a funeral on the day I had planned to set sail. My best friend's mother had died. I had been living with Laura for years and was now about to leave her. She had bought me the new life raft. Her father had already passed away a few years earlier, and, being an only child, she was alone in Ireland coping with her bereavement. The Bay of Biscay would have to wait.

When I returned from the funeral and the wake, some of the jobs which had been farmed out were done and the others quickly followed. I managed to squeeze in enough time to take the boat out for a couple of hours to sea-trial the new gear – not long enough, but I reasoned that if there were any teething problems they could be sorted out along the way. I was now so far behind schedule that the crew who were lined up for the sail to Scotland and down the Irish Sea were no longer available.

Fortunately, Whitby is the kind of town where someone is always available, and a friend of a friend agreed to come with me as far as Inverness in the north of Scotland.

Whitby is also a town with a swing bridge that opens two hours either side of high water to allow shipping to pass in and out. It was 14 August, and I was one month behind schedule and had to get going. I decided to catch the last opening of the bridge that day. The boat was in a chaotic state, with fenders, ropes, engine bits, self-steering gear, fuel containers, gas bottles, and tools littered all over the place. It was 6.0 p.m., and we had 30 minutes to catch the last opening of the bridge. Everything was jammed into lockers on top of everything else. At 6.25, we slipped the mooring lines and motored through the open bridge, out to sea. It was such a frantic departure that it was only as the boat cleared the outer walls of the harbour that I realised I was truly on my way. After all the hectic last few months of preparation, I was too tired to feel anything but relief. There was an empty sense of anticlimax – such are dreams when they become reality.

3. A Night in the Graveyard

ONCE WE CLEARED THE HARBOUR ENTRANCE, ALL I WANTED was a cup of tea and a cigarette. This always soothes the nerves. It would also give me a chance to get acquainted with John, who had joined at the last minute. The first thing I realised was that in the rush to depart I had forgotten to buy tobacco, but I knew that John also smoked roll-your-owns. 'How much tobacco do you have?' I asked. He told me that he had given up a few days ago and didn't have any! This was my first big problem. However, with an expected landfall in just over a day, I had enough to keep me going if I rationed it carefully.

With the wind blowing gently, we hoisted full sail. John had a new girlfriend in Edinburgh, with whom he was madly in love. He was planning to visit her after sailing with me as far as Inverness. As we sat in the cockpit, sipping the tea, John was happy to tell me about the 'good karma' that existed between them, and I was happy to listen. Shortly before dark, I advised him to turn in for a few hours' sleep. He went forward to the forepeak, closed the door, fell asleep, and no doubt dreamed about good karma.

Sitting alone in the cockpit at dusk, everything seemed so simple now that I was at last underway. The wind became a bit fitful, eventually dying away completely. I started the engine. The electronic autopilot was engaged. The motor for this was fitted below decks and couldn't be seen working – the boat gave the impression of being steered by an invisible helmsman, because the wheel in the cockpit would turn as if by magic with fine adjustments this way and that. I stretched out on the saloon berth to read the first book of my voyage. Plunging straight into the rich heritage of seafaring literature, I duly opened *Moby Dick*.

All was calm but I was too restless to make much progress with Melville's classic. I put it to one side and walked about the main cabin and cockpit, checking the engine instruments, compass, charts and navigation lights. Everything seemed to be in order. There was nothing much for me to do. The black silhouettes of a few fishing boats ghosted by, their navigation lights winking at me. None of them came too close to cause concern.

The British Admiralty chart for the North Sea was rolled out on the chart table. I studied its fine detail as if it were a painting in the Louvre. Charts of the sea are wonderful things. They show fishing grounds, shoals, banks, isolated dangers and rock outcrops. Every stretch of water has name, as does each headland and bay. Every aid to navigation, be it a buoy, a beacon or a lighthouse, is clearly marked, as are the contours of the seabed. Even the seabed material is indicated – mud, clay, sand, shingle, rock. Currents, tides, magnetic variation, all are given, along with traffic-separation zones for inshore shipping. But there are few details of the land, apart from those visible from seaward – church spires, radio masts and old ruins perched on cliff-tops. The chartmakers of the sea tend to disregard the land. Theirs is another world, and its priorities and imperatives impose themselves upon the chart.

Each sea is different, and because the North Sea is prone to bad weather, it is one of the biggest graveyards in the world. Wrecks lie all over the bottom. They are shown on the chart by a short horizontal line with two shorter perpendicular lines cutting through. I suppose this is an icon for the deck of a boat and two masts, but it also looks like two crucifixes joined together; one for the soul of the lost ship and one for the lost souls onboard. Each one is an untold or forgotten story. I always felt a strange feeling, sailing over these little marks on the chart. Such a tiny mark, such a big tragedy.

By now people were going to bed in Whitby. A man I hardly knew was fast asleep in the forepeak. Land was out of sight. After checking all the instruments time and again, I lifted the hatch in the cockpit to inspect the newly painted engine. With the help of a flashlight, everything looked fine. All the belts and pulleys were turning smoothly. The beam of the flashlight followed the fuel line, shining through the glass-bowled filter. It dipped down to the rubber engine mountings, which looked in good order, and travelled on to the gearbox at the back of the engine — no problem there. The stainless-steel propeller shaft was whizzing round, catching and reflecting back the brilliance of the light. The end of the shaft then passes through a watertight gland in the hull and out to sea to the propeller. Any through-hull fitting below the waterline is a potential source of disaster because if a leak is going to occur these are the most likely places. I craned my head to avoid the whirling pulleys and allow my eye to catch sight of the watertight gland. It had come undone!

Panic, surprisingly enough, is a response rarely encountered at sea because there is usually time to come to terms with problems. To my great relief, and even greater disbelief, there didn't seem to be any water coming aboard, but it was surely only a matter of time before water seeped though the grease already packed in the gland and came flooding in. But there were plenty of fishing boats around, my VHF radio was working, it was a calm night, I had a brand new life raft. I and was only 15 miles away. No need to panic, I kept thinking, but the engine must be shut down immediately. I pulled the stop handle. All fell silent. I felt a great sense of relief now that the engine was closed down. John, asleep in the forepeak, may have good karma with women, but I have always had bad karma with engines.

I didn't know what was the worst prospect: sinking or turning back? If I turned back to Whitby now, I had doubts that I would ever get going again before the equinoctial gales set in. There were safe harbours further north where I could put in for repairs. The wind was now starting to pick up again, probably the nightly offshore breeze. By making headway under sail and with the propeller not turning, there wouldn't be much strain on the stern gland. I kept a northerly course and a close eye on the gland.

The nightly offshore breeze stiffened, filling the sails. There is a compelling simplicity about making headway under sail: no moving parts, no lubrication or fuel, no noise — just the wind in the sails and the boat in harmony with nature.

Almost imperceptibly, the wind began to increase. With the sea beginning to get a bit lumpy, I shortened canvas. I had given considerable thought to the sailplan: a large headsail was attached to the forestay, which had roller reefing — a mechanism for reducing sail by pulling on a line that winds the canvas around a foil, like wrapping a piece of paper round a pencil. The other sail was the mainsail, which was hoisted up the mast and attached at the bottom to a swinging boom. This sail was short-ened by hauling on a series of lines that pulled the sail down the mast in three stages, known as reefs. All sail control lines, which, for some reason that I have never understood, are called sheets, were led back to the cockpit to allow sail to be reduced without leaving its comparative safety.

Still the wind continued to rise. It was now blowing spray off the top of the waves. I rolled up more of the headsail and put the first-stage reef in the main. None of the new gear for reducing sail had been sea-trialed properly but it was being tested now. It proved inadequate. All the sheets had been re-routed back to the cockpit via a series of blocks. There was a single winch for gaining extra purchase on the sheets, along with a few rope jammers. I had seen this arrangement on other boats, and it looked eminently sensible. What I didn't realise is that each owner had a care-fully worked-out configuration of winches, jammers and control lines that had been evolved and refined over two or three sailing seasons to meet each boat's particular needs. The set-up I had, although it looked fine on paper, simply didn't work in practice. I was finding this out for the first time at sea at night with a steadily increasing wind, a suspect stern gland, and an engine that I couldn't use.

There was no doubt that the weather was taking a turn for the worse, and the warm summer evening and settled sea that had enticed me out of the safety of the harbour in Whitby now seemed like a distant dream. Most of the people in bed in Whitby didn't care a hoot about the wind — the worst that could happen to them is that they might lose a slate from their roof — but the wind held me and the boat in its thrall: it had the power to change my world. I fumbled with the sheets to put the second reef in the mainsail.

When the wind blows hard and the seas build, the most uncomfort-able place on a boat is the forepeak. As the troughs between waves get deeper and steeper, the bow of the boat falls into each one, slamming down hard. The sound of the water crashing against the hull is fearsome, and you start to wonder how the thin fibreglass skin of the boat can stand up to it. Sleeping in the forepeak is almost impossible, so I wasn't surprised when the door to this cabin opened and John stumbled out already fully dressed.

There was a look of anxiety on his face. 'What's going on?' he asked, making his way with difficulty through the main cabin to the companion-way. When he went to bed there was daylight, the sea was flat calm, and there was very little wind. When he woke up four hours later, the whole world had changed. It wasn't surprising that he asked what was going on.

Alarmism is everyone's worst enemy aboard a boat, so I replied very casually, 'The wind's just getting up a bit, stick the kettle on.' John brewed a strong cup of tea, and the time spent doing it gave him a chance to wake up and get his wits about him. With the boat on autopilot, I came below. I smoked a couple of cigarettes with my tea, while John ate a few apples with his.

When the tea was finished, the wind was even stronger. I remembered reading somewhere that if the wind increases by more than three points on the Beaufort Scale in less than an hour, then a full-blown gale is approaching. John asked whether I had heard the forecast before we left. All I could say was, 'No.' Although the BBC issues a regular, comprehensive shipping forecast, it had never occurred to me to tune in. The evening transmission is just before the news at six – at that time I was stuffing gear into lockers. What's more, it had been a very settled summer so far, with hardly any wind at all for the last three or four weeks. The prospect of bad weather never entered my head. What was entering my head right then was the prospect of the stern gland bursting apart. In these deteriorating conditions, it would be no easy matter to launch the life raft and board it should the need arise. It wouldn't have served any purpose to tell John about the stern gland – I was doing enough worrying for the two of us – and there was no need to open the engine hatch to inspect it. It would be easy to establish whether we were taking water by regular pumping with the manual bilge pump, so I mentioned to John that we should pump the bilges every half hour, just to keep the boat nice and dry.

I had first go on the bilge pump, counting 42 strokes. As long as the number of strokes stayed at about this level, things were under control. With the full gale now nearly upon us, the boat was seriously overcanvased. Taking more canvas off the headsail was easy because the furling gear, which hadn't been changed in the refit, worked well. The long foil rotated, rolling the sail up neatly on the forestay until only a small amount remained – enough to help control the boat, but not too much to unbalance her. The seas were now too big for the electric autopilot to work. The invisible helmsman was being overwhelmed and couldn't turn the wheel fast or hard enough to counteract the effect of the waves which were breaking on the boat, knocking her off course.

Although the headsail had been brought under control, there was far too much mainsail up. The third and last reef had to go in without delay. When the new sails had been made, I had decided to opt for a very deep third reef in the main. The reasoning behind this was that it would allow me to carry a minimal amount of sail on the main, even in very bad conditions. It was needed now. When it was first hoisted up the mast a few days earlier in Whitby harbour, local yachtsmen, always eager to inspect any new gear on any boat, had commented that it was very deep and that I would probably never need it. They were wrong. So too was the boatyard owner who had fitted a new boom with all the sail control lines running inside. The arrangement of sliding blocks inside the boom restricted the number of lines available to four. I needed a single line for putting in the first reef, another for putting in the second, one for pulling the sail tight along the boom, and two for the third reef – that made five! That meant one short. I was advised that the best thing to do was not to worry about connecting one of the lines for the third reef – if I ever needed it, I could untie a line that was already used and feed it through the cringle in the sail for reef number three. Sounds great in theory, but now, with the wind blowing at gale force, darkness all around, the boat being knocked off course, heavy seas crashing on the deck and a wildly flogging main about to shred, it didn't seem so easy. The situation was made worse by the inadequate system of jammers and winches that I had installed.

With John's help, I tried again and again to put the third reef in. Even though it was late summer, our fingers became numb from the wet and cold. After many attempts we gave up. We couldn't use the engine because of the broken stern gland, and the boat couldn't be sailed because she had too much canvas. Had I been more experienced, I would have dropped the entire mainsail and lashed it to the boom, but I was so preoccupied with the third reef that this didn't occur to me. I thought, mistakenly, that some mainsail was necessary to balance the boat.

All the exertion of trying to tame the sail had taken its toll on both of us – John was starting to look very pale. He leaned over the side of the cockpit: I held on to his waist while he vomited up the apples and tea consumed an hour earlier. I had seen the debilitating effect that seasickness can have on people and was worried that he would succumb completely. Seasickness is a curse, which, like all curses, afflicts some more than others. It can drain all the life out of the strongest man, making him feel miserable beyond belief. Hypothermia, weakness, lethargy and depression always accompany the wretching. The stomach heaves and contracts violently, almost turning itself inside-out to empty its contents, and the foul bile lingers in the mouth like the after-taste of death. It can get so bad that sometimes a man with severe seasickness can fold like a house of cards, crawling into his bunk, almost wishing for death as a means of release. But there is no escape from it, which only makes it worse. As John wiped the last bits of green apple peel and white vomit from his mouth, he put a very brave face on it, saying almost apologetically, 'I don't normally get seasick.'

It takes real courage to keep going when you're sick. Not wanting to make him feel any worse than he already did, I replied, 'Don't worry, it'll do you good.'

Somehow or other, the boat had to be brought under control quickly. I decided to heave to. A long-keeled sailboat can be made to come virtually to rest in the water by backing the headsail, so that it tries to force the bow round one way, and putting the wheel hard over, to force the bow round the other way. The yacht lies at about 50 degrees to the wind, making slow forward progress, riding the oncoming seas. When the boat is hove to, no one needs to do anything and the gale can be waited out, provided you don't drift towards land. I hove so that whatever progress we made was to seaward. When I went down below to see John, who was recovering from his seasickness, and told him what I had done, I could see that he was a little concerned about drifting further out to sea in the teeth of a gale. He told me that if this was a fairground ride he wouldn't get on, but he was on and there was no getting off. He was somewhat reassured by the relative calm that settled upon us now that we were hove to. When I told him the old adage about land being the most dangerous thing you can see when at sea, we both managed to smile at one another.

The smile disappeared from my face when I suddenly remembered the bilge pump. We had completely forgotten about pumping her out while trying to tie and untie the sail lines. I went out to the cockpit, pump handle in hand, and started to empty her out once more. Sitting there huddled inside my foul-weather gear, forcing the handle up and down, I remembered all the fishing boats we had seen earlier that night. It occurred to me that I hadn't seen one in the last four or five hours. No doubt they knew more about the weather than I did, having picked up the gale warning issued in the shipping forecast. They had headed straight for port. Like a fool, I kept heading out to sea.

Once the weather had started to deteriorate, my consumption of cigarettes had escalated in line with the Beaufort Scale. I was now on my last one. As I finished the wet butt off, we were about level with Newcastle upon Tyne: there was a 24-hour shop in Newcastle – it sold cigarettes! Laura also lived there. She had just returned from her mother's funeral. I had asked her not to bother to take time off work to come down to see me off but to join me for a full week in Inverness to sail through the Caledonian Canal. It always made me sad to think of leaving her, and I couldn't bear the thought of being parted from her for a week, let alone two years. Most of my friends thought she was too good for me, and I agreed with them. She would have tuned in to the midnight shipping forecast and would know that I was out in a gale. She would probably be asleep now – all would be quiet and still. I could be lying in bed beside her, warm and safe – smoking a cigarette.

The wind was howling, the boat was pitching up and down, and the sea was raging about us. Land was out of sight, I was out of tobacco, and I must have been out of my mind. I strained my eyes to try to pick up a light on the shoreline to the west but could see none, and in time with the strokes of the pump, muttered to myself, 'What the hell . . . am I . . . doing here . . . ?'

4. Slow Progress

WE LAY HOVE TO, WAITING FOR DAWN. NEITHER OF US GOT any sleep. The light came slowly at first, as it does in high latitudes, cheering us up a little. But the dawn was a bleak sight by any standards. It was a monochrome world. Everything was different shades of grey: the sky was overcast and grey, the sea was dark and grey, and the breakers on the tops of the waves were more grey than white.

Now that this dismal light was upon us, the best thing to do was to try to get going again. That meant putting the third reef in the main, which we had struggled unsuccessfully with the night before. The key to success lay in threading a line through a heavy cringle in the corner of the sail. Once this line was through, the sail could be reduced and the surplus canvas at the bottom could then be secured to the boom by pulling hard on the line. We zipped ourselves into our foul-weather gear and clipped on our life-harnesses and life-lines, before going out to the cockpit to try again. Life-lines are, in theory, a good idea. They secure you to the ship like an umbilical cord, stopping you from falling overboard, but they also severely restrict your movement and continually get in the way. When undertaking a difficult job, a moment sometimes occurs when you need an extra bit of reach quickly, and you have to unclip the life-line or the moment is lost.

When we dropped the sail it started to flog once more. John was trying to pull the canvas tight while I was trying to thread the line through. He was standing on the cockpit seat in order to reach the boom. His life-line was unclipped. As he struggled with the canvas, it slipped out of his wet, cold hands. He started to fall backwards. There was a hole in his face the size of an Italian tomato where his mouth should have been, but no sound came out. His eyes were open wide, staring straight at me. There was real terror in them – he didn't know where he was going to fall. I reached out and grabbed the front of his jacket. He stopped falling. Another failed attempt! John was visibly shaken by the fall – he had a haunted expression on his face even after the danger had passed. In that moment he was falling, he thought he was going to die. When someone has just had such thoughts they need time to come to terms with them, but there was no time to waste.

We tried again. This time John stayed on the wheel, trying to steer the boat so that the sail flogged as little as possible, while I tried on my own to get the line through. I just couldn't reach high enough for long enough to get it through the damn hole. If I climbed on to the end of the boom, I had a better chance of getting it through.

Above the noise of the wind and the breaking seas, I called out to John, 'Do you think you can hold her in this position?' There was a nod of desperation. I unclipped the harness and clambered on to the end of the boom. 'Make sure you hold her steady,' I yelled, trying, with one hand for the ship and one for myself, to get the line through. The sail, which seemed to be possessed, was thrashing about like a lunatic in a strait-jacket. It was impossible to manage with one hand. There was a big bag of billowing canvas hanging at the bottom of the boom. This was catching the wind, whipping the edge of the sail into a frenzy. I checked once more that John could hold her steady and jumped into the bag of canvas at the bottom of the leeward side of the boom. The thrashing lunatic was pinned to the ground and I now had two hands free to finish him off. The line went through the cringle and was secured. It was the most dangerous and stupid thing I had ever done, but it worked.

Once all the lines were made as tight as we could get them with the hopeless arrangement of winches and jammers I had installed, but never tested, the boat was brought under some sort of control. We swung her on to a north-westerly course and got underway. John remained on the wheel while I went below for a much-needed cup of tea. The tea just wasn't the same without a cigarette, and I craved one. As I sat sipping the tea, all I could think of was tobacco and how stupid I had just been. If the boat had been knocked round by a wave, the bag of sailcloth in which I had been standing would have flipped over to the other side of the boom, catapulting me into the raging sea and eternity. I vowed to myself that never again would I do anything with any risk attached to it without a life-line.

Visibility was poor, and we had made some miles to seaward while hove to. Even though we were now making good progress, land didn't appear for a long time. Shortly before noon, we caught our first glimpse of it off the coast of Northumberland. Bamburgh Castle, majestic and medieval, slowly appeared perched on a cragged cliff. The Northumberland coastline is steeped in history, and it wasn't long before Lindisfarne Priory on Holy Island, built in the eleventh century, came into view. St Cuthbert had once lived, prayed and scribbled away within its walls. He had, no doubt, on many occasions looked out to sea from his cell and seen ships struggling to make a landfall, and had probably said prayers for them.

We decided to try to put in to Berwick upon Tweed. This, the most northerly town in England, has changed hands between that country and its old rival, Scotland, many times. The harbour, like most harbours on the east coast of England and Scotland, has a shallow entrance. It can only be approached by deep-draught vessels at certain states of the tide. The nautical almanac showed that high water occurred shortly after 2.0 p.m. There would be enough water for the *Warrior Queen* to go in up to about 3.30 p.m. We were making good progress and would probably get there in time.

When at sea, things don't go according to plan. By the time we were approaching the entrance to Berwick Harbour it was nearly 4.0 p.m. I hadn't had any sleep worth talking about for over 30 hours, had been through a gale, and the stern gland needed sorting out. I wanted to get into port badly. Berwick Harbour has a long wall that extends out to sea. You approach the harbour by heading for the end of this wall and then creep along the inside of it. The shallowest water is just before you reach the wall, and there is a vicious-looking outcrop of rocks close by. As long as we could reach the wall, we would be OK. We inched forward under power, keeping a close watch on the depth-sounder. With about 50 yards to go, as we were level with the rock outcrop, the depth fell off sharply. With 25 yards to go, we hit ground! There was a sickening, hard grating noise. The boat juddered on the bottom, losing its buoyancy in an instant. The rock outcrop, although still in the same place, now looked twice as big and twice as close.

The tide was on the ebb. If we didn't get off immediately, the ship would be lost. This wasn't a sandbank in a sheltered estuary on a calm day. There were rocks below us, and we were still in the open sea in bad weather. I slammed the engine into reverse. The engine was racing like mad and so was my mind. How could I ever cope with the humiliation of losing the boat at the start of the trip? People would say it was my fault, and they would be right. The local TV cameras would be here in no time, and I would never be able to look Laura in the face again. It would have been better to sink miles out to sea – at least that has a certain romance about it, but there is nothing romantic about piling your boat up at the entrance to a harbour. I could already see people shaking their heads when I tried to explain to them that I thought we *might* have had enough water to get in.

I willed her to come off. With the wind blowing from the bow and the propeller spinning like crazy, she started to move. We were backing off slowly, very slowly. I was worried that we might back into another clump of rocks on the seabed but she kept moving and we came clear. John and I were getting to the stage where we couldn't take much more of this. We couldn't carry on because of the stern gland, and we couldn't get into port because of the tide, but I did have a big insurance policy lashed to the bow of the boat – an anchor! There is a large bay south of the harbour entrance at Berwick. The chart showed that there was plenty of water and indicated that the bottom was sand and mud – perfect holding ground. We motored out to the middle of the bay and let go the anchor. It dug into the bottom, holding her fast with the bow to the wind. I remembered that someone had once told me that the most important gear aboard was good ground tackle. I now knew why.

We shut down the engine and, to allow access to the stern gland, cleared all the gear out of the cockpit lockers that had been stuffed in the day before. Although we were both dead tired, I couldn't go to sleep knowing that she might sink at anchor during the night. I clambered into the locker and lay prone in a space literally the size of a coffin. By removing an inspection plate at the aft end of this locker, I could stick my head through into the back of the engine bay. The stern gland was sorted out in less than half an hour. After a few sandwiches, John and I turned in and fell instantly into a deep sleep while the boat bobbed up and down on the sea, swinging on the anchor chain.

When we woke next morning, the wind had dropped off and was blowing gently from the north. This was bad news. It was now coming from where we wanted to go, but with the stern gland fixed we could motor. I felt an urgent need to make as much progress as possible. It looked as though summer was coming to an early close – the autumn would bring more gales. The evenings were already starting to draw in, so the sooner I got to more southerly latitudes, the better. We started the engine, checked the stern gland, hauled up the anchor chain and got underway. Before clearing the bay at Berwick, I called up the harbour master on the VHF radio to tell him we had hit ground when approaching the harbour entrance the day before. I asked him what was on the bottom. 'Rock covered with sand and mud,' came the disheartening reply, and I wondered how much damage had been done.

North of Berwick lies St Abb's Head, with its bird sanctuary. As we passed, the sky was filled with gannets, fulmers and puffins. The puffins flapped their wings furiously to make very little progress, while the fulmers, with their short tails and stocky bodies, seemed to be able to catch every shift in the wind, skipping over the waves with an effortlessness that belied their appearance. The gannets soared majestically above the rest, folding their wings flat every once in a while, before plunging like arrows into the sea below to catch a fish.

I made sure to tune in to the lunchtime shipping forecast – northerly winds of force four to six were predicted. The force of the wind is measured on the Beaufort Scale, with force 0 representing flat calm and force 12 being a hurricane with winds over 100 miles an hour. Force four to six represents a good stiff breeze, which is ideal for sailing, provided it blows from the right direction. We needed the wind to blow anywhere from east through south to west, but today it was coming from where we wanted to go. The open sea at the mouth of the Firth of Forth lay in front of us, and we had no alternative but to motor across. It was only about 20 miles wide. Provided we made four or five knots, we should make it before nightfall. As the wind picked up to the predicted force six, it whipped up the sea before us. The waves were not particularly big but we were heading straight into them, and the ride was a bit uncomfortable. Engines on sailboats don't have much power. They perform well in harbour or in calm conditions, but when going to windward they have to fight against each oncoming wave and the drag of the wind. St Abb's Head behind us seemed to stay where it was forever – we were not making much progress. By regularly checking our position on the chart, it was clear that instead of doing the expected four or five knots, we were barely making one knot. By nightfall we were only a third of the way across.

As we got further out into the open sea and the wind had more time to stir up the waves, our speed across the ground fell off to about half a knot. Spray broke over the bow, soaking the helmsman. When you spend an hour being soaked with freezing water to cover half a mile and have the prospect of another 20 or 30 hours in store, you start to get a bit demoralised. With the boat pitching up and down, the propeller rises out of the water every now and again and the engine screeches. All the time you struggle with the futility of asking yourself pointless questions such as, 'Why doesn't the wind go round to the west or the east?', because you know that if it did, you could hoist the sails, close down the drone of the engine, and take flight.

John was beginning to miss his girlfriend and I was starting to miss mine. We got the charts out to explore the options. It was now slowly dawning on me that it was pointless to simply look at a destination, in this case Inverness in the north of Scotland, and try to head straight for it regardless of where the wind blew from. There was a small harbour in Dunbar, round the corner from St Abb's Head. We could turn round and sail straight to it. There wouldn't be much progress to show from Berwick but there would be some. At about three in the morning we brought the bow round and started heading back.

At daybreak, we were sailing close along the coast, looking for the entrance to Dunbar. A friend, who had once sailed in there, had told me that it was the most dramatic harbour entrance he had ever seen. The harbour is not visible from seaward but there are two large beacons situated on a hillside near the town which guide you in. The beacons are some distance apart and at different heights. The closest of the two has a triangle pointing upwards and the furthest has a triangle pointing downwards. Having spotted the beacons, we sailed along until both triangles were lined up. I made sure that the two apexes of each triangle kept pointing together as I sailed in. This line took us between pinnacles of isolated rock on either side, along the edge of a tall cliff and seemingly straight to the shore. No harbour could be seen. As we approached the shore, and I was just beginning to say to myself, 'This can't be right', a small gap appeared in the cliff. Sheer rock towered above the mast as we edged in through this gap, whereupon a small, tranquil fishing harbour appeared in front of us. Fishing boats were getting ready to leave as we tied up alongside the harbour wall.

It had been a miserable trip. The newly installed reefing gear hadn't worked, the stern gland fell apart, and John had been sick. We had been caught in a gale, then ran aground, and, finally, had turned back. I had probably come as close to going overboard as I ever wanted to, and we were nowhere near Inverness. It had taken us nearly three hard days to cover a distance that you could do in a car in comfort in less than three hours. Sydney Opera House seemed a very long way away.

Although the harbour is sheltered, it is subject to heavy swell in northerly winds. This swell was running up the side of the harbour wall. The only way to secure the boat was with two very long lines tied bow and stern. The boat was swept up and down the harbour wall with the incoming swell and kept banging up against the side. The harbour master gave us some help in adjusting the lines but there was nothing that we could do to get her to lie steady.

We both climbed up the steel ladder on the harbour wall. The first thing that John did, before we went off to find a telephone, was to kneel down to kiss the ground. He was so serious that he didn't even bother trying to make a joke about it. Laura had, as I expected, been listening to the shipping forecasts. She was full of sympathy and concern but her first words were what they would always be for the time I was at sea. 'Where are you?' she asked. I was hoping that she would join me that day and as often as possible in the future, so I played down the drama of the last three days and lied, saying we had just had one or two minor problems. She said she would get a train up in the afternoon. John, who had also been in touch with his girl, was going to leave at Dunbar. He was good with his hands, and there were a couple of broken hinges and fastenings that he said he would fix before leaving. We both went back to the boat and started work.

It would have been easy for John to pack up his gear and leave there and then, but he spent all morning helping me sort out a few problems. He was as shattered as I was and would probably never sail on the *Warrior Queen* again. But he got stuck in. Nothing pleases the owner of a boat more than having someone aboard who is able and willing to help fix broken gear. I was very touched that he took the time to help. Before leaving round about lunchtime, he told me that the last three days had been the worst and the longest of his life but he was still glad he had made the trip. I think he now had a keener appreciation of everything in life after nearly having lost his own. Just as he was going, he put his hand in his pocket, pulled out a half-ounce of rolling tobacco that was still wrapped in the cellophane, and said as he handed it to me, 'I had this with me all the time.'

'I thought you'd given up?'

'I have, but I just needed it in my pocket for reassurance.'

'But why didn't you give it to me when I ran out?'

'Because I thought that if you didn't have any, you would be more likely to put in sooner, and all I wanted was to get off the boat.'

'Well, why are you telling me this now?'

'Because . . . because I feel guilty about it.' A craving for cigarettes is, like fear, intensely experienced when it occurs but it leaves no memory. We both laughed about it, before shaking hands warmly and saying good-bye. I climbed back down the ladder, stretched out on my bunk and was so exhausted that I couldn't be bothered to take my shoes off before falling fast asleep.

5. *Freshwater and Mountains*

WHEN LAURA ARRIVED LATER THAT DAY, SHE WAS GREETED
by a surreal sight on making her way down to the harbour. It was near
low tide as she approached the edge of the wall. Nothing in the harbour
was visible, apart from the top half of a mast. This disembodied half of a
mast was rushing backwards and forwards along the top of the harbour
wall, carried this way and that by the incoming swell.

'Ahoy, *Warrior Queen*, is anyone aboard?' I think I heard her in my
sleep the second time she called out. When I came up to have a look, she
was standing at the edge of the wall. She had a bottle of whisky in her
hand and a big smile on her face. There was a rucksack on her back and a
large plastic bag by her side.

'How do I get on the boat?' she asked, as it slid back and forth below
her. Always lead by example, I thought, so I climbed to the top of the
steel ladder and asked her to pass the bags and the bottle. When she saw
me make the descent with one free hand, she had a go herself with two
hands. She managed to get to the bottom safely and clambered over the
guard-rail. With both hands now free, she gave me a big tight hug. I was
bruised and stiff from the knocks and exertions of the trip and held on to
her as if she were a feather pillow.

The view from inside the main cabin was every bit as surreal as from
the top of the harbour wall. All that could be seen through the small,
smoked-perspex windows were large granite stones rushing past one way
before flying back the other, like giant tennis balls at Wimbledon.

'Have you got this boat tied up right?' she asked incredulously. When
I explained what was happening with the swell, she looked at me as if to
say, 'Are you sure you know what you're doing?'

Once she'd come to terms with the situation, it was time for
presents. The large plastic bag was produced. First item out was a
melonite plastic mug elaborately decorated with tropical foliage and
green parrots. The galley of the ship was poorly equipped, so every addition was welcome. Three more mugs, four dinner plates and three soup
bowls followed to form a handsome set. These lovely presents would have
pleased me no end at any time, but to have Laura there beside me just

then, lavishing me with something which was the very epitome of gracious living and foretold of fine food and good company in a warm tropical climate, was what my body and soul needed.

I had arranged for an old friend to join us the next day, and the three of us were going to continue taking the boat north. Aidan turned up, doing his best to appear enthusiastic. With no sailing experience, he planned to join me when transiting the Caledonian Canal, but nothing was running to schedule. He loved the Scottish mountains and the idea of sailing straight through the middle of them had captured his imagination when I first talked him into it. The thought of heading out to the North Sea, albeit along the coast, was something that neither he nor Laura looked forward to, but the weather had settled down and the forecast indicated that it would stay that way for a few days.

On passing through the narrow gap in the wall of the cliff, their first sight of the open sea was the gauntlet of rocks that I had passed on the way in. They were both probably too shocked at the sight of them to say anything but quickly relaxed once we left them behind and headed out across the firth. This time it all went according to plan, and we were rewarded with a sighting of a small pilot whale about 200 yards off. It showed its back once then disappeared.

When people travel, most of the time they know where they are going to end up. On a sailboat, you are never quite sure. There is a harbour in Aberdeen where the royal yacht *Britannia* is usually moored in August, while the Queen and her family visit Balmoral Castle in the Highlands. There was an outside chance we might make that by nightfall. The outside chance proved to be no chance at all, so I decided to spend the night anchored in a bay further south. When I put this to Aidan and Laura, they reacted the way someone does when a dentist tells them that they need to have three teeth extracted. You don't relish the prospect but there is nothing you can do but grin and bear it.

I had known Aidan for about ten years, and we had once worked with each other in the same college. He was a much more conscientious academic than I was and was at his best when writing or editing a paper for a journal. Anchoring in a bay at night off the coast of Scotland was not his forte. He had helped me in the past with a software package that I had developed and was going to be my business manager while I was at sea. So for all these reasons and a host of others, I was happy to have him aboard. But, right then, his greatest and most relevant accomplishment was his cooking ability. He went down below while Laura and I sat out in the cockpit drinking whisky. In just over half an hour he produced a sumptuous spaghetti carbonara which we served up on my new dinner set.

We had dinner ashore the next night in Aberdeen but, unfortunately, Elizabeth, the Queen, didn't drop into the Chinese restaurant that night. Laura left the next morning to go back to work for a few days and Aidan and I sailed out past *Britannia*, heading north.

We hugged the coast all the way, putting in at a different harbour each night – small, slightly run-down fishing ports with lots of knocked-about fishing boats and the occasional yacht. There were no problems apart from the fact that the engine kept cutting out for no apparent reason. Aidan was a bit anxious about this, especially when it occurred as we were approaching a harbour in the dark, but it always seemed to start again just in time. The weather was very settled. While sailing, we relaxed in the cockpit, engaged the autopilot, drank whisky and listened to music. Aidan had brought somes tapes along for the trip. In my rush to depart, I didn't have time to organise a tape collection of my own: all I had were a few operatic highlights and some chamber music by Mozart – not much to sail round the world with. Aidan had one tape by Ry Cooder, whom I had never heard of, and we played this over and over again. Sailing along the north-east coast of Scotland in late summer, I fell in love with Ry Cooder's guitar.

Four days after leaving Aberdeen we reached Inverness and were lying in the sealock at the entrance to the Caledonian Canal, ready to pass from salt to freshwater. We had arrived late in the afternoon, and the lockgate wasn't due to open until next morning. Once more Laura was going to join me, this time for a full week. Everything now seemed very civilised: the boat was resting perfectly still in the shelter of the lock, the weather was settled and warm, Aidan was at last going to get to see the mountains, and Laura was on the train heading north.

Aidan started to cook another fine dinner while I went off to meet Laura in a pub a mile or so away. Even though it was less than a week since she left in Aberdeen, I was overjoyed to see her. We walked back to the boat along the canal bank. Neither of us had ever been there before, and it was strange to keep meeting like this in the most unlikely places. The last part of the walk took us along a gravel path towards the sealock. The fresh mountain water cascaded over the gate into the sea below, where it lapped against the hull of my boat. The Tilley lamp was swinging on the boom, bathing the yacht in its warm, numinous glow. Ry Cooder was playing his guitar, and the smell of freshly cooked chicken wafted up through the open hatches. When Aidan heard us coming, he came out to the cockpit, glass of whisky in hand, and invited the two of us to come aboard for supper.

Lock-keepers get up early in the morning in Scotland, as no doubt they do everywhere else in the world. Next morning found all three of us scrambling around the deck in our night attire, tripping over ropes and tying on extra fenders. The open lock to the sea was about to be closed and filled with water. As if by magic, other boats had appeared from nowhere, jamming into the lock, which was in a state of pandemonium. The water poured in from the opened sluices, the lock started to fill and the boats started to rise – the elevator was going up. The resulting slack on the ropes meant that all the boats started to bump into each other but the other crews seemed much more wide awake than we were and managed to fend us off. It was all over in five pre-breakfast, bleary-eyed, chaotic minutes and the sea lay beneath us. We had negotiated the first lock and had 28 more to go.

The canal can only deal with boats up to 48 metres long, which rules out the largest fishing boats and most cargo vessels. These days it is used mainly by pleasure craft and the odd fishing boat. Most go through in convoys and every inch in each lock is usually taken up. This means that you see the same boats and crews on a regular basis and get to know each other pretty well. By the time we reached the next lock, we had fallen in with an old fishing boat and a host of small sailboats. The fishing boat was so dilapidated that it was hard to believe it could be seaworthy. Every metal fixture onboard was rusted right through, and the planking had sprung loose all the way round the hull. The crew were in an equally run-down state and looked like extras from an Errol Flynn pirate movie. Given the condition of their boat, they weren't in the least concerned about taking any knocks while in the locks. This boat probably weighed about 60 tons, and with so much jagged metal sticking out from every corner it was just as menacing as any pirate ship. After one or two close encounters, we hung back to let it go on in front, hoping to have seen the last of it.

In between the locks, the canal meandered through the forests and hills leading into the Highlands. On rounding one bend in the canal, we were greeted with a sight that would have done justice not only to Errol Flynn but also to Cecil B. De Mille. The *Søren Larsen* bore down upon us. She is one of the world's most famous tall ships and is to an old beat-up fishing boat what a racehorse is to a donkey. She was on her way from the tall ships gathering in Boston to the mainland of Europe and towered above us as she squeezed by. There wasn't a rope out of place. Every piece of exposed timber was gleaming with varnish. All the brass work was buffed and polished. The helmsman stood at the huge spocked wheel, concentrating on his task. Set among the glens and woodlands, and passing within a hand's reach of us, she was a truly beautiful sight.

As we climbed higher with each lock, the woodland became more sparse and the mountains more impressive. On the second day we cleared the last lock before Loch Ness and sailed out into the deep water to meet the monster. The Loch Ness monster is a bit like God – a lot of people believe in him but there is no firm evidence that he actually exists. They come from all over the world in search of him but he only reveals himself to a chosen few and is rarely, if ever, caught in the act of doing so. I didn't know what I would find on this trip but I didn't expect to encounter monsters of the deep, so I wasn't disappointed when Nessie didn't turn up. But Loch Ness is impressive even without a monster. It is long, narrow and deep, with rugged mountains on all sides. We sailed along its shore, past the ruins of Urquhart Castle. Other historic ruins and lived-in baronial homes, just a notch down from your genuine castle in real-estate terms, flank its shoreline and nestle into the sides of its mountains. If the monster does exist, it certainly picked a nice place to live.

We made the south-west corner of this fabled loch well before nightfall and tied up to a jetty in the Highland town of Fort Augustus. The *Søren Larsen* was only the first of many tall ships transiting the canal – the rest all seemed to be gathered in this small town. As soon as we tied up, we scampered off my puny little plastic boat and went to have a good look at these beauties. Each one had crossed the Atlantic Ocean. Their crews were suntanned and brimming with good health and good cheer. If ever I needed encouragement to carry on, I was getting it in large helpings. The pubs were crowded with crews of all nationalities, so I went inside, where I sat quietly beside them, soaking up the atmosphere.

The tall ships were going one way and I was going the other. As is ever the case when you come across ships at sea or in port, we parted company and next morning left them behind. In the first lock that morning there was a French yacht similar to mine. There were three people aboard: two men and a woman, or a couple and a man. They had been sailing for about nine months around the Baltic and Scandinavia and were now on their way home to Brittany. The crew handled the boat well, working as a team without anyone seeming to be in charge.

People on a boat close by are like neighbours, and everyone loves to gossip about their neighbours. I couldn't help speculating about the domestic arrangements on the French yacht. Whatever way you looked at it, it must have been tough for the man without the woman. I suppose it was feasible that they might have reached an accommodation whereby both men were happy and the woman was twice as happy but this set-up would be hard to negotiate in a house, let alone a boat, and didn't seem likely. I discussed all these possibilities with Laura and Aidan. Laura pretended not to be interested but Aidan was more forthcoming.

Later that day, we had to negotiate a series of locks close together. While going through one of these, Laura decided to walk along the towpath to the next one. At the same time, the Frenchman without the woman decided to take a stroll himself. It wasn't long before I could see the two of them engaged in a halting conversation. I had tried to have a few words with the Frenchman earlier but he didn't speak a word of English. Laura spoke a little French, though. I had always taken great delight in teasing her, so I hurried through the lock. As the boat drew level with the two of them, I shouted out to her, 'You never know your luck, that frog just might turn into a prince.' The Frenchman smiled an inane grin without knowing why. Laura was mortified.

We carried on through the canal and reached the last Highland loch of the trip, which, believe it or not, is called Loch Lochy. We were now at our highest point above sea-level and about to go down to the sea again. The procedure to adopt when going down the locks is to enter a full lock and tie the boat up. As the water is drained off, the boat descends. It is imperative that the lines are let out steadily, otherwise you could end up hanging in mid-air against the side of the wall. This requires neatly coiled ropes that can be let out as required. Aidan had problems with ropes and Laura didn't have the strength to control them, but the Frenchman was always ready to help her so we managed in the end.

A day or so saw us make our way down. The night before Aidan was due to leave, we were perched on top of Neptune's Ladder. This is a series of locks packed tightly together before reaching the sea. Aidan was due to leave the day after so we all went out for a farewell dinner in Fort William, the main town on the western side of the canal. He certainly enjoyed the platter of fresh seafood, and I think he enjoyed the trip. He left early next morning, wished me luck and gave me his Ry Cooder tape.

Laura and I bumped the boat down Neptune's Ladder later that day. She was on the wheel in the cockpit of the boat in the lock below. I was at the top with two ropes over my shoulders. The Frenchman was nowhere to be seen.

6. Serious Talking

THE BOAT DROPPED DOWN THE LAST LOCK OF THE CANAL. Once again we were in saltwater. If everything went according to plan, the next time freshwater would lap against the hull would be in the Panama Canal. Laura still had a few more days' holiday left. She wasn't happy about going out to sea with just the two of us aboard, but I was anxious to make as much progress as possible. I got the charts out and showed her how well sheltered the Scottish sea lochs on the west coast are. She mumbled something about it being a bad idea but came round to it in the end.

The passage through the canal had been a good one, and I was hoping that the sailing would be easy and help bolster Laura's confidence. Loch Linnhe, the first sealoch you enter when leaving the Caledonian Canal, is as close to a Norwegian fjord as you get anywhere outside Norway. The Grampian mountains rise up out of the sea on one side and the North-west Highlands plunge into the sea on the other. The wind usually blows up this loch from the open sea, bouncing off the side of the two mountain ranges as it funnels through. Its direction and strength, as we were about to find out, can change very suddenly and in unpredictable ways.

At first the wind was light, which allowed us to hoist full sail. The small villages on either side floated past, and Laura scrutinised each one with the binoculars, which she hung round her neck. They looked better on her than any necklace I had ever seen. The wind began to pick up, just a little, and a few clouds darkened the sky. I took some canvas down to be on the safe side. There was a dark patch of sky ahead. It looked like rain advancing up the loch. Before I had even thought of taking more sail down, a rain squall was upon us. It was so sudden that it knocked the boat right over, putting the headsail in the water. Laura is always expecting the boat to sink and has great faith in life-jackets. While I worked on taking the sails in, she rushed down below to put her jacket on and get one for me. As she was doing this, a bottle of red wine, which was sitting in a side locker, became airborne. It flew straight past her head, crashed into the other side of the cabin above the chart table and smashed. The red wine flowed over the chart on the table, whereupon Loch Linnhe became a deep shade of burgundy. The wine then seeped through the hinged opening of the chart table before percolating through the Sound of Jura, the Irish Sea (North and South), the Bay of Biscay, and on down to Cape Finisterre, where the remains of it were soaked up by the Atlantic Ocean.

I managed to bring the boat under control fairly quickly and thought it diplomatic to put on the life-jacket that Laura insisted I wear. The squalls continued for most of the day, with the rain coming down in bucketloads. When it was at its most torrential, the visibility dropped to less than 50 yards. Laura remained remarkably cheerful, but there were a few 'I told you so' glances.

By late afternoon, the squalls had all but passed and we decided to put in to the town of Oban, where we tied up alongside a classic 60-foot wooden yacht. We hung the charts up to dry like washing on a line inside the cabin before going ashore to see the sights. Oban has plenty of shops that sell red wine, and it also has a railway station. We walked about the town, bought some wine, then checked out the times of trains going south.

When we returned to the dock and climbed over the classic 60-footer, we bumped into a frogman about to jump over the side. There was lots of commotion, and it turned out that this beautiful ship had run aground on rocks earlier that day. The frogman had been hired to dive down to inspect the damage to her keel. You say odd things to strangers on other boats, and I asked this man in a rubber suit, as he was just about to jump off, to have a look at my bottom. He came up after about five minutes, reporting minor damage to my boat and serious damage to the big 60-footer.

I had a lot of sympathy for their skipper, but I couldn't understand how they had run aground. Oban opens up to a wide bay, and the entrance is easy from every direction. Although there is a submerged rock ledge to the south of the town and a rock shelf to the north, they are both well buoyed. The buoys are also shown on the charts and in sailing handbooks. The rock ledge in the south of the bay is marked by a buoy at either end, and you can go round the ledge anyway you like. Apparently, they had misread the chart and the buoys. Instead of going round the ledge, they had gone straight on to it. Somehow they managed to get off. You learn not to be judgmental at sea, and when I had a word with the skipper, who had chartered the boat for a two-week sailing holiday, I quoted Gorbachev's words to him, when, after the failed coup that eventually led to his downfall, a hostile reporter asked whether he thought he had made any mistakes Gorbachev snapped back, 'It's only people that don't do things that don't make mistakes.'

Laura's stay was coming to an end. We had some serious talking to do. My plans for the trip were in tatters, and she knew it. I was fast running out of money, and the crew arrangements, which I thought would be so easy, were giving me a real headache. I was so far behind schedule that the time had come and gone for those who said they would join me in the early part of the trip. My brother and one of his friends had been waiting for me in Ireland for weeks. I had been phoning him up every time I was in port to explain the delays. He had never done any sailing and couldn't understand why I wasn't where I was supposed to be. Once Laura left, I would be on my own in Oban with no crew to get to Ireland. I told her that I was going to do the trip on my own, but she refused to consider it. She kept reminding me that I had never done any sailing on my own and that Aidan had told her that the engine wasn't even working properly (I told him not to). When she pointed out that it was unfair of me to cause her any more worry than I already had, I knew the argument was lost, so we worked out between us what I would say to my brother to get him and his mate over to Oban.

The crew arrangements for the next week had been sorted out but that still left the rest of our lives. 'What about you and me, John?' she asked. I had dreaded this moment for a long time and came up with a string of facile platitudes which convinced neither of us. I knew that once she got on that train, I wouldn't see her for a long time and that she and I would have to cope with the pressures of our diverging lives on our own.

When friends had asked me if I was frightened about making the trip, I had glibly stated that there were three things that I stood to lose. I could lose the boat, and had already nearly done so when running aground outside Berwick. That would be a financial setback, but if it happened I could accept it. I could lose my life, and had already nearly done so when I jumped into the sail. Although I would probably go kicking, screaming and crying, I could accept it as a theoretical possibility. The famous passage from James Joyce's book *Dubliners*, which begins 'Better to go bravely into that other world . . . ', always came to my mind when I considered this theoretical possibility. And, finally, I could lose Laura. This was the most likely thing of all and the prospect that frightened me most.

She had just got a new job and would be taking up the appointment in a week or so. She would be moving to another city where she knew no one. She would meet new, interesting people, and I wouldn't be around. I knew that there were lots of male sexual predators about and that some of them would already have their eye on her. There were probably two or three just waiting for me to leave before they pounced. With the recent death of her mother, and with no brothers or sisters to fall back on, she would be lonely while I was away. I also knew that she would have a host of problems settling into a new job and finding a new home and from time to time she would pine for a shoulder to lean on. I knew all these things but had answers for none of them.

We had no conventional ties binding us, which up until now I had always thought was a sign of a strong relationship – no shared property, no children, no wedding certificate and no in-laws to appease. We both had our financial independence and exercised it. We had been together for a long time and there had been ups and downs but we always stayed together. Neither of us knew what would happen in the next two years, and we were both unhappy about the thought of being separated. I felt I had to make the trip because I knew I would never get another chance, but I didn't want to lose her. She thought there was a strong possibility that I would disappear at sea and didn't want me to go. We talked, half-jokingly, about the idea of me pretending to go, and Laura suggested that she could hide me. We could fly out to exotic places, from where I could send postcards home. There were no real answers or solutions, only pretend ones: it looked as though this might be the end of the line. We were both desperately sad and resolved nothing.

The next day, the big yacht cast off in a clumsy manner, banging into my stern in the process. The second shelf of submerged rock was as clearly marked as the first but they headed straight for it – right between the buoy and the shore. Five minutes later the boat was lying over on its side and the lifeboat had been launched to haul it off. Laura and I left the scene of the drama to walk the short distance to the railway station. The train was already waiting on the platform, ready to leave. She boarded it and leaned out of the window. I held on to her hand as the train started to pull out. When her hand slipped from mine, I felt like running after the train to jump aboard, but I just stood there, watching it disappear.

The reality of what I was doing came crashing down upon me. I had a good job, sound health and a woman who loved me. Most men would have given their eye teeth for her, but here was I, selfishly indulging my whims, leaving her and taking off in a beat-up boat going nowhere slowly – all because of a book I had read as a child.

But there was more to it than that. I knew that life, which can be snuffed out in an instant, is very short. I also knew that it is very easy to fall into a comfortable routine that leads inexorably to the grave. Most men are forced to lead lives of subdued frustration and end up getting stuck in a groove. The only difference between being in a groove and in a grave is one of depth. Along the way to that grave in the comfortable groove, you might get a new car or a greenhouse or, if you really hit the big time, a holiday home – but these things are palliatives, the opiate of a materialistic lifestyle that is impoverished through lack of meaning. I wasn't interested in the trappings of material success – all they lead to is entrapment in spiritual failure – and the conventional rewards of career advancement meant nothing to me. With each passing year, I knew I would become more enfeebled and the mad passions of youth would give way to the cautious sobriety of middle age. Whatever happened, I didn't want to end up slumped in an armchair in an old people's home looking back on a life of comfortable but frustrated existence.

I also knew that the world is a big, beautiful place, and I wanted to experience as much of it as I could in the split second of eternity that was allocated to me. I had seen too many of my friends die young to wait any longer to fulfil my dream. It was self-indulgent and it wasn't working out as planned – but what the hell. Life was too precious to be squandered in denying dreams, even if they turned out to be sour. I was determined to try to take hold of my life and squeeze every drop out of it. There is no God, no meaning, no purpose – all we have is love and existential experience. The sea was where I might lose one but where I knew I would find the other.

7. *Roy and Walko*

I WANDERED ROUND OBAN AIMLESSLY. I HAD NO STOMACH to go back to my own boat nor any interest in seeing what remained of the classic wooden yacht that had fetched up on the rock ledge. Anyway, I had another appointment in the station later that day. My brother, Roy, and his friend, John Walko, were due to arrive.

This time the train wasn't on the platform, so I sat on the side with the sunshine, smoking a few cigarettes. The train turned up more or less on time. I could see my brother, Roy, who is much taller than I am, from a long way off. He was wearing his best casual summer gear, had a suitcase in his hand and a guitar slung over his shoulder. Walko, with his shining, bald head, was walking along beside him, and they were engaged in animated conversation. It was clear they had both been drinking – and why not? They were on their holidays, had left their worries behind, and for the next week or so were determined to do everything they could to enjoy themselves.

Roy greeted me with the usual brotherly banter, complaining about me messing him around over the last two or three weeks. I tried to explain that it was all beyond my control but he wasn't really interested. He thought that I had been hanging back to spend more time with Laura. Walko played the peacemaker straight away, saying, 'Now come on boys, you're brothers, I hope you're not goin' to fight all week, 'cause if you are, I'm gettin' back on that train and goin' home.'

I offered to buy them a drink. They readily accepted. We went into a small bar near the harbour, from where we could see the boat through the window. Neither of them had ever been aboard a sailboat before, and they were both dying of curiosity. After one drink, I took them down to the *Warrior Queen*.

When they climbed aboard, I could see that they were taking everything in. Walko went below first and asked, 'Where's the bedrooms?'

I showed him the forepeak cabin and told him that they could share it. Nearly every sentence Walko spoke contained at least one swearword. The next one was no exception. 'I'm not sleeping in there with that bastard of a brother of yours.'

Roy had already sized up the aft cabin and said he would sleep there. This was my one private space on the boat and, big brother or no big brother, he wasn't having it. We worked out that Roy could sleep in the main cabin, Walko would have the forepeak, and I would stay where I was.

The tour continued. Walko opened the door to the head and said, 'Jesus Christ, Roy, have you seen this wee toilet?'

They both squeezed in to have a good look. 'Can I ask a serious question now, John?' Walko said, pointing his finger at me.

'Go ahead.'

'Where does all the stuff go when you do something?'

'Straight out to sea.'

'You're jokin', aren't you, you're jokin'?'

They both looked rather shocked and somewhat disgusted. 'How do you flush it then?' asked Walko.

I pumped the handle beside the bowl up and down. The water in the bottom bubbled a little as I did so. Walko recoiled in horror with visions, which he graphically described, of the 'stuff' bubbling back, splashing into your face. While walking through the main cabin, Walko bumped against the cooker, which was resting on its gimbals. These allow the stove to swing freely, remaining horizontal when at sea. It rocked from side to side after he knocked into it. 'I think you'd better fix this, John,' he said, stopping it with his hand.

He then sat down at the chart table to have a quick look at one of the British Admiralty charts. After a short while, he exclaimed, 'Hey, John, there's no friggin' roads on this map.' He noticed the chart-table light, which was fixed on a flexible mounting that allows you to alter its position, the way you do with some microphones. Walko pulled the light down towards his mouth and said into the bulb, 'Eyes down, Ladies and Gentlemen, the bingo game is about to start.'

The various navigational instruments above the chart table fascinated him, and he asked, 'John, seriously now, do you know how to use all this stuff?' When I assured him that I did, he replied, 'Well, it's a good job somebody does, 'cause I haven't a clue.'

They unpacked their clean, smartly pressed summer clothes, which they put away neatly in the lockers. Roy asked me to show him how to use the cooker so that he could make a cup of tea. Walko sat in the cockpit with me, cracking a few more jokes while admiring the boat. Roy then came up with three steaming mugs of tea. They had been drinking all day and needed the tea. Roy was the first to take a big mouthful. His eyes bulged, nearly popping out of their sockets. He then spat the tea all over Walko. 'What the hell's wrong with you?' asked Walko, showing genuine concern.

All Roy could say was, 'Taste it, go on, just taste it.'

Walko took a small sip, spat his tea over Roy, and spurted out, 'It's bloody seawater!'

There were two hand pumps in the galley. One of them was installed to draw water directly from the sea for washing dishes when on long passages. It had not been intended for use when making tea. 'You just think about it, Roy. All these boats are crappin' in this water and we're makin' tea with it and drinkin' it,' were Walko's last words on the subject.

That evening, we went out for a few drinks. I did my best to catch up with them. Walko was telling anyone that would listen that he was a sailor, helping me to take the yacht to Ireland. By the time we got back to the boat, it was past midnight and everyone was well oiled. Roy got his guitar out to gave us the first song, which was an Irish sea shanty about a ship called the 'Irish Rover'. Walko was busting to have a go. He picked up the gas lighter – a plastic spark-making implement about ten inches long – it would do as a microphone prop. John Walko then crooned a sad song into the gas lighter while Roy gently strummed his guitar. The sing-song tradition in Ireland is that the singer who has the floor (and the microphone), has to do two songs. Walko gave us a second. It was my turn next. I took the gas lighter from Walko, began with 'Some Enchanted Evening' and finished with a Paul Robeson spiritual called 'It Takes a Long Pull to Get There'. The gas lighter was passed from hand to hand. When Roy was singing and playing the guitar, Walko sat beside him, holding it under his face. The good order that was present at the start of the sing-song, with each singer being allowed two songs at a time, didn't last. It wasn't long before certain people in the company were insisting on doing a third song. We resolved these temporary difficulties by agreeing to do duets, where two of us each had a hand on the gas lighter. As the night wore on, the gas lighter became a microphone. It was impossible to sing without it and impossible not to sing when you had it in your hand. We danced around the cabin in between scuffles for the gas lighter and beat out rhythms on the chart table. There was a stainless-steel pole down the middle of the cabin which Walko took to in a big way. He kept sliding up against it, declaring his undying love. 'I love this pole, John, I just love it – I can't help myself. Can I take the pole home with me?' I told him I'd get him another pole but he wasn't interested. The quality of the singing and the songs deteriorated with each extra drink, and we ended up singing maudlin ballads by Barry Manilow and Neil Diamond. It was a good party.

The wind was blowing fresh from the south-west next morning, which meant that it would be dead in front of us. The plan was for the three of us to get the boat to Dublin. With the right conditions we could make the passage in about 30 hours but south-westerly winds were not the right conditions. We hung about for a day or two, waiting for the wind to shift or drop off. Neither of these things happened, so we had no alternative but to get going under power. On the day we left, I waited for the lunchtime shipping forecast while Roy and Walko went ashore to have a few pints of Guinness. After they returned, we motored out past the buoys and headed towards the Sound of Jura.

Roy, who had decided to assume the role of cook while at sea, busied himself preparing a late breakfast of bacon and eggs. Neither of them had any idea what to expect. Roy was struggling with the gimballed stove as the boat made erratic and bumpy headway against the advancing choppy seas. By the time my breakfast was served up, I was ravenous and thoroughly enjoyed it. Walko watched me eat it, screwing up his face a little. He then shouted down to Roy to tell him that he was going to skip breakfast. We were now well out of the relative shelter of Oban Harbour, and Roy was beginning to have second thoughts about being cook. There was lots of mumbling going on over the stove. It took him some time before he managed to prepare his own breakfast, which he brought out to the cockpit to eat. When he came up, he got his first view of the open sea. He looked at his breakfast and lost his appetite. I was still hungry and ate it for him.

We had to motor down a long, narrow channel where the wind strengthened as it squeezed through. The seas got bigger. It was an uncomfortable passage, but not too difficult. John Walko was already beginning to look a bit dodgy even before he got drenched by a wave that broke over the bow. I saw it coming from a mile off and ducked at the last minute. John just stood there in disbelief as it poured over him. He went down below to change his clothes and called out that he would be using the toilet for a short while. He went into the head, closing the door behind him.

Roy and I were now in our waterproofs, and he had learned to duck when a wave broke over the bow. Progress was so slow that I could only convince Roy we were actually moving by showing him how to take a compass bearing on a headland and checking the bearing some time later. Walko was still in the head. When we reached the end of the channel after a couple of hours, the sea opened up to the full blast of the south-westerly wind and the passage became even slower. The engine revs were rising and falling, which is a bad sign. Roy picked up on this immediately. 'Is this engine alright?' he asked anxiously. I told him not to worry, saying it was just an effect of the movement of the boat. My fingers, in the pockets of my waterproof trousers, were crossed, and I hoped it wouldn't cut out. It droned on, the revs rising and falling, for another hour, and then stopped. I let some headsail out straight away to give us some control, because if a boat is not making way there is no steerage. Roy steadied the boat very skilfully, while I dug out a large jerry can of fuel from a locker to top up the tank. Whatever the problem was, it always seemed to cure itself when I topped the tank up. The engine started again and we carried on. Walko was still in the head.

Roy wanted to know where we were going and how long it would take to get there, but I was keen to make as much progress as possible and keep going for as long as we were able. I showed him the charts and explained that when we got in the lee of the Isle of Jura, we would get a lot of shelter and it would be much easier. He accepted this but was still unhappy about not knowing where we were going.

The narrow entrance to the northern end of the Sound of Jura is a mysterious place. The tide rushes past the northern tip of Jura, forming the infamous Corryvreckan tide race. Many small boats have foundered there – George Orwell nearly lost his life in an open boat when he was caught in this helter-skelter of water. It was strange to think that if the sea had taken him that day, 1984 would be a year just like any other and there would be only one meaning for the term 'big brother'. Roy quickly learned to read the charts and helped me navigate this stretch of water. As we went through the narrows, it was as if three or four rivers were all meeting at the same place, pushing each other to one side. When we had passed through safely, I knew that my brother had done well and that he was pleased with his work. We stood in the cockpit, surveying the narrows as they fell astern. Roy was beginning to enjoy himself. Walko was still in the head.

The next major obstacle was rounding the Mull of Kintyre. We would have to put in somewhere for the night before having a go at this, but with persistent south-westerly winds, it was going to be very difficult to weather this headland. Roy and I had both gone down to talk to John in the head from time to time. He was clearly not well and could not be coaxed out. He assured us that he was alright and we let him be. He stayed in the head.

By now Roy was studying the charts and cruising guidebooks, coming up with suggestions about where we should go. Instead of sailing round the Mull of Kintyre, it is possible to cut through the Crinan Canal to the Firth of Clyde. The Clyde is very sheltered and can be sailed down all the way to Stranraer, from where it is only a short hop over to Ireland. Roy convinced me that this was the best option. Late that night we edged into the sealock of the canal. Once again the boat was about to re-enter fresh-water — so much for Panama.

Conditions had settled down as we approached the canal entrance. John came out of the head. He had been in this small toilet compartment for over ten hours. He looked drawn and pale but said he felt alright. There was a small hotel nearby. After climbing up the vertical wall of the sea-lock, we went there. All John Walko would have to drink was a Coke. My brother and I sat down at a table but John wanted to stand. He stood with his back to us, his face close to a wall, upon which hung a painting of a sailship. He stood like this for a long time before Roy said, 'Come and sit down, John. Come on . . . pull a chair up, join in the conversation. Sit down and make yourself more comfortable.'

All Walko said was, 'I'm alright.' He stood where he was without moving or saying another word. He kept his back to us and his eye on the painting of the sailship.

We entered the canal early next morning. Walko was much improved for a good night's sleep. The Crinan Canal wasn't a patch on the Caledonian but it was a restful day and just what Walko needed. We managed to get through in a day and entered the sea again in the Firth of Clyde. I no longer had any interest in thinking about the next time the boat would be in freshwater. The Clyde is a popular cruising ground, with quite a few marinas, and a short sail took us to a newly built one.

The forecast for the next day was once again south-westerly winds. Now that we were in the Firth of Clyde, the course was southerly so we just might be able to sail some of the way. My plan, for what it was worth, was to sail straight to Dublin. Roy and Walko weren't interested in night sailing, but I knew that if the weather was settled and we were making good progress I could talk them into it.

Once we left the marina and started heading due south, it was clear that the wind had shifted from the south-west – it had shifted to the south! Dead on the nose once more. This time we had more shelter, so the passage was not as uncomfortable as when we left Oban, and we were able to make slightly better progress under power. Walko had his sea legs by now and was back to his usual self. By late afternoon we were approaching more exposed water, and the wind once more began to pick up. Roy wanted to know where we were going to put in. I suggested that we keep going all through the night. Our destination was Ireland and I saw no way of getting there other than staying at sea until we reached it. I knew that Roy and Walko had a very tight schedule and were running out of time. They were the only crew I had and I needed them to get across the Irish Sea.

Roy didn't like it but Walko resigned himself to it very well and was content to keep the peace between the two of us. He kept telling Roy, 'John's the captain, you know. We have to do whatever he says, that's the way it is on boats.' At dusk I lit the paraffin lamp in the main cabin. Roy and Walko stayed down below and had private mumbled conversations while I stayed out in the cockpit. The wind was building all the time and it started to rain heavily. I went down below to arrange a watch-keeping routine for the night but it was clear that there was very little enthusiasm. Roy hadn't given up and was urging me to put in. I compromised by saying we would just keep going for the time being and make our minds up later on. It was a very dark night. Rain squalls started to come through. After the second squall, we were making so little progress that it was hardly worth carrying on, so I decided reluctantly to head for harbour. After studying the charts, Roy and I eventually agreed on the port in the town of Ayr. This was slightly further south than where he wanted to go, but I was anxious to make good every mile. There were 14,000 more to get to Sydney – each one gained was one less to go.

The south coast of the Firth of Clyde, all the way down to Ayr, is well developed, and the whole coastline was ablaze with lights. Identifying the harbour lights is very difficult if you have never been there before. There is an off-lying, uninhabited island close to the town. This has a lighthouse on it, which we could already see, so we headed in its general direction. The squalls now gave way to continuous torrential rain. At times the rain was so heavy that all visibility was lost: the lights along the coast and on the uninhabited island went out as if turned off by a switch. To add to the general gloom, thunderclaps and flashes of lightning accompanied the heavy downpours.

Roy was out in the cockpit with me during one of these. He was moaning a bit, saying that I'd never told him it was going to be like this. He then turned to me and asked very seriously, 'Why are you doing this? This is *wick*.'

I thought for a long time before answering him and said, 'I'm not really sure. But I do know that for all this shite I have to go through, there will be moments of pure rapture later on.' He didn't believe me.

The thunderstorm intensified, and I tried to put out of my mind what would happen if we were struck by lightning. The lighthouse kept disappearing from view. If the engine cut out now we would be finished. The island was close and we were passing it on the windward side, which meant we would be driven on to it in no time. Roy was plotting our position every five minutes. By the time we were level with the island, everyone's nerves were getting close to breaking point. I looked down into the cabin to see Roy standing beside the chart table with the VHF microphone in his hand. I thought he had cracked and was trying to call the coastguard for help. 'Put that down, you don't know how to use it,' I yelled.

Roy looked at me and then at the microphone in his hand. He then said, very quietly, 'It's just come loose and I'm putting it back where it came from.'

I felt deeply ashamed. I had raised my voice in anger to my own brother, who had done nothing wrong. He was my big brother, who as a child was always better at things than me, and here I was shouting at him simply because it was my boat and I thought I knew a little more about it than he did.

There wasn't much talking after that. Instead we all stood in the cockpit like drowned rats, peering into the dark to try to pick up the harbour lights. As we did so, a strange, shadowy shape came into view on the starboard beam. I was the first to see it and pointed it out to Roy and Walko. It looked like a half-submerged, large whale moving slowly through the water. We examined it with the binoculars and

could see a bow wave and a wake – it was a submarine! The Clyde is
one of the main submarine-training grounds for the Royal Navy. There
have been numerous reports over the years of fishing vessels disappearing mysteriously at sea, and the finger of suspicion has been
pointed at these submarine exercises. When Walko exclaimed, 'That's
all we need, a bloody submarine!' the comic dimensions of the situation became apparent and everyone laughed nervously. I switched on
every light that I had, lighting the boat up like a Christmas tree. The
submarine moved slowly away amid the rumble of thunder and flashes
of lightning.

After several hours searching for the harbour lights, we eventually
picked them up, entered the river in Ayr, and tied up opposite the fish
quay. Everyone was wiped out. It was 2.0 a.m. and the streets of the town
were deserted.

Next morning, the wind was blowing at near gale force from the
south-west, which meant there was no possibility of going anywhere. The
forecast indicated that these conditions were likely to persist for a few
days. Roy and Walko wanted to go home, and I couldn't blame them. The
berth opposite the fish quay was very uncomfortable, but I had noticed on
the chart that there was a more sheltered basin just inside the harbour
entrance. A fisherman in the boat alongside called the harbour master on
the VHF to ask if we could move up to the basin. The harbour master said
it would be OK for a day or two, so I asked Roy and Walko to do me one
last favour and help me move the boat.

The basin turned out to be a dismal place. There were no ships in it
and it seemed to have accumulated all the flotsam and jetsam of the west
coast of Scotland. Huge piles of coal and scrap metal were stacked up
along its edges. Gantries stood idle while a few lorries deposited more
coal and scrap metal. The open sea was on the far side of the basin wall
that we were tied up against. The wall itself was so high that the top of it
was well above the masthead. Although it took all the sting out of the sea,
which battered against it, the wind came straight over the top, blowing
coal dust everywhere.

Roy and Walko took their unused, freshly ironed summer clothes out
of the lockers and packed their bags. We struggled to pull the boat in
against the wall to allow us to get to the ladder and passed the suitcases
and the guitar up to the top. They were both feeling very sorry for me.
Roy asked, 'What are you going to do here all on your own?'

I tried to put a brave face on it, saying I would just wait till the
weather changed.

Walko then asked, 'Aren't you depressed, John?' When I said not

THE BREATH OF ANGELS

really, he promptly replied, 'Well, I'd be friggin' depressed,' and Roy and I both laughed.

I left them to the railway station and was sorry to see them go. If the weather had been better or the wind had gone round to the west or north or east, we would all be in Dublin now, sitting in a bar drinking Guinness. But they were on the train home. I was on my own and I was depressed.

8. *An Englishman, a Scotsman and an Irishman*

AYR IS AN ATTRACTIVE, PROSPEROUS TOWN, DESPITE THE dismal, semi-derelict industrial basin. It also has a yacht club for small, bilge-keel boats that can take the ground and sit in the mud on their twin short keels. After spending the afternoon in town, I strolled down to the club in the early evening to try to find some crew. It was more of a social club than anything else, and although everyone was very friendly they were not able to help. I tried the bars in town later on, asking anyone who I got talking to if they would like to sail with me to Ireland. They probably regarded me as some sort of a nutcase, which I may well have been, and I had no luck.

After midnight, I picked my solitary way through the scrap metal and slag heaps before climbing down the ladder to the boat. I kept hanging on to those moments of pure rapture that would surely come and went to bed in reasonable spirits. It was hard to sustain these in the morning because the wind was still whistling in from the south-west and the whole deck of the boat was covered in thick coal dust. The debris in the basin had found a new object to cluster around, and there was all sorts of rubbish jammed in between the now blackened hull of the boat and the wall, including a tree trunk about 20 feet long with sharp branches sticking out in every direction. Even the lorries that had been around the day before seemed to have deserted the place.

Crew or no crew, I had to get out of there. There was a marina about five miles back up the coast. Although I had never gone out in a boat on my own before, it would be quite simple to motor to the marina because the wind would be behind me. I could even hoist the sails and sail there. It was straightforward motoring out of the harbour, but when I tried to hoist the mainsail I got the main halyard hopelessly entangled. Eventually, I managed to get into Troon marina without too much bother. I could see people looking at me and the boat strangely. My clothes were covered in coal dust, and although the hull had been washed clean by the seawater, the decks were still black.

It was like going into a five-star hotel after having spent a few nights in a dosshouse, but instead of jumping into the bath in the hotel room, I used the water hose on the pontoon to give the decks a good scrub before having a shower in the clubhouse. Laura and I had been keeping in touch by telephone, so she knew that I had no crew and that the wind was forecast to continue blowing hard from the south-west. She suggested that I just leave the boat in the safety of the marina and catch the next train to Newcastle. It didn't take much to persuade me. When we said goodbye in Oban, I had not expected to see her again until Christmas. We had talked about the most likely place I would be at that time – Panama, that old favourite of mine, was the number-one contender.

It took me three-and-a-half hours, on a slow train, to cover the ground that had taken me three-and-a-half weeks by boat. I wondered whether you could buy such a thing as a round-the-world rail ticket. The train journey gave me an opportunity to consider the progress, or lack of it, I had made so far. I tried to be as objective as possible – there was no denying that I had been a bit unlucky. Since leaving Whitby, the wind had either been gale force, non-existent or dead ahead. There was nothing I could do about that. I hadn't been able to sail towards my destination for more than an hour or so at any one time and I had, and still had, serious gear problems. Most of these could have been averted if there had been more time to sea-trial the boat but there was no point worrying about that now. The crew arrangements had been difficult to organise, with people joining me for a very short time, and all of the crew had very little, if any, experience. Given all these problems, I had probably done as much as I could have reasonably expected.

When I got to Laura's place, she took good care of me. All I wanted to do was stay in bed in the morning and sit on a sofa in the evening, watching TV. I had never appreciated the sheer luxury of it all before. It occurred to me that maybe I should leave the boat in Troon and call the whole thing off. I could rationalise it by saying that the boat needed a lot of work (which it did) and that by the time all this was done, it would be too late in the year to cross Biscay. But I didn't seriously consider it. I also had to think about the newspapers. The press officer at the university where I worked had put out a press release before my departure. I had been plastered all over the local papers. A NIGHT AT THE OPERA FOR CAPTAIN CULTURE ran one headline. There was worse. The local paper in Whitby, whose most famous son is James Cook RN, described me as '. . . following in the footsteps of Captain Cook' (ha ha).

I decided to stay with Laura until the persistent south-west wind changed, using the time to try to sort out crew. Of the two people who expressed a serious interest in joining me in response to my advertisement, one had signed up with the Royal Navy at the last minute, and the other one signed up with me. He had arranged to meet me in Ireland, where he already was, staying with some friends in Dublin. He was going to join me for eight months, by which time I hoped to be in Tahiti. As long as I could get to Dublin soon, my crew problems would be well on their way to being taken care of. After a lot of phone-calls, I found my crew: a good friend called Tim from England and a stranger called Kenny from Scotland, whose telephone number I got from a noticeboard in a yacht club. They could both join me for a weekend, which should be time enough to make the passage.

Laura travelled with me to the boat the night before I was about to sail. We went through the same agonising about our future that we had been through in Oban but still managed to make a good night of it. Kenny, who struck me as being a rather earnest young man, was the first to turn up the next morning. Tim weighed in about an hour later, greeting me with the customary, 'Well then, Johnnie Boy, how are you doing?' He had the same million-dollar smile on his face that I had seen so many times before and which I always told him was his best asset. Tim and I had been on a few sailing holidays in the past and there had been plenty of good times together.

It was now September, which can be a time of unsettled weather. The forecast was somewhat uncertain. The wind was currently light and had shifted to the south-east. With the rapid advance of an Atlantic low-pressure system, it was expected to increase to possibly gale force in 24 hours. As the sun was shining brightly, I didn't really believe this forecast, and in any case we could probably be across the Irish Sea, snug in harbour before the bad weather came. There was a little weather window, which I had to take. Being the weekend, I tried to persuade Laura to come with us but she had more sense. She stood on the end of the dock, waving us off as we headed south towards the Irish Sea. I didn't know where or when I would see her again.

The sail down the last stretch of the Firth of Clyde was very pleasant. Kenny quickly learned how to handle the sails. Tim and I let him get on with it while we sat up at the bow drinking a few beers. I was quite optimistic. Once we reached the end of the firth, it was less than 20 miles across to the coast of Ireland and another 80 down to Dublin. We had supper late in the afternoon, by which time the sun had stopped shining and the wind had freshened. Kenny turned out to be a committed Scottish nationalist, and the dinner conversation revolved around politics. By nightfall, we hadn't cleared the firth. The wind shifted to the south, continuing to increase in strength. It raced through those three tell-tale points of the Beaufort Scale in less than an hour, and I thought about putting into port. But it wasn't far across to Ireland. With a good crew we should make it before the weather got much worse.

When we entered the Irish Sea, the wind was blowing straight from the south, which meant that we could forget about going to Dublin. But we could just manage to sail a south-westerly course which would bring us to the entrance of Belfast Lough, where there is plenty of shelter and places to moor. It did mean sailing close to the wind, which is always difficult and is probably why it's called beating. Little did we realise just then the beating we were about to take that night.

The forecast had said that there *might* be gales in 24 hours. In less than 12 hours after leaving, the full gale was upon us. The weather window had closed. Kenny emptied his supper out of his stomach, the sight of which had Tim doing likewise, but they both managed to keep going. There was no more talk of politics and Tim's million-dollar smile turned into a two-bit grimace. The boat was being pounded by the seas, which were building all the time, as we tried to sail the south-westerly course. Our speed dropped right off. The gale intensified. The wind was so strong that it became difficult to control the movement of your arms and body. We took turns of one hour on the wheel, making sure that we were clipped in at all times. By the end of the hour, the helmsman was all washed up and had to go below to try to rest. The noise from the pounding of the seas, as they crashed against the boat, was amplified in the cabin. It was impossible to rest with all the racket; it was like being inside a drum. Each loud bang and thud jarred the nerves and shook the body. Only the dead could have slept through it.

From time to time, we glimpsed lighthouses on the Irish coast but they never seemed to get any closer. White spume was being blown off the top of the waves, and the decks, fore and aft, were awash with water. The cockpit was permanently flooded with breaking seas that can easily dump a ton of water on top of the boat in less than a second. The companionway boards had been removed briefly, to allow access, when one such sea broke over us. Bathtubs full of this water poured down into the main cabin: for each bathtub that came in, 50 bucketfuls had to go out. Inside the main cabin, shoes, tins of food and pencils floated in the water, swept from one side to the other. With the boat thrown all over the place by the colliding waves, anyone trying to rest down below had to jam their bodies into a corner and wedge themselves in with their feet. As Tim was walking through the narrow aisle of the main cabin, a violent lurch to one side threw him off balance. He fell backwards towards the chart table, smacking his head against a piece of solid teak. The sound of that smack could be heard above the din, and for a moment Kenny and I feared the worst. I cupped his head in my hands to examine it. Within minutes he had a lump on the back of it like something out of a Tom and Jerry cartoon.

Tim probably thought it was safer in the cockpit and squeezed himself in beside me when it was my turn on the wheel. We spent about five minutes trying to light a cigarette, and only got it going after Tim buried his head inside my waterproofs. There is something profoundly intimate about sharing a cigarette with a friend in a full-blown gale at sea. I found the presence of his body beside me and the sight of his face close up to mine very reassuring. The little red glowing light at the end of the cigarette kept lighting up his face each time he took a drag. I could see that he was looking at me very intently for any outward sign of anxiety – the way that a passenger on a plane might look at the air hostess after the pilot makes an unexpected announcement – so I did my best to keep smiling.

While sharing that cigarette, I noticed something strange going on just behind the stern of the boat. There appeared to be a large fish jumping out of the water every now and again. When I mentioned it to Tim, he said that he had seen it as well but thought it was the after-effects of the smack on the head. It's easy for one person to hallucinate, but when two people see the same thing it's not hallucination. Whatever it was, it wasn't likely to be a fish. As we caught more glimpses of it in the white froth, it suddenly came to me what it was. My wind self-steering gear had an auxiliary rudder that could be detached when not in use. This rudder had been left on the aft deck, where it was secured by a strong rope. It had been washed overboard by the waves flooding the deck and was now being trailed along behind us. It was about four feet long with four sharp corners. There was a strong possibility that, as it flew out of the water, it could bash against the fibreglass hull, doing serious damage. It had to be retrieved or cut free.

The *Warrior Queen* has a centre cockpit and a small deck behind the aft cabin. The stern of the boat is about ten feet from the cockpit. To catch this big flying fish, I had to make my way back to the stern. Tim checked my harness and life-line by tugging it violently. I climbed over the side of the cockpit to crawl along the deck. Pulling myself along with my hands, I made sure that all of my body was pressed down hard and flat on the deck. The freezing-cold water from the breaking waves washed over me. Tim and Kenny stood in silence, watching. It was the longest ten feet I ever crawled. When I got to the stern the line on the rudder was so tight that I wasn't able to pull it in right away. No real fish ever struggled as hard as that self-steering rudder but, bit by bit, it came in.

That night, each hour seemed to last forever as the sea raged about us. White masses of water rushed past on every side, and the mast shook with each violent gust of wind. The blades on the wind generator were turning so fast that it sounded like a helicopter. The generator was mounted on a pole, and the vibrations set up by the spinning blades shook one of the supporting stays loose. The whole contraption wobbled backwards and forwards, threatening to disintegrate at any moment. We were cold, wet, tired and frightened. Although I was beginning, in a strange way, to resign myself to this sort of thing, I'm sure the other two wondered why on earth they had come in the first place. The one consolation I had was that I had not been able to persuade Laura to join us.

By dawn, with visibility closed in, we had lost sight of the lighthouses. There was hardly any progress to show for all the long hours of bashing into the sea, and it was clear that we couldn't make Belfast Lough. Everyone was devastated. Tim was becoming more and more irritated, which is a sure sign of exhaustion. Both he and Kenny had been seasick several more times. Tim was on the wheel while I was poring over the charts, which were soaked through, when he shouted out, 'Where's Kenny, tell him to get up here.' Poor old Kenny, who looked a bit punch-drunk, was just trying to have a rest, but he struggled to his feet to go out to the cockpit for more punishment. Tim could no longer shout at Kenny, so he had a go at me, 'What are you going to do, John?' I didn't like being shouted at, and told him so in no uncertain terms, without raising my voice. But he was right: we had to change our plan and stop trying to beat into this wind and sea. We altered course towards the port of Larne, which allowed us to sail with the wind coming more behind us, and immediately we started to make better progress. It was still hard going but at least we could make port. Tim's irritation gave way to determination once he knew that port was only a few hours away. Now that we were heading for a port we could make, everyone dug deep and found extra reserves of energy.

Larne Harbour only came into view when it was less than a mile away. I had travelled by ferry from this port many times in the past but I had never seen it look anything like it did now. Even inside the harbour, the water was boiling like a cauldron, and we were lucky to find a mooring buoy to tie up to. It was mid-morning – all we wanted to do was sleep. The passage to Ireland was the hardest I had ever made. The boat had sustained yet more damage, and I never wanted to be out at sea in conditions as bad as that ever again. Tim and Kenny were just glad to be alive.

9. *A Troubled Land*

AFTER SLEEPING FOR THE REST OF THE MORNING AND ALL of the afternoon, we caught the train into Belfast. I wanted to show them both round the city of my birth and take them to my favourite bar. Neither of them had been to Belfast before, and Kenny, as a Scottish nationalist, was particularly interested.

I like to believe that all problems have solutions, but no one had yet found one for the Irish question. As an adolescent, I was living in Belfast at the start of the latest troubles and found it all very exciting. The first petrol bomb that I saw arched its parabolic way through the night sky before bursting into flames. It sent a thrill through me and all of my friends who saw it. The boom from the first real bomb was even better. But once the killing started, I lost interest, and when the sectarian internecine warfare got going, I wanted out.

As long as you know your way around, Belfast is no more dangerous than any other place, but being on the wrong side of a road can put you in the wrong part of town. Tim looked and spoke like an English soldier, Kenny had more than a little sympathy with the cause of Irish nationalism, and I was a Belfast Protestant. We had had plenty of aggravation the night before; none of us wanted any more. It was important that we navigated the politically troubled waters with care, and the best way to achieve this was to stick to the city centre.

We found ourselves an American-style upmarket hamburger restaurant – which every city has – and a bar which only Belfast has – the Crown, in Great Victoria Street. This was the first pub where I got well and truly smashed, as a boy of 16, and it was as magical as ever. There isn't much left of old Belfast but the Crown is the crowning glory of what there is. Engraved gilt mirrors, original working gas lamps, elaborate Italian tile work, and hand-carved mahogany snugs make it a Victorian masterpiece of functional architecture.

We got a snug to ourselves and stacked up the Guinness. The strain of the previous night and the relief of being free from it made us full of life. The conversation was rich – politics, sailing, old friends and women each jostled for a place. I confided to Tim my fears about losing Laura. He gave me advice which was sound but hard to take. 'Well, it's a possibility, John,' he said, 'but if she does go off with someone while you're away, you just have to win her back when you come home. You can do it if you want to.' I wasn't prepared to look at it in these terms and told Tim so. Tim told me I was full of male crap.

The first ferry left Larne early next morning with Tim on it. Kenny took him in the dinghy and returned wearing Tim's good-quality waterproofs, which he had been given as a present. They weren't really Tim's to give away, because he had nicked them from work, but Kenny wasn't worried about that. Kenny was getting a later ferry so we had a chance to talk between ourselves. He told me that he was really glad that he had come on the trip and had enjoyed it tremendously. He said he would love to have stayed aboard but had commitments at home. It's amazing what a difference a bit of sleep makes.

I was once again on my own but at least I was in Ireland. I phoned the chap waiting in Dublin to ask him to travel up north. While I had been struggling to get to Ireland, I had managed to put out of my mind the worries I had about him joining me. Eight months is a very long time to spend with someone you hardly know in the cramped confinement of a small boat. I already had misgivings. He came to Whitby for a week to help get the boat ready before I left, and I wasn't overjoyed with the way things worked out. I had already confided to several friends that, deep down, I thought it was going to be a disaster, but made up my mind to sweep all these thoughts away and start with a clean slate.

We met in the Crown and had a drink in the same snug that I had been in the night before. His name was Terry and he was in his late twenties. He had been working as a building contracting supervisor since leaving college and had saved up enough money to have a few years off work. The conversation was awkward, in stark contrast to the night before, but we were strangers to each other and he was probably worried as much about me as I was about him.

The gale had passed, and we sailed next day for Bangor, just outside Belfast. It was a short trip and gave Terry a chance to get to know the boat. When I brought the boat into the new marina in Bangor, Terry stepped on to the pontoon to secure the bow and stern lines to the cleats. The standard and universally used way of doing this is to put a few figure-of-eight turns around the cleat, before locking it off with a loop in the last turn pulled tight. The locking off with the loop is essential for the rope not to come undone. I noticed that Terry didn't do this but passed no comment. An hour or so later, when we were going ashore, I put the locking loop on each cleat and said to Terry, very casually, that it was always a good idea to do this. He just huffed and said there were lots of ways of doing things. This was not a good start.

Now that I was in Bangor, I took the opportunity to invite all my close relatives down to see the boat. My sister and her husband, along with their two children, were the first to arrive. Tea and cream buns in the cockpit followed the tour of the boat. The kids loved it, and Laura, my little niece, asked a thousand questions. The one way to keep her quiet was to embarrass her, which I could do very easily by singing to her at the top of my voice so that everyone could hear:

> Tell Laura I love her
> Tell Laura I need her
> Tell Laura not to cry
> My love for her, will never die

She buried her face in her hands and tried to disappear.

My brother turned up with his daughter and two of her giggling teenage schoolfriends. I now had a crew of nine. We had a little trip round the bay before anchoring in a nearby cove to save the marina fees. All the kids had a go on the wheel. It was quite a performance getting everyone off, because I had to ferry them ashore in the dinghy in parties of two or three. The older girls were the last to go. It had started to rain heavily, so I fished out all the waterproofs to keep them dry. Each set was about four sizes too big, and the girls, ever conscious of their appearance as all teenage girls are, cracked up at the sight of each other and them-selves dressed in the bright orange-and-yellow outsize suits.

My father had died when he and I were both young men but at the time I didn't fully realise just how young 47 is. My mother had since remarried, and she and her husband came down the next day. I hadn't seen her for about a year, during which time I had been growing my hair long. It was at that awkward stage where it was neither one thing nor the other, and I was worried about what my mother was going to make of it. My worries were well founded because her first words to me were, 'Oh my God, that hair of yours is a sight. How does Laura put up with you runnin' about like that. If I was her I wouldn't be seen dead with you.' She was also shocked at the Spartan conditions onboard. I think she ex-pected a more luxurious boat – something along the lines of a big cabin cruiser. I had been a bit wild as a boy and had given her some trouble, so she wasn't entirely surprised when I told her I was going to sail round the world. She couldn't understand why anyone would want to do such a thing but she was as tolerant towards this hare-brained scheme as she had been towards every other foolish thing I'd done. She was no doubt very worried for my safety but tried her best not to show it. We went to lunch in a little restaurant, and while I was making a telephone call I glanced over my shoulder to see her looking straight at me. There was a distant expression in her eyes that I had never seen before: she seemed to be looking at a little boy, whose hair she quiffed and whose cheek she kissed as he stood at the front door before leaving for school, instead of a 41-year-old man with a beard that was going white. That look unsettled me. There was a finality about it, and I knew she was wondering whether she would ever see me again.

Terry and I hung around for a few days. When the wind shifted to the west we hauled up the anchor. We sailed out of Belfast Lough and along the coast of County Down, where I had spent many childhood holidays. I scanned the coastline with the binoculars, picking out places steeped in memories: the little harbour at Donaghadee, where I had boarded my first boat, along with my brother and father, for a fishing trip; rock pools along the shore, where I had caught and killed crabs (I still felt bad about that); and a stretch of beach, where I had nearly drowned one summer's day. It was low water that day when three of us waded straight out as far as we could. As the tide turned, flooding in behind us, it filled up all the depressions in the sand. We now had to wade through these to get back to the shore. None of us could swim, and I was the smallest. The depressions became pools which got deeper and deeper. The two taller boys in front of me were up to their necks in water. I had to stand on tiptoes, craning my head back as the water lapped over the top of my chin and dribbled into my mouth. Death always seems distant to a child but I knew it was close then. If any one of the depressions had been a few inches deeper, I would have dropped out of sight and drowned. It was a strange feeling to look at that shoreline – from the deck of a boat on which I was now planning to sail across oceans – and think about such things. It was almost like dreaming, as if I was sailing past my own life.

The wind once more swung round to the south-west, checking our progress. We put in to the fishing port of Portavogie. Before the lines were secured, we heard the grunting of seals beside the boat. A whole gang of them had colonised the place. They popped their heads above the water, looking at us in an almost interrogative way, as if to say, 'Who the hell are you?' Terry had never seen seals before and was much taken by them. He kept photographing the creatures, repeating over and over again the word bizarre. It was pronounced in such a way that the 'zarre' syllable was about ten times as long as the first one.

I left Terry with his camera and the seals to have a look around. Just up from the outer harbour, there was an inner basin which was so packed with fishing boats that it was impossible to see how any at the back could get out. I had never seen so many fishing boats – they were jammed into the basin as tight as the fish jammed into their holds. It would have been easy to cross to the other side of the basin by walking from one deck to another.

It was now early evening and time for a quiet drink but I couldn't see any pubs. I stopped the first passerby to ask where the best bar was. He told me that there were no bars in Portavogie. I couldn't believe it – a fishing port with hundreds of fishing boats and no pubs! This really was bizarre! Portavogie may not have had any pubs, but it had plenty of artists. The town was covered with political graffiti. It was on the side of buildings, down the middle of the main road through the town, and plastered on the harbour wall. GOD SAVE THE QUEEN – from what, I wondered. REMEMBER 1690 – as if anyone in Ireland could forget it. UP THE UDA – with a kick in the arse, I thought. And ULSTER SAYS NO – just for a bit of positive thinking. But there was one slogan that I had always liked, and it seemed to fit my circumstances. It gave me heart, and I punched the air with my fist when I looked up at it. In ten-foot-high white lettering on a gable wall were the words – NO SURRENDER.

There were hand-painted images of all the icons of loyalism: King Billy crossing the Boyne on a white stallion, paramilitaries with hoods on their heads and guns in their hands, and the severed Red Hand of Ulster – the symbol of Protestant defiance. Ulster unionism, with its strains of religious fundamentalism and teetotalism, takes many forms, but when you get a town full of fishermen and artists that doesn't have a pub, there is something seriously wrong.

Just down the coast from Portavogie is the holiday town of Newcastle, County Down. We dropped anchor there the next night. After our stopover of the night before, this place seemed like sin city – neon lights all along the front, hamburger joints, amusement arcades and pubs everywhere. The main street had cars parked all the way along it, and in every car there was a boy and girl snogging like mad. The divisions in the North of Ireland run deep: Protestants and Catholics, loyalists and republicans; the yacht-owning, well-heeled middle classes of Bangor marina and the unemployed workers of Belfast; and now, the abstemious artists and fishermen of Portavogie and the wild, life-loving youth that poured into Newcastle. Terry found it all very bizarre.

I was about to leave this land of contradictions behind and sail to that other land over the border – the Republic of Ireland. As we sailed along the coast past the Mountains of Mourne, it was sunny and warm. I looked inland to the hills and peaks that I roamed as a boy: a boy who had read about sailing ships and had once stood on these hills, looking out to sea. It was time for a song. A song about Ireland and about its emigrant navvy workers in London and about these mountains.

> Oh, Mary this London's a wonderful sight,
> where the people are digging by day and by night.
> They don't grow potatoes or barley or wheat,
> but there's gangs of them digging for gold in the street.
> At least when I asked them that's what I was told,
> so I just took a hand at this digging for gold.
> But for all that I found there I might as well be,
> where the Mountains of Mourne sweep down to the sea.

On crossing the stretch of water that separates the North of Ireland from the South, a high-speed commando launch, with two soldiers riding shot-gun on the bow, came out to have a look at us. With their painted faces and camouflage fatigues, they were like something out of a Vietnam war movie. I shouted out to them to come aboard for a drink but I don't think they heard me. Goodbye to Ulster.

10. *Escape*

IT WAS CLOSE TO MIDNIGHT WHEN WE MOTORED INTO THE crowded marina in the town of Howth. This is the southern counterpart to the new marina in Bangor in the North. Howth, which lies just outside Dublin, has effectively become one of its suburbs. And Dublin had a fond place in my heart because it was there that I had met Laura 14 years earlier. We had both been postgraduate students at Trinity College, and I was attracted to her the first time I set eyes on her. She had no interest in me. After three months of getting nowhere, I gave up. Her parents, who came from the North, had been burned out in the troubles of the 1920s, and she viewed any northern Protestant with suspicion, especially one who was only interested in getting her into bed. It was only after I gave up and showed no more interest in her that she began to have a little time for me — such is the way of wooing.

Dublin, for me, also symbolised escape. I had married in Belfast as a young man of 21 and spent six years living in matrimonial misery. With two young daughters, there seemed no way out. Things got so bad that at one stage I even thought of suicide. When I came to Dublin to study, I knew I was never going back, and we split up and subsequently got divorced. It had been difficult over the intervening years to keep in touch with my daughters but I never gave up and always managed to see them regularly. They were now fully grown. I liked to think that they loved me as much as I loved them, but I knew it must have been very hard on them.

Dublin became my solace. I walked its crowded streets, sat in its lovely parks, read in its well-stocked libraries and drank in its incomparable pubs. I got to know it almost as well as Belfast. The only down-side was the course of study I was engaged in, which was something of a joke. The professor responsible for the dreadful course was a complete charlatan and a nasty piece of work into the bargain. On his bookshelf, he had a copy of a thesis I had written. For years I had an abiding fantasy of walking straight into the office and taking my thesis from the bookshelf. If he demurred, I would knock him to one side, before throwing the thesis in the River Liffey nearby, to show my complete disdain. The thought of the headlines back home in the local press — CAPTAIN CULTURE ASSAULTS EMINENT PROFESSOR — dissuaded me from carrying this through right now, but I resolved to do it on the way home, after I had sailed round the world.

Now that I was back in Dublin, I wanted to visit all the old places. The first of these was a bar called the Palace. When Laura showed that initial interest in me, I suggested going there for a drink. We sat all night in the back room; she drank hot ports while I stuck to the Guinness. People came and went but I managed to keep her there, giving it everything I had. I think I even told her about my plans to get a boat someday and sail off. When it comes to really big things in life, you usually only get one chance, and it has to be seized. There truly is a tide in the affairs of men which must be taken at the flood. I took that tide, and it did lead on to fortune.

Everyone should have a back room in the Palace in their lives. The only problem now was that Laura was in Greece. It was now mid-September, and she had arranged a short holiday there some time ago because she thought that I would be long gone and far out to sea. Most of her friends in Dublin were on holiday with her, so there was no big reception committee waiting for me. I did track down an old friend called Doreen, who turned up after work to share a drink with me in the Palace before inviting me back to her place to have dinner with her and her son.

There were one or two possibilities for finding crew in Dublin. Doreen let me use her phone to call round. Each phone-call drew a blank, but I had a friend who lived in Westport, in the west of Ireland, who might be interested. He had become quite a celebrity in recent years, ever since his release from four-and-a-half years of captivity at the hands of Islamic fundamentalists in Beirut. His name was Brian Keenan. We had grown up together in Belfast, had gone to the same school and walked together as boys in the Mountains of Mourne. A few days before I was due to get married in 1972, I bumped into him in the street in the centre of Belfast, and he agreed to be my best man. After moving to Dublin, I saw very little of him and didn't even know he had gone to Beirut until I read in the newspapers about him being taken hostage. Once he was released, I dropped him a line to wish him all the best, and that was the end of it until a few months ago. At that time I was in Dublin with Laura visiting her mother, who was then ailing, and we all went out to the country for lunch. Later in the day, while sitting in a hotel bar in County Wicklow, I looked across the room and saw Keenan.

It was a good reunion, meeting like that across a crowded room, and I was very happy to see him after so many years. He was in good form and, as far as I could tell, had recovered from his terrible ordeal and seemed to be enjoying life. We spent the next day together in a bar in Dublin, talking about old and new times. He was genuinely interested in the sailing trip and said he might like to join me for part of it, once he finished a book he was writing. He wasn't on the phone in Westport but I had the number of the pub he drinks in and managed to get hold of him. He sounded as though he had had a few and asked me for instructions on how to get to the boat. He said he would drive over from the west of Ireland. I didn't expect to see him.

Doreen drove me back to Howth, and she and her son came aboard to have a look around. Her son, Gareth, was a fine boy – had he been a few years older, I would have taken him with me. Terry and I were planning to leave the next day and went to bed shortly after they left.

'Ahoy, *Warrior Queen*. Beattie, are you there?' It was Keenan's voice and it was 2.30 a.m. The daft bugger had driven all the way from Westport. Brian came below and I opened a bottle of Bushmills which my mother had given me in Belfast. He had big news. His book was finished and due to be published in hardback in a few days. I was dying to have a copy but all he had was the dust-jacket, which he gave me, and I put it away in the chart table. He was calling it *An Evil Cradling*. He wanted to escape from all the pre-publication hype. That explained the mad dash across the country. We carried on talking in low voices, so as not to disturb Terry, and drank too much whiskey before going to bed.

Brian was fast asleep in no time after stretching out in the saloon berth. I lay awake in my bunk, unable to get to sleep because of Brian's snoring, laughing out loud about the incongruity of the whole situation. It seemed like only yesterday when he was unemployed in Belfast and I was working as a welder in Harland and Wolff shipyard – how things change. He was now the only Protestant saint in Ireland, and I was on my boat about to leave home waters behind me. Brian's snoring was deep and regular: he sounded like a bear in hibernation. I was smiling to myself, thinking that it must have driven those friends of his, with whom he was held captive, up the wall, when I heard a much more disturbing sound. From the forepeak, Terry yelled out, 'Shut up,' in an aggressive and ugly tone. Patience and tolerance are mandatory virtues in the confined spaces of a small boat. If the weather is bad, you put up with it; if gear fails and you can't fix it, you do without; and if a shipmate snores, you accept it. Brian didn't pay a blind bit of notice. Terry continued to yell out through the night. I was very angry.

Brian had some business to attend to in Dublin next day, and Terry went with him to get some provisions. While they were gone, I took the opportunity to sort out some of the problems with the boat. We had two large rubber freshwater bags, which allowed us to carry 80 gallons. One of these had ruptured beyond repair in the gale in the Irish Sea. A replacement for this was hard to come by. The marine-supply shop could have ordered one but it would take about two weeks to arrive. For most yachtsmen, based in their home port, this would be no problem, but in two weeks' time I hoped to be in Spain – no water bag.

When Terry and Brian arrived back, we cast off to sail to the south-west of Ireland. I gave Brian the wheel straight away. He took the boat round the Howth peninsula and out into Dublin Bay. The sun was on its way down. Dublin was a grand sight surrounded by the broad sweep of the bay, with Howth astern and the Wicklow Mountains to the south in front of us. If it had been in my power to turn the clock back 14 years, it would have been hard to choose between the back room of the Palace and sailing on.

Keenan had never sailed before but he certainly looked the part, standing at the wheel with his grizzled beard and sturdy frame. He had changed a bit since our Belfast days. His laugh wasn't as loud or outgoing, his conversation was more deliberate than it used to be, and his manner was a touch more introspective. We had already had words on his years as a hostage when we met in Dublin some months ago and I didn't see any point in going over it again. Anyway, I could read the book, which would say all that he wanted to say. Instead, the conversation centred around our school-days and friends. I had forgotten, a long time ago, many of the things that he remembered, but when he brought them up they came flooding back. He also knew more about what these old friends were up to now, and we went through the whole gang of them.

'Do you remember Stansfield?'

'It was a real shame about Bunting . . .'

'Have you ever heard from Laird?'

'Did you know that Scamp went off to America and he's now working in a bank.'

'Scamp, working in a bank! In Minnesota?'

'Jim Wilson went to Australia!'

'Sidney Wilson joined the army!'

'Do you remember that day, me, you, and Rainey swam in the River Lagan?'

'Were you there?'

'Of course I was.'

'I don't remember you being there.'

The light on Wicklow head flashed 3 times every 15 seconds as we left Dublin behind, making good progress through the night. On the afternoon of the next day the wind swung round to the north-west and the boat took wing. She hurtled along faster than at any time on the trip so far, throwing out a huge wake behind her as she forged forward. The Tusker Rock, a large, menacing piece of granite sticking straight up out of the sea at the south-east corner of Ireland, came into view before nightfall. With the tide running in our favour, we flew past it, and I was glad to leave it astern. This was sailing, but just when you think everything's going great, something goes wrong. A clanging noise was heard from the masthead – the VHF radio antenna had come loose. It was hanging on the thread of its cable, slapping against the side of the mast. This meant that our radio was out of action, but it wasn't a big problem and could be sorted out when we put into port in a few days.

With the boat charging along, I got my head down for a few hours. When I awoke just before nightfall of the second night out, Terry told me about a vibrating noise he could hear. The first sign of trouble with a boat is usually a strange noise. This one was a low-pitched flapping noise that seemed to come from the hull of the ship. Terry wasn't in the least bothered, Brian couldn't be expected to be, but I was concerned. I put my ear to the side of the hull and heard it get louder. I lifted up all the hatches to the bilges, sticking my head deep in each one to try to trace the source. As I worked from the bow of the boat to the stern, with my ear down as close to the water below as I could get it, the noise became louder still. In the aft cabin it was loudest of all. When the cover over the compartment where the rudder shaft comes through the hull was removed, not only could I hear the noise but I could feel vibrations through the hull. There must be something caught in the rudder. What the hell could it be? Probably a fishing net.

The wind that had flung us down the coast dropped off with the onset of dusk. A few hours after dark, as we were ghosting along, Terry called out to tell me that the wheel had jammed. I took the wheel, trying to turn it. It went halfway round freely but came up hard when going the other way. We had lost steerage! It was like trying to drive a car that could turn one way but not the other.

We were close to a large outcrop of rocks. The Coningbeg lightship is permanently moored near these rocks to warn shipping of the danger. The light was clearly visible. There was no immediate crisis, but whatever was fouling the rudder had to be freed if at all possible. I sat down in the lowest section of the aft cabin, watching the part of the rudder shaft that comes through the hull, and asked Terry to gradually force the wheel. The inboard end of the rudder wasn't fouled but it stopped in the middle of its cycle for no obvious reason. 'More pressure, Terry,' I called out. There was no movement. 'Give it more.' Still no movement. 'Keep going, give her a wee bit more.'

'I'm applying an awful lot of bloody pressure to this damn wheel,' Terry shouted.

'Hold it, hold it, no more!' I could hear a crunching sound from underneath the hull. The rudder was not free.

I couldn't figure out why it was jammed and was sitting in the aft cabin looking at the linkage, when Brian called out, 'Hey, John, the light on this lightship seems to be getting a bit fainter.' He was right but it wasn't because we were getting further away from it. With the tide and what little wind there was, we were getting closer all the time. Within half an hour the light had completely disappeared. We were enveloped in thick fog. The visibility closed right in, and it wasn't long before it was less than 20 yards. It felt as if the ship was entombed in an immense ball of black cotton wool. The foghorn on the lightship went into action, blasting out its doleful sound 3 times every 60 seconds. A foghorn at sea at night is an eerie sound that floats in the air with an almost supernatural presence. The fact that it signifies an unseen but known danger and repeats itself with monotonous regularity gives it a mysterious, spectre-like quality. You imagine that it is speaking to you, telling you that you are doomed. AAHHUMMN . . .

AAHHUMMN . . . AAHHUMMN . . . On and on it droned, its words of woe seeping through the opaque blackness. As if that wasn't enough, the fog played tricks with the acoustics. One minute the horn sounded a long way off and you could hardly hear it; and the next minute it nearly deafened you.

Whatever was fouling the rudder might also be fouling the propeller. I thought for a long time about whether or not to start the engine. There were three outcrops of rock in the immediate vicinity: the Coningmore rock, the Coningbeg rock and a clump of three or four known as the Brandies. With each one of these threatening to loom out of the fog at any moment, it was worth a try. I could start the engine in neutral, gingerly engage gear and hopefully free the obstruction. I turned the key in the switch. The engine turned over once, groaned and died – flat batteries! I couldn't understand it. We had conserved our electrical power and the wind generator had been whirling around like mad since we left Dublin.

We had no rudder, no engine, no radio, no wind, and no visibility. All we had was the drone of the foghorn. This was getting ridiculous. Rocks stood out of the water somewhere beyond the edge of the fog, and the horn droned on to tease and torment us. The rudder now began to play tricks with us. All of a sudden it freed itself and then it locked up again. It was bloody infuriating but of little consequence, because with no wind and no engine the boat could not be made to move, and steerage wouldn't have helped anyway. The crisis was now very real. The fog thickened.

A heavy fog hanging over the sea at night is like a suspended, oppressive dome. It forces the mind in upon itself, inducing thought – deep, dark, disturbing thought. Sitting in the cockpit with Brian, I wondered what he was thinking about. But the stillness of fog also induces silence and I didn't ask him. We hardly spoke a word. If I hadn't rung him up in Westport, he could be sitting in the back room of the pub sipping Guinness, and if the media was pestering him, somebody else could take the calls. I felt like telling him that I was sorry for getting him into this mess, but somehow the words would have been as hollow as the fog itself. He no doubt fully appreciated just how serious the situation was but we all knew there was nothing any of us could do about it other than wait and hope.

As I strained my eyes to try to see through the encircling dome of dark fog and looked down at the oily sea, I was struck by the black humour of it all. I couldn't help chuckling a little quiet chuckle to myself and thinking that, for all the danger, discomfort and frustration, I would rather be here than getting into bed, setting an alarm clock to wake me up for work the next morning. Even the bad moments like these had an edge to them which was sharper than anything I had known. Whether this sharp edge was to Brian's taste or not, I couldn't tell, but there was one thing for sure — we were both going to remember this night even more clearly than we remembered the day we all swam in the River Lagan.

It was too deep to anchor. We drifted at the mercy of the tides for the rest of the night and into the early morning. There was a macabre irony in the fact that we didn't have to worry in the slightest about what sailors most dread when in fog — collision with another vessel. Nobody else in their right minds would be as close to the rocks as we were. Unless, of course, they were also in a boat with no rudder and no engine, but somehow this didn't seem likely. The lightship was never less than a mile away, and at times we came very close to it without ever seeing it. The foghorn never missed a beat. Like a ghost, it haunted us through the night, but unlike any ghost I have ever heard of, it stayed with us after dawn, wrapped in a thick grey shroud. The rocks that were close by were anything but apparitions though — they were jagged pieces of unyielding granite, and they would tear the bottom out of the ship, ripping the keel right off her if we hit one of them. Had the Coningmore, the Coningbeg or the Brandies materialised in front of us, we could have done nothing other than take to the life raft.

It occurred to me that if we did hit any of the rocks and were all lost at sea, Brian's publishers would have a field day and his book would sell out overnight. Brian, who had joined us to escape the attention of the media before the publication of his book, had done it in style. Nobody was going to find him out here.

A few hours after dawn, there was a little puff of wind. The fog began to lift and the puffs got stronger. They got stronger still and turned into a breeze which rolled up the fog with it. The Coningbeg lightship stood before us and the rudder was free. All the sails were hoisted in an instant and we sailed off towards land.

11. *Nuts and Bolts and Death*

AS WELL AS BEING A HOME, A BOAT IS A MEANS OF TRANS-portation and a life-support system. It's more than a house, a car and all the insurance policies in the world rolled into one. When it doesn't work the way it's supposed to, it causes nothing but heartache. You can't call up a builder to come out to fix it, or drive into a garage to have it repaired, or take out extra insurance. If things go badly wrong your whole world can vanish off the face of the earth in seconds, claiming the lives of everybody aboard at the same time. My boat was giving me real heartache, and we needed to put into port for repairs without delay. The town of Dunmore East was only a few hours' sail away, so we set a course for it. No sooner had we got underway than the rudder started to play its tricks again. It jammed up, then freed itself, and the vibrating noise under the hull could be heard at some times and not others – I was completely lost for an explanation.

The sailing guide showed that Dunmore East has a row of skids – big wooden sleepers – up in the far corner of the harbour. We could go in there at high water and wait for the tide to go out. If everything went well, the boat would dry out and rest on the skids, allowing us to examine the rudder and do any repairs that were necessary. Yet again, the wind was from the wrong direction and we had to zig-zag, or tack, to make port. This proved very difficult with a rudder that seemed to have a mind of its own but in about three hours we had made enough progress to bring us within sight of the houses in the town. With less than half a mile to go, the wind that had spirited us away from the Coningbeg light-vessel deserted us once more, and we drifted in the bay outside the harbour.

After sitting in the bay for a couple of hours, Terry volunteered to go over the side with a face mask to have a look at the rudder. The mystery was about to be solved. He stripped off and dived in. Brian and I waited with bated breath to have everything revealed. I expected him to find half-a-dozen lobster pots and yards of fishing net wrapped around it but when he came up the first time he said there was nothing there. He went down again. This time he came up with an answer. Taking a gulp of air before he spoke, he shouted out, 'The propeller was jammed up against the rudder. I just pushed it with my hand and it moved back.' I checked the wheel – the rudder was completely free. The propshaft had come out of the gearbox at the back of the engine! This explained everything. The vibrating noise was the propeller banging against the rudder, and the crunching sound below the waterline, when I had asked Terry to force the wheel the night before, was caused by the blades of the propeller digging into the fibreglass of the rudder. Sometimes, as the boat turned in the water, the sea would push the propeller and shaft back into place and the rudder would be free.

With the rudder now free, we were able to use the few little puffs of wind that came along to sail up to a mooring buoy in the harbour. The radio antenna needed sorting out, the batteries had to be charged, the reason for them going flat established, and the propeller and shaft had to come out. I would then need to find a marine workshop to have new transmission bits made and reassemble the whole lot. This was going to take at least a week, which meant crossing Biscay even later in the year. It also meant that Brian would have to leave to return to Dublin.

We rowed ashore and found the nearest pub, where we had a few drinks. My entire consciousness was focused on the boat and the mechanical setbacks. I was talking non-stop about the gear problems when Brian pulled me up short, asking, 'Do you have the engineering skills to do all these jobs?' I wasn't sure if I had but there was no one else to do them. He then took another drink from his glass and said, 'A boat's a very selfish thing, isn't it? It makes a lot of demands.' There was no denying that he was right. But although the problems seemed to be multiplying by the day, I was somehow able to tolerate the selfish demands of this boat and my only concern was to patch her up and keep going.

Waterford was the nearest town with a railway station, and Brian and I boarded the bus later that day. After locating a marine workshop that was willing to machine the parts, Brian and I then found a bar for a last drink. I wished him luck with his book. He wished me luck with my trip, before leaving to catch the train back to Dublin. I had had enough of saying goodbye to good friends on the platforms of railway stations so I stayed in the bar.

When I arrived back in Dunmore East, I found a small marine supply shop whose owner turned out to be very helpful. He had a boat of his own and arranged, at high water next day, to tow me into the corner of the harbour where I could dry out to do the repairs. I didn't want any confusion, so I made it clear to Terry that this man was doing us a favour and was in charge – we had to do whatever he asked us without question. It was a tricky manoeuvre but he clearly knew what to do. He lashed his boat tightly to the side of mine and drove the two boats right up into the corner of the harbour. It was like taking a sick person to a hospital bed.

He gave me good advice about how to settle the boat down on the skids when the tide went out, and I made sure to pay attention to his every word. We could see the wooden sleepers on the harbour bottom, and it was important to rest the keel on two of these with the centre of gravity of the boat between them. Failure to do this would result in the boat falling over. When a yacht with a heavy keel is out of the water it's like a beached whale – it can't be moved. If it falls over and gets its mast and rigging entangled in an obstruction, the damage can be terminal. As if this wasn't enough, the side of the harbour didn't have a wall to rest up against. Instead there were wooden piles driven into the ground about 15 feet apart. We had to rest against the side of these piles. He suggested hanging a long piece of timber over the side of the boat, on the outside of my fenders, so that this piece of timber would rest up against the wooden piles. Finally, he told me to make sure that the boat was as close in to the side as I could get it, just before it touched bottom, to stop it leaning over too much and fouling its mast on the road above. Some hospital bed, this!

I asked Terry to go and find a long piece of timber. He came back empty-handed after 15 minutes. There isn't a harbour in the world that doesn't have timber lying around, and I scampered off the boat and found a piece right away. I then took all of the anchor chain from the chain locker and laid it along the side of the deck closest to the vertical wooden piles. The weight of this chain on one side altered the trim of the boat, ensuring that it would lean into the harbour side rather than fall over the other way. I also took a line from the top of the mast and secured this to a strong point on the roadside. By tensioning this line, we could make the boat lean over in the right direction even more, just to be on the safe side.

As the tide started to go out, I kept adjusting the lines, the fenders and the long piece of timber on the outside of them. The boat came to rest on the skids, leaned up against the long piece of timber, which, in turn, pressed against two of the wooden piles. So far so good. There was still the possibility that the centre of gravity was not between two skids. The only way to find out was to wait for the tide to drop some more. An hour or so later, when I was thinking everything was fine, the boat started to tilt at the bow. I moved to the stern as fast as I could. It slowly righted itself. Its centre of gravity was perched bang on the forward skid, and the slightest movement made it go one way or the other. It was just like the famous scene from Charlie Chaplin's film *The Gold Rush*, where the log cabin is perched on the edge of the cliff. I didn't dare move and remembered that in *The Gold Rush* Charlie and Big Jack manage to get a rope on to a stake at the edge of the cliff. I didn't have a rope to hand but there was something even better – a big, heavy chain, the end of which was lying at my feet. I slowly pulled the chain from along the side of the boat, piling it up on the aft deck. The centre of gravity of the boat moved back, and the little log cabin didn't go over the cliff.

This carry-on would need to be gone through twice a day with the approach of low water but it would be much easier the next time and there would be no more guesswork about where the centre of gravity of the boat was. When the boat dried out, we were able to get to work. The propeller came off the shaft, the shaft was pulled out of the back of the boat, and the gearbox coupling was unbolted. It wasn't easy working with Terry. Unlike most other people with whom I had sailed, he had nothing to teach me on the nuts-and-bolts side of things and wouldn't let me teach him what little I knew. When tackling a difficult job, it always helps to be able to talk it through with someone and consider all the different options. Two minds and two pairs of hands are more than twice as good as one but I found that Terry didn't have much interest.

With the next low water, I moved her back a touch and settled her down with no bother at all. There were 12 hours before it would need doing again, so I jumped on a bus to Waterford with a five-foot propshaft and a propeller between my legs. The parts were made that day, and I was back before nightfall in good time to catch low water around midnight.

Space in the engine compartment, where the reassembly of all the new parts had to be done, was severely restricted. The only access to it was from inside the coffin-sized locker, through a tiny inspection hatch. You could only use one hand and your eyes, or two hands and no eyes. Two hands were essential, and I began to appreciate how blind people cope. By feeling all the parts, bolt holes and nuts, I ended up almost seeing them with my hands. But hands are very sensitive to pain. Particularly so when that pain is caused by heat. Because all the new bits fitted very tight, we had to heat them up in the oven to get them to expand a little. Terry passed the hot pieces of metal into the locker in a heavy cloth, while I fumbled with them, trying to connect everything up. After three or four attempts, it all went together and the job was finished the same day.

We still needed to do some more work on the bottom and had to stay on the skids for a couple more days. We established a rota for settling the boat on the skids at low water. It was Terry's turn to do it on his own for the first time at about two o'clock the next morning. I emphasised to him how critical it was to adjust all the lines the moment before she touched bottom, and the need to get the boat in as close to the side as possible.

Shortly before midnight, I went to bed. I lay awake, listening to the water around the boat ebb away. It wasn't long before I felt the keel touch the skids. There was lots of action as Terry ran about the decks. If there was any problem, he would call me, I thought, so I stayed where I was. The first sure sign of trouble, a few minutes later, was a muffled 'shit' from Terry. I jumped out of my bunk. The boat had come to rest on the skids a long way out from the wooden piles at the harbour side and was leaning into them at a severe angle. The long wire stay from the top of the mast was pressing hard against the roadside and had a kink in it like a tightly pulled bowstring. With the angle at which the boat was leaning increasing every second, it was only a matter of minutes before the stay snapped, bringing the mast down with it. I thought of cutting it there and then with heavy-duty wire cutters but got the tools out instead and frantically dismantled the bottle-screw at the bottom of the stay. Terry and I didn't speak a word. Before going back to my bunk, I said, 'You should have got me up straight away.' Terry didn't reply.

The work continued for a few more days. I hoisted Terry to the top of the mast where he bolted the VHF antenna back into place. I stripped the fuel-line down and found a clogged filter that I never knew existed – this was the cause of the engine cutting out for no apparent reason. The electric bilge pump, which was bought less than two months earlier, had also packed up. I took the pump apart and found an internal electrical short in the sealed motor. The replacement motor cost more than I could afford but we had to get one nonetheless. It took Terry a full day to hitch-hike the 100 miles, there and back, to the nearest supplier. He returned with the wrong motor and had to make the trip again the following day. Despite checking everything, I couldn't figure out why the batteries kept going flat. We would just have to go very easy with our use of battery power in the future.

Dunmore East is a friendly place. Since arriving, I hadn't been able to think of anything else apart from the mechanical problems with the boat, but the mood in the town, and in my own mind, changed when a tragedy at sea occurred in our last few days. A small fishing boat from the town had gone out for an overnight fishing trip and had been run down in the middle of the night by a big French trawler. The small boat was cut in two, sinking in seconds. Three men were lost. Two bodies were picked up soon after, and there was a search party out looking for the third one. I didn't know the men but we had probably sat beside each other a few days earlier in one of the two bars in the town. As the funerals of the dead men took place, it was a very disturbing feeling to think of these men sitting in a cosy bar, maybe even right beside me, having a quiet drink one night before perishing at sea the next. What with all the gear problems I was having, the bad weather, and now this, I began to wonder if someone was trying to tell me something.

We left Dunmore East after a week, by which time the search for the body of the missing fisherman had been called off. The man in the marine shop had been very kind to us, and I thought that someday I would like to come back to this pleasant small seaside town with Laura. The boat was in better shape than she was when we came in, and I had found out a great deal about how she worked. I had also been reminded how dangerous and unforgiving the sea can be.

12. *Haute Cuisine and Fish and Chips*

AT THE BACK OF MY MIND, AS WE LEFT THE HARBOUR, WAS the thought of coming across the body of the dead fisherman. This was a very unlikely possibility but a gruesome one nonetheless. We would be sailing over the ground where the boat went down but the chances of coming across anything as small as a body in the open sea are extremely remote.

The weather was settled and it was a good feeling to be sailing again after having spent a week in dirty overalls. The coastline along this part of Ireland is rugged and wild. I commented on this to Terry. He replied, 'Yes, it's very pretty.' When Terry was visually pleased, he invariably described the source of his pleasure as 'pretty'.

We decided upon Kinsale as the port to head for. In recent years this has been developed for upmarket tourism and has a thriving yacht-charter business. It would be as good a place as any to find crew. The harbour lies about ten miles inland from the Old Head of Kinsale. Once we picked this headland up, we turned in. I had spent a few idyllic days in a small cottage near the Old Head of Kinsale with Laura in the first spring after we got together. In the early evenings, round about the same time of day as it was now, we came down to the little shingle beach, lit a fire and cooked dinner. I could see the beach very clearly with the binoculars but there was no one on it.

Kinsale is the gastronomic capital of Ireland, with more French bistros per square mile than Paris. Even in late September in mid-week, they do a good trade. After tying the boat up I went ashore. I walked through the narrow streets, stopping at each restaurant, where I studied the menus posted outside and peered through the windows at the people inside. There were couples everywhere. Some exchanged loving glances across the tables, others were engaged in lively conversation and some just sat in silence, drinking their wine and eating their food. Eating good food in fine restaurants is Laura's favourite pastime. If she had been with me, we would have visited a different one each night, and I would have enjoyed it as much as she would. But I hadn't the slightest interest in putting another hole in my budget if it meant eating alone in an expensive restaurant in the midst of so many couples, so I settled for a bag of chips from a roadside van instead.

Next day I stuck up several notices on various shop windows, which read:

Passage to spain on 35 foot yacht departing in a few days – crew needed. Leave name and telephone number if interested

We didn't get any interest and busied ourselves with the outstanding jobs. Hurricane Bonnie, which had recently lashed the eastern seaboard of the USA, had turned east and was tracking across the Atlantic. As it moved across the ocean, it gradually dissipated itself but the tail-end of it was expected on the south coast of Ireland in a few days. We thought it wise to wait until it passed before sailing to Spain. That allowed us to spend the weekend in Kinsale, and on Saturday night Terry and I went to the local disco.

Terry was quite a bit younger than me but even he was an old man compared to the kids in the disco. These kids had come in, as they did every Saturday night, from the outlying farms and villages. This was a completely different set from the professional city-dwellers in town for the haute cuisine. The music was intolerably loud but I found the spectacle of adolescent courtship rituals fascinating to watch and stuck it out to the end to keep Terry company. The really serious work of pairing off was left to the last minute, and most of the young women were playing hard to get.

When the hall finally closed, the stragglers wandered off through the town towards a fish-and-chip shop that stayed open all night. Terry and I stopped in to get something to eat. The queue at the counter was three deep and stretched to the door. There was a big red-headed fellow directly in front of me. In front of him was a small, good-looking young woman who refused to acknowledge his presence. He clearly fancied her like mad but he didn't have a clue about how to chat her up.

'Hey, hey you, you,' he said, poking her in the shoulder with his long, bony, freckled finger. She paid no attention. He sulked. While he was poking her in the shoulder, a dark-haired lad further away was watching his every movement.

I didn't want to miss the show so we got our fish and chips and sat down to eat them along with everyone else. The good-looking young woman was with a girlfriend sitting not far from us, when a chip, covered in tomato ketchup, flew past. The big red-headed fellow, who was seriously drunk, was telling her that he loved her. The ketchup-covered chips were his love letters. When she refused to answer his letters, he came up behind her and dumped the rest of his chips over her head. It looked like things were about to erupt before the owner told him to leave and he skulked out. Terry and I left shortly afterwards. As we walked down to the boat, the big red-headed fellow and the dark-haired lad were squaring up for a fight – they had to do something with their testosterone.

The tail-end of Hurricane Bonnie had come and gone by Sunday, which was our last full day in port before we set out for Spain. We were both a little hungover from the high jinks of the night before but a good three-course dinner would soon put that to right. It was going to be our last dinner in port, and I was looking forward to preparing it. Most of the shopping had been done but I wanted to get some fresh strawberries for dessert and a bottle of red wine to go with the main course.

While walking around Kinsale at lunchtime in the late autumn sunshine, with the newspapers, wine and strawberries under my arm, the world seemed a good place. I rang Laura, who had returned from her holiday in Greece, to tell her of our plans to leave the following day. She was concerned that we would be making the trip with just two of us aboard but I lied to her, saying it was no big deal. Anyway, I had one last chance to get extra crew with a plan I was going to put into operation later that night.

Terry was still feeling a bit rough when I returned to the boat but I was in good spirits. I told him of my plans for finding crew, showed him the strawberries and red wine, and gave him the newspapers. He was not happy about something and eventually said, 'You can have the wine for yourself.' There were very few hard-and-fast rules on the boat, but one that I had insisted on to make domestic and shopping arrangements work was that the cost of all provisions consumed aboard would be split equally by everyone, regardless of who had what. Every time somebody bought provisions, the cost went in a small notebook. Terry was telling me that he didn't want the cost of the wine to go in the book.

We had served wine with some of our other meals in port. Terry always drank it. Once the principle was conceded that someone could negotiate their way out of orange juice, breakfast cereal, fresh fruit, wine with dinner, or anything else for that matter, the scope for disputes would be unlimited. The law would have to be laid down.

'I'm cooking dinner tonight, it's our last meal in port before we cross the Bay of Biscay, and if I, as cook, decide that wine should accompany the meal and you are too hungover to drink it, that's your problem,' I said. These were the harshest words we had had so far but there was more to come.

'I don't think that's reasonable,' Terry said.

'Well, it doesn't matter whether you think it's reasonable or not, there have to be rules, and I'm saying that wine with meals in port is part of the way this ship is run. If the person who is cooking wishes to serve up wine, then it goes in the book.' Terry wasn't happy, and neither was I. He continued, 'I don't see why I should pay for your drinking.'

This was the last straw. Pointing my finger at him, but trying to keep my voice down, I said, 'I'm not going to discuss it any more, other than to say that wine on occasions is as important with food as the salt and pepper that flavours it – and nobody pays for my drinking.' Terry picked up the newspaper. I went out to the cockpit to smoke a cigarette.

Dinner was served up later that day and the table set with napkins and Laura's dinner service. The wine, quite a nice Rioja, was uncorked and we both drank it. There would be no more wine until we reached Spain. But before we got to Spain, we had to visit the Spanish Galleon. In the sixteenth century, when England and Spain were forever at war with each other, Spanish galleons often landed on the south coast of Ireland. Although none of them remain today, a large bar on the edge of Kinsale is called the Spanish Galleon. There is a good turnout on a Sunday night, when they have a resident folk-singer, and I was going to ask him to make an announcement over the PA system about us looking for crew. It was a crazy idea but it might work. The folk-singer thought I was taking the mickey at first but I managed to convince him I was serious. After a couple of ballads and a few rousing 'Come all Ya's', he put the announce-ment out. The idea might appeal to some of the local young men or one or two of the German hitch-hikers who were in town. There were no takers apart from three teenage lads who had never been on a boat in their lives. They said that they wanted to come but would have to get permission from their parents. I told them to turn up at the boat the next morning if their parents agreed.

They didn't show up. Terry and I prepared the boat for our departure. While waiting for the tide to turn, I went ashore for a last look around town. There was an oyster bar that I had been eyeing up for some time, which, for a modest charge, served half-a-dozen live oysters with a half-pint of Guinness. I bought the newspaper on the way to the bar, where I settled myself down in the corner beside the peat fire. The fire warmed me while I read a rave review of Keenan's book in the *Irish Times*, sipped the Guinness, and sucked the oysters from their shells. I could have stayed there forever, but the tide was turning and it was time to leave.

I had hoped to be across Biscay by mid-August to avoid the equinoctial gales but it was now the first day of October. There could be no further delay. We were able to sail up the estuary and out towards the open sea. As we approached the Old Head of Kinsale, I looked over to the small shingle beach where Laura and I had had picnics. There was a woman sitting on it. I waved to her and she waved back to me.

Farewell my native land.

PART TWO

Ocean Waters

SHIP OF FOOLS

We are those fools who could not rest
In the dull earth we left behind
But burned with a passion for the west
And drew a frenzy from its wind
The world where small men live at ease
Fades from our unregretful eyes
And blind across uncharted seas
We stagger on our enterprise

ST JOHN LUCAS

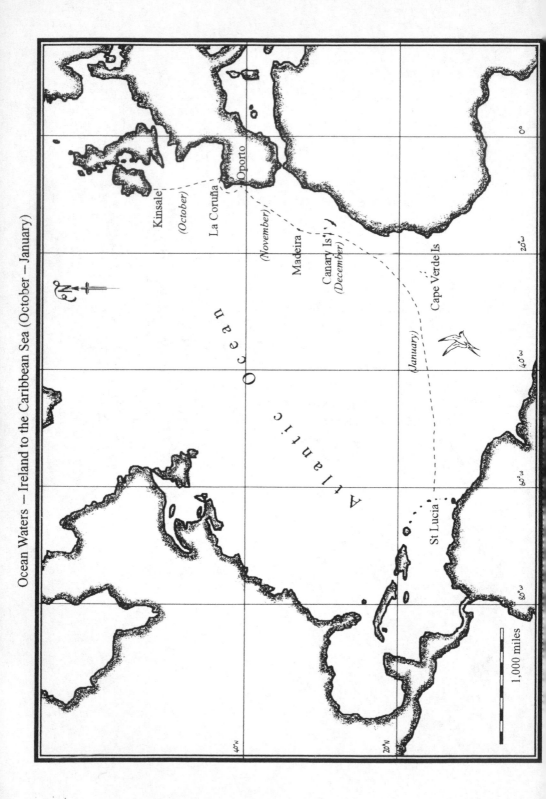

Ocean Waters — Ireland to the Caribbean Sea (October – January)

Kinsale
(October)

La Coruña

Oporto

(November)

Madeira

Canary Is.
(December)

Cape Verde Is

(January)

St Lucia

Atlantic Ocean

N

1,000 miles

0°

20°

40°

60°

4°N

20°N

13. *Bay of Biscay*

IT IS ABOUT 600 MILES FROM THE SOUTHERN COAST OF Ireland to the northern coast of Spain, and for most long passages it is reasonable to assume an average run of around 100 miles a day. The longest trip I had ever made before was 350 miles to Norway. That was in mid-summer and I had a crew of five. There were now only two of us but I had newly installed self-steering gear, and if this worked well a crew of two should be sufficient. I hadn't figured out why the batteries kept going flat so it was important for us to use as little battery power as possible. That ruled out using the electric autopilot but we had the wind-operated system.

We spent the first day rigging this up, experimenting with different settings. It worked remarkably well. There is virtue in simplicity and this device proved it. The business end of the contraption is an auxiliary rudder that is moved by a wind vane. When the boat veers off course, the vane is deflected by the wind to one side. This, in turn, moves the auxiliary rudder which brings the boat back on course. The unit worked perfectly, provided the boat was balanced with the right amount of fore-sail and mainsail set to ensure that the ship was inclined to stay on course in the first place. The device consumed no power, and we could use it day and night. We would need to adjust it from time to time, but that would be much easier than having to helm 24 hours a day.

The Bay of Biscay is covered by the BBC shipping forecast, so if the weather took a turn for the worse we would have plenty of warning. The immediate forecast was good with fresh westerly winds, which were perfect. By starting from as far west as Kinsale, the course was due south. This avoided the need to make any more headway to the west, which can be a big headache in this sea, should a gale whistle in from the west with the rapid advance of an Atlantic low. Before nightfall, the coast of Ireland had been left well astern and for the first time on the whole voyage we were making real progress. The Atlantic swell, which was bigger than I expected, rolled in, but with the wind on the beam, the boat rode every wave comfortably, surging ahead, while the wind vane deflected this way and that, keeping her perfectly on course.

The first dolphins of the trip appeared at dusk and escorted us for several hours. There were about 15 of them, including a few baby ones, and they swam in the bow wave of the boat, surfacing in twos and threes with perfect timing – each one coming out of the water at exactly the same moment as its immediate companion. The pairs and trios split up from time to time, swapping partners as they performed their exquisite aquatic ballet. Terry, who had never seen them before, was bowled over. It was the happiest I had seen him on the trip so far, and it gave me almost as much pleasure to watch Terry as it did watching the dolphins themselves. They vanished as quickly as they had appeared but, unlike professional ballet troupes, refused to come back for an encore.

Terry cooked a fine supper and we lit the Tilley lamp to save power. The nights were now cold and the lamp had the added benefit of warming the cabin, the area of which was not much more than a large broom cupboard. After supper, we worked out the watch-keeping routines. With the memory of the fishing boat lost from Dunmore East still fresh in my mind, I didn't want to take any chances with a collision at sea, so it was important to keep a constant watch through the night. The evening forecast indicated continuing winds from the west. They were expected to increase a little.

We saw no shipping the first night, during which the barometer started to fall. The next day's forecast talked about a new low-pressure system developing 200 miles west of sea area Biscay. On the evening of the second day, the forecast began with a warning: a severe gale was expected in less than 24 hours. The announcer's doom-laden words crackled out of the radio set. He was reading them off a piece of paper in an air-conditioned studio somewhere in England and they meant nothing to him. Nor did they mean anything to the tens of thousands of other people who would be hearing them. But as Terry and I listened in silence, we knew they spelled big trouble for us. I also knew that Laura would be hearing the same words, and I could see her burying her head in her hands. The advance warning gave us plenty of time to prepare. We checked everything to ensure it was securely lashed in place and took the precaution of hoisting the storm jib on the inner forestay and putting the third reef in the main. Once these, and all other preparations we could think off, were complete, we waited for the wind to come. It built up, as it always does, slow and sure, the seas growing steadily in advance of its coming. The chart showed that we were approaching the continental shelf, where the depth changes from about 100 metres to over 4,000 metres in a matter of miles. With a gale roaring in from the west, driving the Atlantic swell before it and piling up the ocean on to that shelf, the seas were going to be very big. They were already bigger than anything I had ever seen. This was a yachtsman's nightmare – crossing the continental shelf in the Bay of Biscay in late autumn with a westerly equinoctial gale. No matter how hard I tried, I was not able to see anything good about the situation. For the first time since leaving Whitby, I felt a tinge of self-pity. We were already nearly exhausted and the gale was not yet upon us. I expected the worst.

Terry had never been on a long passage before. Nor had he ever been at sea in a gale, but he showed great composure and I was very glad to have him with me. The seas were now so big that every now and then they knocked the boat to one side. The self-steering gear did not have the power to bring her back on course. If a wave broke over the beam when she was off course, we could be knocked down on to our side. The prospect was not a pleasant one, so we had no choice but to helm the boat ourselves in shifts of two-hour watches. This would be as long as anyone could manage and it meant there would be very little time for anything but a catnap in between.

Before nightfall on the third night out, the skies were an ominous shade of dark grey and there was 100 per cent cloud cover. There was no possibility of heading to any port to seek refuge. We could not avoid the storm, which was rapidly advancing and would be upon us soon. It was imperative to try to keep dry and warm, and I was thankful I had invested in a good suit of foul-weather gear. I wore a woollen hat that pulled over my whole face, leaving only two small holes for my mouth and eyes. A thick scarf was wrapped around my neck, and I zipped up the hood of the foul-weather jacket over the whole lot. Underneath the jacket I wore a T-shirt, a thick brushed-cotton walking shirt and two sweaters. Long johns, heavy socks and corduroy trousers were worn beneath the bottom part of the waterproof suit, the legs of which were tied around a heavy pair of gum boots. The safety harness was clipped on and adjusted to fit tight. The life-line was secured to it and fastened to a strong point on the deck at all times.

We took turns at the helm through the night and tried to sleep in between watches. The wind grew steadily, and the wire stays supporting the mast hummed all night long and sounded like a banshee wailing. Every now and then, one of them twanged when the mast shook with an extra-strong gust of wind. I was on the watch before dawn. My mouth was parched. The air was laced with saltwater, which stung my lips. The exposed skin of my face around my mouth and eyes was pricked, as if by needles, with the tiredness and the driving spray. The wind had now blown us off course and we were right on the edge of the continental shelf. It was very dark but all around us I could just make out shifting walls of water towering above the boat.

When the sickly light of dawn came, the full fury of the sea revealed itself to me. It was a terrifying sight. The dark dawn sky was unlike any daylight I had known. It loomed above, glaring down on the black, boiling water with a detached air of brooding menace. There was chaos everywhere on the surface of the sea – it was as if the laws of physics had been stood on their head. I stood with my mouth agape and eyes wide open, staring at the waves in disbelief. I was struck dumb by the size of them, never imagining that there could be seas as big as this. I tried to swear but was unable to. Instead a guttural sound, from somewhere deep in the pit of my stomach, worked its way up my windpipe and oozed like slow-motion vomit out of my gaping mouth. The seas growled and roared like tortured monsters as they crashed against one another, and hissed as the wind ripped the crests off the tops of them. One moment, the boat was perched on the top of a wave; the next second, it went careering down the side into the trough below. It was worse than any rollercoaster because as well as going up and down she lurched violently from side to side. Forget about your fairground white-knuckle rides, this was a Bronco Billy ride. As the boat hurtled down the side of the waves, I kept looking over my shoulder, expecting, every second, to see the wall of water collapsing on top of us. She threatened to spin out of control, while I turned the wheel frantically to try to hold her steady. There was no pattern to where the seas were coming from. It seemed as though they were growing in size every minute.

I began to think that we couldn't survive this and even darker thoughts came into my mind. This is nature unbounded, I thought. This ocean has been here since time began and I am but a fleck of dust upon it. My boat is nothing. I am nothing. If we go down it will mean nothing. No one will ever know what happened, very few will care, and all will forget. Maybe this is the way it's meant to be. As these dark, fatalistic thoughts filled my mind, I began to see my boat on the ocean from afar. I was looking down upon her being tossed disdainfully by the sea. It felt as though my whole being was part of these mighty waves. Everything was now very quiet. I was no longer in the boat struggling to hold her on course. My spirit was slowly being absorbed by the elemental grandeur and fury that surrounded me. I wasn't aware of Laura or my daughters or even myself. It was a warm, comforting feeling. I was being seduced by the temptress of death and began to swoon.

A breaking wave knocked the boat to one side and I fell off balance, but the fall was welcome because it broke the spell. I was back in the boat, holding on to the wheel for dear life and trying to fight the sea. The waves roared once more. I was glad to hear them. I wanted to see Laura again. Fear flowed through my veins but it was better to feel fear than the seductive caress of fatalistic abandonment. I screamed a primordial scream at the top of my voice to banish whatever it was that was trying to take hold of me. Exhaustion was not far away, and I knew that it was pointless to try to keep going. I backed the storm jib and put the wheel hard over to make her lie hove to. She settled down very quickly, riding each oncoming wave better than she had when I was at the helm. I was breathless with agitation and excitement and went down below to tell Terry that the boat was hove to. I told him to stay in his bunk for as long as he wanted and that I was going to do the same. The woollen hat was still on my head, and I could see him look at my eyes and mouth through the holes in it while I ranted and raved at him about the importance of sleep and the fact that we were no good without it, no good at all without it. He didn't take much persuading to stay where he was.

My bunk was wringing wet but that didn't bother me in the slightest. I collapsed on to it. I remembered thinking that it had always surprised me how soldiers could sleep through battles and bombardments and that I now knew how they did it. The hatches of the aft cabin were locked in place, and I fell into a deep sleep while the boat took care of Terry and me. Throughout that sleep I heard, from time to time, a loud banging at the stern. I was too exhausted to do anything about it and drifted back to sleep. Eventually the banging stopped and no longer disturbed me. I don't know how long I slept for but Terry woke me up with the words, 'Hey, John, there's a big battleship here.'

I struggled out of the aft cabin to see a large French warship about a quarter of a mile away. It wasn't moving and had obviously been standing by, watching the boat for some time while Terry and I slept. We made sure they could see us, by waving to them, and they moved off. I felt a completely different man for the sleep. Gone was the terror, as was the sense of helplessness and insignificance that had preceded it. In its place was a determination to do something practical. We were still hove to on the edge of the continental shelf, and the seas were crashing all around us. I looked at the mayhem of the ocean, turned to Terry and said, 'Right, Terry, let's get the fuck out of here!' It was life-affirming to be able to speak the word again, and I spat it out with venom. It gave me control.

We got underway without delay, setting a southerly course. Once we were out beyond the edge of the shelf and in deep water, the seas would be less disturbed. Terry went aft to set the self-steering gear and called out, 'We've lost the self-steering rudder!' I went back to check. It was gone. The auxiliary rudder had somehow detached itself from the shaft and was now at the bottom of the continental shelf. As a safeguard against its loss, I had made sure that a strong line was always attached to this rudder but all that remained of this line was the frayed end where it had parted. The banging that I had heard in my sleep had been the detached rudder hanging in the water on the line, bashing into the back of the boat. The banging stopped when the line eventually parted and the rudder was lost. This was a serious setback. It meant that Terry and I would have to helm the boat all the way to Spain, nearly 400 miles away. I didn't dare use the electric autopilot for fear of flattening the batteries. But at least the wind was dropping a bit as we left the continental shelf behind, and the seas, although still intimidatingly massive, were less confused.

I had been pleased with Terry's nerve during the worst of the storm and was optimistic that, after having been through this together, things would improve as we began to understand and trust each other more. This optimism was short lived. The only way to keep going 24 hours a day in these rough conditions was to have watches of two hours on and two hours off. When you are on watch and steering the boat, the thought of the two hours off keeps you going. You have little reveries in which you imagine yourself to be stretching out, reading, listening to music, smoking, drinking and eating. And you know that all your dreams are going to come true at the end of the two hours. Every minute of the two hours' break between watches is precious. The only problem is that there are often jobs which require two men, and these tasks have to be done at the change of watches. Sometimes the jobs only take a few minutes and at other times they can take an hour. This means that someone loses a bit of their two-hour relief time, but it all evens itself out in the end.

At the end of one of my relief periods, I came on watch and needed to rig a pole on to a sail on the foredeck. I could do this on my own but Terry would need to remain at the wheel to hold the ship steady and keep an eye on me in case I got in trouble. It was a difficult job that took about 15 minutes. I had to shout instructions to Terry in the cockpit. Throughout this 15 minutes he kept making exaggerated gestures with his right wrist as he looked conspicuously at his watch. When the job was done and Terry was relieved, he said that in future if jobs had to be done at watch changes, the person who was on relief should come on early to do them. I explained that it made no difference in the long run and the problem with his idea was that it required the person on relief to estimate how long a job would take and this was just not feasible. Terry wouldn't accept this and we ended up getting into a long, pointless discussion about the pros and cons of each approach. At the end of my next watch period, Terry came to relieve me. It was time for my break but it was also time to get the storm jib down. I went forward to do it. It took me over an hour to finish the job off. Terry didn't look at his watch once.

The wind had gone round to the north-west, which was good for a southerly course, and the miles ticked off. It was always difficult to climb out of your bunk in the middle of the night to come up to relieve the person on watch. The nights were long and cold. At first there was virtually no shipping but our course was due to take us across a major shipping lane. All the commercial shipping on passages between northern Europe and the Mediterranean or the Cape of Good Hope sticks to a tightly defined lane that runs from Britanny in northern France to Cape Finisterre at the north-western extremity of the Iberian peninsula. This is a lot of ships. We had to sail right through this highway of the seas. We approached the shipping lane in early evening about 100 miles from the coast of Spain. There was a long line of ships, as far as the eye could see, all going in the same direction. They gave the impression that they were all tied together with each one towing the one behind. It was hard to tell how far they were apart but they were probably further from each other than the naked eye suggested. But the visibility was good, and when we saw a larger than usual gap between two of the ships we sailed through the middle of them.

Crossing a busy shipping lane is like crossing a road   the traffic comes from both directions. A traffic-separation zone is clearly marked on the chart, and ships steaming one way stay on one side, while those going the other way stay on the other. Once we were in the traffic separation-zone I felt like a little bug on the grass bank in the middle of a motorway with juggernauts thundering past on either side. The only difference was that the juggernauts came upon you silently. With the tiredness that we both felt, it was very easy to get confused by the navigation lights on these ships and almost impossible to tell how far away a ship was. Most of the ships would be steaming at about 15 knots, which may not sound that fast, but it means they cover a mile in four minutes, and there are lots of four-minute periods in a two-hour watch. It is easy to nod off for one or two of them. As we were leaving most of the shipping behind, I saw the red navigation light on the port side of a ship some way off. Large vessels must show port and starboard navigation lights as well as a white light at the bow of the ship. Small boats, like the *Warrior Queen*, are not required to show a light at the bow. Whatever this was, it was someway behind us and had no white light at the bow. It was probably not very big. No need for concern, I thought.

The navigation light didn't seem to get any closer. Even though it was some way off, I started to have an uneasy feeling and kept a close eye on it. I was beginning to wonder if the light was playing tricks with my eyes, when I heard a faint but very deep rumble. 'That's an engine,' I said out loud to myself. The rumble grew louder. Out of the darkness, the long shadow of the bow and deck of a supertanker appeared. In my semi-exhausted state it reminded me of the big, black shadow of the monster from the 'Night on the Bare Mountain' in the film *Fantasia*. It even had the red eyes. But there was no white light on its bow, and it was bearing down on us. I started the engine immediately, revving it up as fast as it would go. As the 35 feet of the plastic-hulled *Warrior Queen* scuttled to the side, the 800 feet of the steel-hulled tanker came clearly into view. Its superstructure passed by with its engines now thundering away. With its enormous bulk, it seemed almost close enough to reach out and touch. As the bridgehead passed, I raised my fist and shook it at them, yelling, 'Get your bow light fixed, you bastards.' I don't think they heard me.

We raised the coast of Spain later the next day and set a course for the port of La Coruña. This is a popular stop-off place for yachtsmen and offers good shelter. It also boasts the oldest working lighthouse in the world – the *Torre de Hercules*, which was built by the Romans. Lights at sea from a lighthouse have been a source of comfort to generations of sailors. They tell you that land is near and guide you into a safe port. Each light has its own signature, and the *Torre de Hercules* flashes 4 times every 20 seconds. We were able to pick up the loom from the Hercules light, as it swept through the night sky, long before we could see the flashing itself.

The Bay of Biscay now lay behind us. My self-steering rudder lay on its seabed. We had made it in one piece, and I was looking forward to entering my first non-English-speaking country. The trip had taken us seven days, and we had covered more ground in that time than I had in the preceding six weeks. I felt that the worst was behind me and for the first time began to feel that I was well and truly on my way. I had the perfect song for the occasion. A song which was sung to a fast rumba tune and which I had heard on an old Dean Martin LP. It was about the port of Barcelona, but any port would do for the rhyme in the song, as long as it ended with an 'a'. At the top of my voice, I sang out:

Nearly ready to leave

Big brother beginning to enjoy himself

Peter, who loved the Lord and women

Tony, skipper of Potlatch – Make it Happen

Warrior Queen *hauled out in the Canaries*

Warrior Queen *in mid-ocean*

We sailed into port at La Coruña
And I could see her standing there
She smiled and tossed a gardenia
Which she did pluck from her hair

Oh, olé, that girl from La Coruña way
I kissed her and Oh, olé
I knew that I would never stray

Ahh muh cha cha
She had a lot of muh cha cha ahh
I kissed her and ohh cha cha
I knew that I was here to stay

Oh, bonita, you were such a sweet-ahh
Oh, bonita, you were so petite-ahh
Eyes inviting very amarou-so
Lips enticing, real deliciou-so

The Tower of Hercules was now clearly visible, its bright arc of pulsating light sweeping over our heads. It illuminated Terry's face 4 times every 20 seconds. He grinned a broad smile and said, 'Where do you get them from, John?'

14. *Brown Sludge*

THE PEOPLE OF LA CORUÑA SET ASIDE ONE DAY A YEAR FOR Our Lady of the Rosary, which happened to be the day we arrived in town. We tied the boat up at about 4.0 a.m., and by the time we had got some sleep the fiesta had already started. There was plenty of work to do on the boat but no one was working this day, so Terry and I took a bit of time off to go and party.

The flags were out and brass bands marched up and down the main thoroughfares of the town, playing everything from military tunes to Beatles numbers. Traditional black-and-white costumes adorned the more serious participants in the town's fiesta, while the less committed of the populace hung around marquees, drinking red wine in terracotta saucers and eating octopus stew. Terry and I headed straight for the marquees, where we ordered saucers of wine and big helpings of the calamari stew. It was a warm, sunny day. The red wine was a bit on the rough side, but then so were we after our seven days at sea in the Bay of Biscay.

Sitting on rickety stools, stacking up saucers on the tables beside the marquee, Ireland seemed a long way away. The music was different, the people, although no doubt the same as people everywhere, looked different to the people of Ireland, and the food, for all of the inventiveness of Kinsale's chefs, was the genuine Spanish article. The luxury of having someone else prepare food and serve it up for us to eat at our leisure was not lost on either Terry or me. It was a good feeling to be in port.

La Coruña is a big port. Having spent much of the afternoon at the marquee, we set out to explore it. Most of the shops were closed for the fiesta but the bars and cafés were doing a roaring trade. We found one bar which was very popular with old men who sat around all day playing dominoes. It had always struck me as odd that in most societies it seems to be children and men who play games. Girls somehow lose interest when they become young women, rarely rediscovering the simple and wholesome pleasure that game-playing gives. The passion that the old men displayed, as they smashed the dominoes down hard on the tables, was a joy to watch. Terry and I stayed there for a long time, talking about the trip across Biscay. I asked him directly how he thought things were working out between us. He said he was very happy and was pleased to have got to Spain. He then asked me how I thought things were going. I told him that at times I found him difficult. He wanted me to elaborate, so I gave him one or two examples. He conceded some of the points I made and we argued in a friendly way about a few others. I didn't know whether it was a good idea to try to clear the air or to bottle up things that were bothering me, and the conversation only went as far as both of us wanted it to go. There was no doubt that it was much easier to deal with each other when sitting in a bar in Spain than when coping with life at sea, but I was glad that we had at least talked about a few problems.

Later that night we found ourselves in one of the many squares in the town. A platform had been erected for the performance of traditional music and dance. Troupe after troupe of Spanish dancers entertained us for hours on end. The men wore tight trousers, waistcoats and big, black leather boots. The women wore swirling skirts that fitted tightly about their waists and deep-cut blouses that made their breasts stick out like the horns of a bull. Sometimes there were over 30 of them on the platform, which shook as they stamped their feet. I had a grandstand view right in front of the platform, but despite the noise from the musicians and the thumping feet of the dancers, I eventually fell asleep while sitting on the ground with my back leaning up against a tree.

When the show was over, Terry and I started to make our way back to the boat. As we did so, we heard two female English voices. It was the first spoken English, apart from each other's voices, that we had heard since leaving Ireland. We soon put faces to the voices and started up a conversation with two sisters. The eldest, who was about 35, worked in La Coruña. The youngest was in her late twenties, visiting on an extended holiday. You have a fair amount of credibility with women when you meet them in a foreign land which you have sailed to on a small boat, and they were duly impressed.

The bar at the Club Nautico was still open when we walked past. The four of us went in and ordered a few drinks. I was very tired and didn't participate much in the conversation but Terry was flying and making a big impression on the younger of the two sisters. I kept nodding off to sleep, waking up from time to time when things became lively. The bar was busy, and I woke up at one point to find a boisterous Terry saying something to a middle-aged German woman. She didn't speak very good English, and Terry, who I knew didn't like Germans for some reason, seemed to be having a joke at her expense. The German woman was very polite but a bit nonplussed. I asked Terry to give it a rest. There was a very unpleasant atmosphere. The bar had gone quiet and people were looking at us. I thought it best that we all leave.

By the time we got aboard, I had had enough and was ready to crash out, but Terry and the two sisters sat out in the cockpit, laughing and giggling. I sat down below. I think the eldest of the two might have been interested in flirting with me but all I could think of was Laura. I closed my eyes and realised just how desperately I missed her. The Bay of Biscay had taken its toll on me, and I wanted, more than anything in the world, to be alone with her. I resented other women aboard my boat, and their idle chatter and silly laughter irritated me. It took all the control I could muster not to storm out to the cockpit and throw all three of them off the boat. The incident in the bar troubled me almost as much. Something had happened at the Club Nautico – I didn't know what it was, but I didn't like it.

Next day we set to work. The boat had sustained more damage in the Bay of Biscay. Apart from the lost self-steering rudder, the mainsail was showing signs of serious wear and much of the stitching had come undone. A new leak had developed through the side of one of the deck-level perspex windows, and the leak through the rudder gland, which had been with me since leaving Whitby, was getting worse. There were about 20 other jobs to do, and I had to figure out why the batteries kept going flat. I also had a mystery problem which was eating away at both me and the boat. All along the deck, and especially in areas where there were different kinds of metal, there was a permanent growth of thick, brown sludge. I had noticed it in Ireland and continually scrubbed it off, but it was getting out of control. Immediately next to the brown sludge, the aluminium toerail was severely pitted and was slowly being dissolved. None of the other boats tied up on the pontoons had any brown sludge or corroded aluminium toerails. I dipped my finger in the sludge to taste it – it was very bitter and acidic. The only acid aboard was in the batteries, so I thought that this sludge might be connected with them going flat all the time. Before setting sail, a friend had bought me an electrical multimeter and shown me how to use it. When the meter was used in the vicinity of the sludge, it indicated a voltage of anything from zero to four or five volts. There was electricity flying all round the boat! I tried the meter on various parts of other boats: no volts anywhere! Ours was the only electrically charged boat in the marina.

Terry was now spending most nights with one of the sisters, which gave me the evenings free. The bar at Club Nautico stayed open late. I liked going there because it was a good place to meet other yachtsmen and swap yarns and advice. One English sailor confirmed my suspicions about the sludge, saying it was probably a voltage leak, but he couldn't be expected to have any idea where it came from. He and his wife were taking their boat down to the Canary Islands for the winter and they had made a transatlantic trip a few years earlier. I was eager to get as much information as I could about this trip, and he gave me plenty of tips and much encouragement.

We talked some more about gear and the weather. Shortly before I was about to leave, he asked me, somewhat hesitantly, 'How do you go about finding crew?'

I found this an odd question and answered it casually. Then I asked him, 'Why do you ask?'

He said it didn't really matter, but I pressed him and he went on, 'So that I can avoid making the same mistakes.'

I knew that he was thinking about the incident in the club a few nights ago. I explained that I had been very tired and didn't catch all that was going on, and I asked him to tell me how he saw things. He was reluctant to go into much detail but made it clear that he thought Terry had been very rude to the German woman. He also told me that if he had been the German woman's husband, Terry would have got a thump in the face before leaving. I was very upset to learn this and made what excuses I could for Terry, pointing out that he probably had a bit too much to drink.

It was expensive to take up a mooring on the pontoon so we moved the boat out to the bay to pick up a mooring buoy. The jobs were slowly being ticked off the list, and I kept scrubbing the brown sludge. There was a particularly stubborn patch at the base of the pole supporting the wind generator, which I had to take a piece of wire wool to. As I scrubbed away, I suddenly noticed lots of little sparks leaping across between the pole and wire wool. The voltmeter confirmed an exceptionally high voltage that rose and fell as the wind caught and spun the blades of the generator. All the current from the generator was leaking out from the electrical deck-fitting at the base of the pole. It was then conducted round the decks by seawater. When this electrically charged seawater came into contact with two dissimilar metals, usually stainless steel and aluminium, an electrolytic reaction took place, which corroded the less noble of the two metals, leaving an oxide behind in the form of a sludge. With seawater, electricity and dissimilar metals all combined, I couldn't have designed a better electrolysis bath if I had tried. I leapt to my feet with glee because the mystery was solved.

Every electrical deck-fitting was removed. I installed new water-proof deck-glands, making all connections anew under the deck, well away from any saltwater. I was very pleased with my work and decided to become a real electrician. I would make and install a new instrument panel with voltmeters, ammeters, switches, fuses, resistors and light-emitting diodes to monitor the output from the wind generator as well as the state of charge of the batteries. These parts, along with a replacement for the burst water bag and a host of other bits of gear, might be difficult to find but I had to get them somewhere.

I got what I could in La Coruña before travelling to the regional capital of Santiago de Compostela for the rest. Terry was left to look after the boat, and I gave him a few jobs to get on with. While in Santiago de Compostela, I took time out to visit the cathedral. It is one of Spain's most famous, and rightly so. Like any cathedral, it is a historical statement of the political power of a culture and a testament to the dreams, follies and fears of long-dead and still-living men and women. I went inside. It was quiet and still — a place of grandeur as far removed from the Bay of Biscay as it was possible to imagine. There were a few people dotted about the pews, engaged in silent prayer. What troubled them? Whatever it was, be it a sick child or a dying parent, they were looking for solace of sorts, and some of them may have found it. Their woes, silently expressed in the vaulted enormity of the cathedral, helped me put my own problems in perspective.

When I arrived back in La Coruña, Terry wasn't aboard and I noticed a couple of odd things right away. My bedding, which I had given to Terry to have washed in the flat of the two sisters, was missing and there was new bedding in its place. The deck-level window, which Terry was to remove and re-seal, was cracked. Finally, a little beat-up wooden dinghy, which didn't seem to belong to anyone and which we used in addition to my dinghy to provide independent means of transport for going ashore, was missing. There was a note from Terry saying that he had gone off with the two sisters to a house in the mountains for the weekend.

When Terry returned, I asked him how things had gone while I was away. My bedding had been washed, but when he hung it out to dry on the rigging the wind got up after he had gone ashore, and when he returned it had gone – the new bedding was a replacement. The window cracked as he was trying to ease it off but only a small corner was affected and this was glued back in place. The dinghy was left tied to one of the cleats on the aft deck and had come free during the night while Terry was asleep. Ever since we met up in Ireland, he had refused to lock off the figure-of-eight turns on a cleat. I asked him if he had done so on this occasion. 'I knew you'd say that,' was his reply.

'Well, can you blame me?' I responded.

The difficulties with the boat and with Terry were compounded by the lack of money, which was now becoming a serious problem. I had thought that there would always be at least two other people aboard and that their contribution towards safety gear and charts would keep me ticking over. It wasn't working out like this, and the cost of replacing or fixing broken gear was proving much more than I expected.

The self-steering rudder would be very expensive to replace, and I pondered over the pros and cons of getting a new one. It had proved itself in the Bay of Biscay, and I didn't want to be without it. But I still had the electric autopilot. With the battery problem sorted out, I could use this as long as power consumption was monitored very closely. What's more, I had arranged for two more crew to join me in November for the Atlantic crossing. With four aboard, we could estab-lish a two-hours-on, six-hours-off watch-keeping routine and helm the boat all the way. It would keep everyone busy and be good for morale. With the bank balance about to go into the red, I decided against replacing the self-steering rudder.

The two crew joining me for the Atlantic crossing were expecting to meet up with the boat in the Canary Islands on 1 November. Getting there in time was going to be tight. It took over two weeks to finish off the jobs and make and install the new instrument panel. I was delighted with this and looked forward to fully charged batteries in the future. The weather had turned cold and wintry. We waited for the barometer to rise before trying to round Cape Finisterre. The barometer stuck where it was. Once again, I found myself in the position of having to make headway to rendezvous with crew and, as a result, left La Coruña with a less than favourable forecast.

We sailed at 6.0 a.m. to take full advantage of the daylight and with any luck could be round Cape Finisterre before nightfall. The coastline along this part of Spain is known disconcertingly as *La Costa de Muerte* — the Coast of Death. The wind had gone back to the south-west and rose steadily as we headed for the Cape. After 12 hours of trying to beat into the wind, I turned back to La Coruña. I had never turned back to where I had come from at any other point in the trip, and it was deeply depressing to pick up the same mooring buoy in La Coruña that we had slipped 20 hours earlier. It was beginning to look as though we wouldn't get to the Canary Islands on time — but maybe we could make Lisbon.

Next day, with the barometer still low, I phoned up one of my intended crew to tell him the rendezvous port would be Lisbon in the south of Portugal. I was worried that they might be having second thoughts about making the Atlantic crossing and came over as cheerful as I could. He was clearly concerned about the schedule as he only had a certain amount of time available in which to make the crossing but we agreed to meet in Lisbon. The barometer began to rise slowly the day after and we slipped the buoy for the second time to set sail once more for the Coast of Death. Cape Finisterre, with its powerful lighthouse, came into view shortly before nightfall. With the wind coming from the north-west, we made good headway.

On our first attempt to round Cape Finisterre, I had noticed that the wheel seemed a little stiff. At the time it was hard to detect this but on our second attempt there was no doubt that the wheel had gone stiff and was getting harder to turn by the day. I had also noticed a squeaking noise from the propshaft when the engine was running. Both of these things troubled me as we slipped passed the vague outline of Cape Finisterre at 3.0 a.m. The coastline along this part of Spain is well indented and has many natural harbours worth visiting. When I planned my trip, I had hoped to spend about a month visiting all these anchorages, with time out to go walking in the mountains. But all I got to see of this cruising ground were black shadows in the night.

15. *Comets in the Sea*

NYLON, NYLON, NYLON – THAT WAS ALL I COULD THINK
about after we left Cape Finisterre astern. Up until two months before
I set sail, I had thought it was only used for making ladies' tights, but
ladies' tights were the last thing on my mind now. The wheel was getting
stiffer all the time. I examined the linkages in the steering system to see
if anything was being fouled but could find nothing. It looked as though
the rudder itself had become stiff. This was not unlikely because it was
stiff when I first bought the boat, and I had traced that problem to a
seized nylon bush in which the rudder turns. I had a new one made but
after the boat was relaunched someone mentioned to me that there are
different kinds of nylon, some of which are more hygroscopic than
others. I had no idea what the technical specification of the nylon I had
used was, but if it absorbed too much water it would swell up and seize
again. If it got any worse, the boat would have to be lifted out of the
water to allow me to replace the nylon bush.

I seemed to be dogged by endless mechanical problems but at least
it was starting to get noticeably warmer as we sailed further south. I
knew that the two crew joining me in a few days would want to get
going as soon as they arrived. If I pressed on for Lisbon there would be
no time to sort out these problems, so we decided to put into Oporto
halfway down the Portuguese coast.

Electricity was my next obsession. The new instrument panel
showed that all the power output from the wind generator was going
into the batteries but the voltage was not as high as it should have been.
A fully charged 12-volt battery should show a voltage of about 13.2
volts, and the battery is effectively flat when it drops below 11 volts. I
was now able to monitor the battery voltage at a glance – it was on the
low side. I took the new panel apart and checked it but couldn't see any
obvious cause for it not working properly.

On the last full night before reaching Oporto the sea itself was alive
with electricity. It was glistening with phosphorescence. The wake from
the boat looked like a big, V-shaped neon sign. Each edge of the V was
bright green with thousands of specks of brilliant light. Marine phos-

phorescence is caused by electrical and chemical reactions occurring around microscopic organisms. The light emitted is similar to that produced by fireflies, but instead of one or two sources caused by individual flies, there is an abundance of tiny specks caused by tens of thousands of micro organisms. In the right conditions, movement of any object through the water stimulates the reactions and produces the light. If you reach over the side and trail your hand in the water, the specks of phosphorescence stretch behind it for four or five feet and linger in the sea. I was playing with my hand in the water when, as if from nowhere, two underwater comets streaked towards the boat. Dolphins at night in a phosphorescent sea! They surfaced beside the boat. The water rolled off their backs, and it was as if they were covered in stardust, with the brilliant green specks of light clinging to their smooth, silky skins. Within seconds, there were more than a dozen of them. The comet trails of phosphorescence criss-crossed under the keel and made figures-of-eight at the bow. No fireworks display in ancient China has ever compared with the spectacle of these dolphins in such a sea. Here was a moment of pure rapture I had been waiting for. My spirits were lifted by the glorious sight of these beautiful wild creatures tearing through that sea of sparkling fire.

We picked up the harbour lights of Oporto at about 2.0 a.m. The city, Portugal's second, lies at the mouth of the Douro River. Unlike other places I had been to, it was badly marked for night-time navigation. The channel, which was very narrow, snaked its way right up to the old part of the city. On each bank of the river there were large illuminated signs of famous household names: COCKBURN'S PORT — THE BEST IN THE WORLD, WELCOME TO OPORTO, THE HOME OF DOWS VINTAGE PORT. There was a silhouette of a caped figure with a broad-rimmed hat under the logo for Sandemans. Large wooden dhows, like overgrown gondolas, were tied up to pile moorings near the river's edge, their decks stacked high with big oak barrels.

The Louis I bridge came into view as we negotiated the last bend in the channel. It is one of Oporto's most famous landmarks. Conceived by Alexandre Gustave Eiffel, who also designed the tower in Paris and the Statue of Liberty in New York, it spans the river at a great height where two large rock outcrops jut out of the steep sides of the city. There was a customs office to the seaward side of the bridge, and a solitary small yacht was already tied up to the wall nearby. Unlike La Coruña, which had a large marina and hundreds of yachts, we were the only other sailship in Oporto. It was a magic feeling to sneak up the river in the dead of the night. We sailed right up into the middle of the city. Old pantiled houses perched precariously on ledges of rock, and a twelfth-century Romanesque cathedral rose above them. Portuguese voices carried across the water, mingling with the sound of dance music and Fado singing from a harbour-side nightclub. After three days at sea we could smell the place and scented the unmistakable odour of grilled sardines. We didn't need to ask anyone for directions or find a taxi or look for a hotel. All we had to do was tie up to the other boat and we had arrived in Oporto.

The customs house was a small affair with one officer in charge. I went to see him first thing in the morning. He was sitting behind his desk, building an elaborate model of a sailship with matchsticks and glue. Once the match he was sticking into place had set, he looked up and said, 'You Kapeetan.'

This was the only English he had, and I, thinking that he might understand Spanish, replied, 'Si, si,' which was the only Spanish I had. There were some forms to fill out, which took a few minutes, before Terry and I and the boat were officially cleared.

It was a Saturday morning, and the market along the harbour-side was bustling with people, flowers and fish. I love looking at fish and was excited to see that they had plenty of fresh *esphada*. This is one of the ugliest fishes anyone is ever likely to see. It is black and oily, resembling the inner tube of a car tyre, but its firm flesh tastes like heaven. I bought a piece for dinner that night. If Laura had been there, she would have bought flowers and arranged them on the folding cockpit table while I cooked the fish. We would have selected a bottle of vintage port from one of the specialist suppliers to have after dinner. But she wasn't there, and she didn't even know that I was, so I left the flowers behind and went to telephone her.

'Where are you?' were the usual first words of every telephone conversation, and this one was no exception. I told her I was in Oporto in Portugal with the boat tied up in the centre of the city under the Louis I bridge. She had always wanted to visit Oporto and had been with me and my two daughters about ten years earlier on a holiday to Portugal. We didn't make it to Oporto but had seen the pictures in the glossy brochures. I told her it was better than the pictures, and we agreed that someday, when my voyage was over, we would have a holiday in this beautiful city.

My next call was to instruct the two crew joining me to travel up to Oporto by train from Lisbon. They had already booked their airline tickets, and I was looking forward to their arrival in two days' time. Perhaps with four aboard there would be less tension between me and

Terry. I was unsure what to do though when they did turn up. The main rudder was very tight, and I was worried that it might get worse. The best thing to do would be to sail the boat down to Lisbon and have it craned out to allow me to fix the rudder. This would cause a delay of anything up to two weeks. They probably wouldn't accept this, leaving me short-handed for the Atlantic crossing. The alternative was to sail to the Canary Islands, about 1,000 miles away, as soon as they arrived and have the boat lifted out there. They would then, most likely, be prepared to accept the delay and remain aboard for the ocean crossing. We could break the trip to the Canary Islands by stopping off in Madeira if the rudder packed up altogether. Whatever we did, we had to get out of Oporto soon because in winter the port can be closed for months if strong winds come in from the west and the sea breaks at the entrance to the river.

My decision not to replace the self-steering rudder, to save money, turned out to be a mistake. This could have been used to do most of the steering, and we could have got away with hardly ever touching the wheel. The new crew joining me wouldn't have time to buy one in England, from the sole supplier in another part of the country, before their departure. Somehow or other I had to try to make a new self-steering rudder.

The best thing to make it from was solid hard-cast nylon but I wouldn't have known where to get this in Britain, let alone Oporto. Everywhere was closed for the weekend and very few people spoke English. I wasn't going to find nylon and have some sort of a rudder made by the time they arrived. Getting one fabricated in stainless steel was also out of the question. That left wood, and I spent the rest of the weekend searching the boatyards along the river-banks for something suitable. I couldn't find anything that looked right, and even if I had, I didn't have the tools to shape it or drill large-diameter holes in it.

The new crew arrived late on Monday night and were already aboard when I returned from one of the harbour-side bars. They were both members of Whitby Yacht Club and had done a considerable amount of inshore sailing. The dream that brought the two of them to Oporto was the prospect of sailing the Atlantic Ocean. The older one was about my age and owned a fish-and-chip shop in Whitby, called Siggies. His name was Bob Sigsworth and he had his own boat back home. The younger of the two was a 16-year-old lad called Alex.. He was still at school but his father had given him permission to join me, and I had cleared it with his headmaster by writing a long letter saying how much he would learn from such a trip. I didn't know either of them very well but within a few days I would know a lot more.

It was obvious right away that they were both concerned about the schedule. Siggy made it clear that he wanted to leave the next day. I said that it would be a shame if they didn't get a chance to see the town. Siggy's reply was brief and to the point. 'I've seen the town,' he said.

I knew that he was disappointed not to be joining me as arranged in the Canary Islands and was worried about making the crossing within his time-scale. This curt response was a way of articulating these concerns, so I just shrugged my shoulders in agreement. Terry was standing to one side and chipped in with, 'Oh, you've seen the town, have you?' Before Siggy could reply, I came up with a matter-of-fact list of the jobs to be done tomorrow if we were to leave later the same night. The jobs were delegated without dispute and we all went to bed.

The passage to Madeira was likely to take about seven or eight days. With four aboard we needed to stock up with extra provisions. Terry had taken on the role of quartermaster and had drafted a list of food and drink. I wanted to check this before the shopping was done and noticed that there was no wine on the list. Cheap wine is good wine in Portugal so I asked Terry to make sure to get some for us to have with our main meal each evening. There was a long discussion about whether everyone wanted this. I maintained that it was immaterial who wanted it as long as one of us did. The list already contained 24 cartons of fruit juice, which I hardly ever touched, and 24 bottles of mineral water, which I personally saw no need for. I insisted on wine being added to the list.

Terry and Alex went off to do the shopping while Siggy and I were going to take care of the fuel and the jobs. I still had to solve the problem of the self-steering rudder. The mainsail also needed stitching. Siggy got busy with a palm and needle and I found a piece of marine-grade, half-inch-thick plywood to make a rudder. It wasn't the best solution but it would probably get us to the Canary Islands. I cut a piece about the right size and, working from the dinghy tied up to the back of the boat, bolted it on to the self-steering gear shaft with U-bolts. If there had been time, I would have covered it in epoxy resin and fibreglass to give it extra strength and seal it from water penetration.

By nightfall, all the jobs had been done and we were well stocked with fuel, food, fruit juice, mineral water, and two big flagons of cheap red wine. It was nearly midnight when I tried to start the engine. It cranked over slowly. After three days in port we had used up a fair amount of battery power – the batteries were low. For a moment, I thought it wasn't going to start. Everyone held their breath as the cranking got slower and slower. Just when it looked as though it wouldn't start, it fired into life and I revved it up. The lines were cast off and we motored out to the

open sea past the illuminated signs for the port wine. I had looked longingly at the old shops specialising in the best of this fine drink, but I was
now nearly broke and had to content myself with just looking.

16. *Running Repairs*

SIGGY AND ALEX WERE FULL OF EXPECTATION AND IN
good humour. They were embarking on what, for them, was the trip of
a lifetime and had high hopes. I had mentioned to them that the steering was stiff, and they could feel it themselves when they took the
wheel. I advanced my theory about the hygroscopic nylon bush. Alex
wasn't very interested in the mechanical side of things, but Siggy was. It
was wonderful to have someone to discuss all the problems the boat was
giving me, after having dealt with them for so long on my own – it was
like talking to a marriage-guidance counsellor.

After motoring for long enough to charge the batteries, we shut
down the engine and set the sails. The home-made self-steering rudder
worked well. It steered the boat without any need to touch the main
wheel – this was a big relief to me. The watches were apportioned, and
everyone got a decent sleep on the first night. With lots of fishing boats
about, we kept a constant watch and showed a masthead navigation light
throughout the night. Progress was slow and the coast was always in
view.

Shortly after dawn, the wind left us. After waiting for about an hour
in the vain hope that it would return, I cranked up the engine. It turned
over very slowly and refused to start. I left it for five minutes and tried
again. This time it turned over even more slowly before grinding itself
to a halt – flat batteries yet again! This was a bad start for a new crew. I
just couldn't understand why the batteries refused to hold a charge.
They were new when I left Whitby, and I was sure that I had fixed the
wind generator. The engine had been running for several hours. The
only battery power we had used was a tricolour masthead light which
drew two amps, and that wasn't enough to drain the batteries in one
night.

Not long after the engine failed to start, the visibility closed in and
light fog settled around us. The situation was nowhere near as serious as

the occasion in the Irish Sea, when we drifted around the Coningbeg rock. I was not unduly concerned. There were no hazards about. If we drifted in towards the shore, we could drop an anchor in the sandy bottom before being swept up on the long beaches that run for hundreds of miles along the Portuguese coast. With a long, gentle swell running and no wind in the sails to stabilise the boat, she wallowed and rolled from side to side. Siggy and Alex hadn't been to sea for a few months and had yet to acquire their sea legs – it wasn't long before both of them were throwing up over the side. I had seen enough of seasickness in other people to know what an awful condition it is. If ever I needed a fair wind, it was now, with the new crew aboard and their morale already beginning to plummet, but the wind owes no sailor any favours and didn't oblige. They were both sick again. In the end they found it more comfortable to sit in the cockpit than to try to sleep in their bunks.

There was no mistaking that we were drifting towards the shore. Every now and again we could hear the sound of motor traffic along the coastal highway. Alex, full of the impatience of youth, kept shouting for the wind to come, but Siggy kept his counsel. He also kept his eye on the echo-sounder and his ear towards the shore.

We never got into dangerously shallow water before the wind picked up later in the day, dispersing the fog. The shoreline was about three miles away when the fog lifted. With the wind coming from the north, we headed out to the open sea. The boat leaned against the breeze, heeling over slightly, balanced by the weight in her keel. The pendulum stopped swinging, and Siggy and Alex recovered from their seasickness in less than half-an-hour. When the coast dropped below the horizon and the wind stiffened to a good strong breeze, Siggy and Alex's spirits were restored, and they began to take a keen interest in sailing the boat.

Neither of them had been on passages as long or as hard as I had, but they had more experience than I on how to get the optimum performance from a sailboat. Siggy had sailed for 20 years, starting out with dinghies and working up to yachts and had raced with the local yacht club – something that I had never done. Alex was also an enthusiastic racer and something of a speed freak. They both had slightly different ideas about how to trim the sails to get the best performance from the boat, but it was clear that they knew more about this aspect of sailing than I did. I was happy to let them get on with it and learn from them.

Bob (I had taken to calling Siggy by his first name) was interested in learning how to use the sextant to fix our position. I had studied and mastered this before my departure and was able to teach him. I set him exercises to do, and he sat at the chart table, working through them. It was almost like being back at work at college for me as I stood over his shoulder, correcting his mistakes. Celestial navigation is one of those arts that is very difficult to study in abstraction but is much easier to do in practice. There are many concepts to grasp – declination of the sun, local hour angle, altitude and azimuth, parallax errors, and corrections for dip and refraction, to name only a few. But he picked it up quickly and made good progress.

With four aboard, the evening meal was always something to look forward to. We all sat round the small table in the cabin for this daily dinner party. Terry's big interest was environmentalism; Alex's was sailing and speed; Bob's was sex. I was interested in all three. Around these broad themes the conversation was liable to go off on tangents, and we would end up spending hours talking about the most unlikely subjects. Sex was the most popular topic of conversation. Terry regarded himself as something of a gigolo: his ultimate dream was to make his way to New Zealand, where he hoped to find and marry a rich widow with plenty of land. Bob had put it about a bit in his younger days, but I think he realised on this trip, for the first time in his life, just how much he loved his wife. Bob missed her a lot and I was pining for Laura all the time. Alex seemed to have no problem finding women and had a steady girlfriend back home.

Every now and then I would put on one of my opera tapes. Most people usually retired to the cockpit. I knew this wasn't to everyone's taste and never played more than one a day. Terry got particularly agitated when I played these. In the end I told him that I loved the music so much that I had to listen to it from time to time. I myself hadn't liked opera as a young man but had come round to it in time and felt that everyone should at least give it a chance. Terry was unconvinced, and I said, rather pompously, that if he didn't like it he could go outside because I adored it and it sometimes brought tears to my eyes. As he climbed the companionway steps to go out to the cockpit, he replied, without turning his head or looking at me, 'It certainly brings tears to my eyes alright.'

We were now on a large-scale chart of an area that stretched from Freetown in Africa to Lisbon in Portugal, encompassing the Canary Islands and Madeira. It was stained with the red wine that had smashed into the cabin roof above the chart table when Laura was aboard in Scotland. As I worked at this chart in the middle of the night, while everyone slept soundly, I thought of Laura sleeping in her bed and the operas we had gone to see. For my 40th birthday we went to Covent

Garden to see *The Magic Flute* — we had a box that night and were able to take a bottle of wine in with us. The main cabin of the boat was about the same size as the box at the opera. One of the flagons of red wine was jammed behind the companionway steps. I poured myself a large glass and drank it before waking up Terry and turning in.

Sailing conditions stayed good as we knocked off the miles to Madeira. In three days we were about halfway but the home-made self-steering rudder was beginning to show signs of wear. All the stress was concentrated on the corner that was bolted to the shaft. This corner was now waterlogged and bent like a piece of soggy cardboard. Instead of the rudder turning to keep the boat on course, the main body of it stayed amidships and the soggy, cardboard corner bent to one side. We were having to use the main rudder, and the wheel was now virtually solid. It was too risky to keep forcing it. The improvised self-steering rudder had to be fixed somehow.

If we could get it off and turn it round, it could be bolted back on to the shaft using the other corner, which would keep us going for a bit longer. We hove to in order to get the boat lying fairly still in the water. Terry went over the side to try to undo it. I leaned over the guard-rails and passed him the spanners. With the stern of the boat pitching up and down, it was impossible for him to work with spanners in hand and swim at the same time, and I was worried about him getting injured. Alex was worried about sharks but we hadn't seen any and the chances of an unprovoked attack were negligible. I was pleased though that Terry had tried.

There was a chance that I could reach the bolts from the aft deck of the boat. Alex held my legs as I leaned out over the aft deck with my crotch on the aluminium toerail and my torso hanging vertically down. I could just reach the bolts, but my head kept being dunked underwater as the boat pitched up and down. Bob wedged a cushion between my crotch and the boat, while Terry stood by with the tools. The three of them found the sight and sound of me lying upside-down being dunked in the water, with spanners in each hand and a mouth full of seawater and swearwords, hilarious, but I didn't see the funny side of it. Bob had brought a video camera along with him, and he ran off to get it to film the whole pantomime. I heard him say to Alex in a low voice, 'They're never going to believe this back at the yacht club without evidence.'

The home-made rudder was in a sorry state when it came off. What had been rigid, high-grade marine plywood a few days ago was now completely waterlogged. We drilled holes in the opposite corner and put the U-bolts through prior to reassembly. I once again assumed the punishment position while Terry relieved Alex on leg-holding duty. By the time it was all finished, I had swallowed a lot of seawater and was very cold and tired, but at least we were underway again without the need to use the wheel. The steering wheel was one of the few items on the boat that didn't move. It made a first-rate clothes line, and we hung our washing on it to dry.

The sea never ceases to surprise, and it wasn't long after that we spotted an odd-looking object on the horizon. As we sailed towards it, scanning it with the binoculars, it puzzled us even more because we could make out all sorts of different bright colours – blue, green, yellow, red and white. The excitement rose as we got closer, and the mystery deepened as the colours became more vivid. Alex, who had the sharpest eyesight, was on the bow and called out, 'I think it's balloons.' Within a few minutes there was no mistaking that it was balloons. I grabbed the boathook to scoop them out of the sea as we passed close by. They were all tied together with string and I picked the whole lot up on the first pass.

We were about 300 miles from land and had found over 50 balloons. There was drawing and writing on all of them. The writing appeared to be in Spanish or Portuguese, and we could make no sense of it, but the drawings were perfectly clear. Almost every balloon had a large penis and a pair of testicles drawn on it. The ones that didn't have a penis had women's breasts and buttocks – pornographic balloons in the middle of the ocean! We decorated the boat with the balloons and hung them from the rigging. They were of no practical use to us but they certainly raised morale. We must have looked a strange sight, sailing along in the bright sunshine with underpants hanging from the wheel and the rigging festooned with pornographic balloons, while the boat was steered with a piece of soggy cardboard and 'Rock Around the Clock' blasted out of the ship's stereo.

The repaired self-steering rudder lasted little more than a day. I took it off again and reinforced it with a few pieces of mahogany. The batteries were almost completely dead, and with the relatively light winds there wasn't enough output from the wind generator to restore them to a level of charge that would start the engine. To provide light at night we lit the Tilley lamp and only switched on the electric navigation lights when we saw other shipping.

With about 150 miles to go, I woke one morning to be told that the Tilley lamp had caught fire the night before. The fire was brought under control quickly but the glass globe of the lamp was broken in the process. Things break on boats all the time, and you learn to accept it, but when I went below to make some tea I found the broken glass from the lamp lying in the sink. I wasn't going to moan about it being broken, even though it was a Christmas present from Laura, but I was annoyed that jagged glass had been left lying in the sink for five or six hours. I cleaned up the galley, discarding the broken glass over the side. The headlining in the cabin was also covered in thick, black soot, and I cleaned this mess up as well. The other three had all been up for a couple of hours – somebody else should have sorted it out straight away.

The island of Porto Santo, where Christopher Columbus had once kept a mistress, is about 50 miles from Madeira. I had been here on holiday with Laura and knew it had a large sheltered bay. Even without an engine, we could sail into the bay and anchor. We sighted it next day and by midnight were lying at anchor just outside the harbour walls. Next morning we rowed ashore with the batteries to take them to a local garage. Bob and Alex were anxious to ring home but the phone system gave us a lot of problems. It was difficult to get an operator, and Alex was all wound up by the delays. I tried to talk to him in a support-ive way, telling him that he just had to be patient, but he didn't seem to know what the word meant. Bob was missing his wife and kids, from whom he had never been separated before, and when he did get through he was on the phone for a long time.

It was eight years since Laura and I had spent a few days on this island, and I called her up to tell her I was there. She was intrigued to learn that I was making the call from right outside the small boarding house we had stayed in. She asked me how things were going. I didn't mention the fire, the engine or the rudder, but I told her about the balloons and said that everything was going well. Things were not going well at all, because, in addition to the gear problems, it was obvious that Bob and Alex were very anxious about being home soon, and it was imperative that we got the boat repaired as soon as possible to make the Atlantic crossing within their time frame. When we first talked about the trip, I emphasised that they needed to set aside at least eight weeks, which would take us up to the end of December, but it was clear that they both only had a maximum of five weeks available to them. Alex had already booked a skiing holiday just after Christmas, and Bob wanted to be home well before Christmas.

After collecting the batteries we set sail for Madeira. The cliffs at Cabo Giroã are the tallest in Europe, standing at over 1,900 feet. They were a fine sight as we sailed into the capital of Funchal and tied up in the marina.

17. *Plan Overboard*

THE BOAT NEEDED TO COME OUT OF THE WATER AS SOON AS possible. After we tied up I went to see the marina manager to try to arrange a lift with the dockside crane. The crane was already in use, with another yacht in the slings, and I wasn't surprised when he told me it would be at least ten days before he could lift my boat out. But the Canary Islands, which are about 300 miles further south, had many marinas, and it would be much easier, I hoped, to be lifted out there. In the meantime, we had to do something about the self-steering rudder. I asked Terry, who was going into Funchal for extra provisions, to keep his eye out for a timberyard that could supply us with a solid piece of hardwood.

The marina was crammed with boats, and the harbour walls were painted with the names and pictures of hundreds that had made the Atlantic crossing in the past. Some of these were minor works of art, ranging from the standard depiction of a yacht to cartoon caricatures of the crews aboard. Many of the paintings also had little aphorisms beneath them. There was one in particular that struck me. It read:

> If you want to be happy for a day – get drunk
> If you want to be happy for a week – get married
> But if you want to be happy for a lifetime – get a sailboat.

At the time, I thought it must have been written by some idiot who had never done any sailing, because the way I was feeling, I would have been ready to trade my boat there and then for a bottle of whisky and a wife.

Bob decided to leave our mark on the harbour wall. Alex helped me improve the way the boom poles were rigged up, before trying to catch a fish and hooking a girl. Terry returned with the good news that he had found a timberyard that cut and supplied hardwood. I had noticed another boat in the marina with the same self-steering system, so I gave Terry a tape measure and asked him to go and get the dimensions from the rudder. When he came back, we both went to the timberyard to select a piece of mahogany. It seemed very large and weighed a ton.

I spent the rest of the day working on the rudder, but the more I worked with it the more I was convinced it was the wrong size. I asked

Terry if he was sure that he measured the one on the other boat correctly and he assured me he had. It just didn't look right, and after working on it for a few more hours, I insisted that he check it again. He was gone a long time and came back with a miserable expression on his face – it was about two feet too long. This required more work to put it right. It also involved me in needless expense, which I was carrying myself, as I had always held that it was my responsibility to cover maintenance and breakages. The rudder was eventually finished off by about ten o'clock that evening.

I knew Madeira was a beautiful island which, because it has no beaches, has not been spoiled by mass tourism. The Portuguese settled it in 1420, and the slave and convict labour that was brought in over the next few hundred years worked miracles on the steep, fertile, volcanic landscape. They carved terraces into the hillsides, irrigating the entire island with an elaborate system of watercourses known as *levadas*. The *levadas* are the lifeblood of the island's agriculture. Each one has a pathway that runs alongside through lush, sub-tropical vegetation. It's a walker's paradise, and when Laura and I came here, we spent days exploring the island and hiked to the top of Pico Ruivo, the highest mountain.

They were happy days. When the voyage was planned, I had intended to spend about two weeks in Madeira and visit the interior of the island once more – maybe even get Laura to come out – but we had to leave that night, so I didn't get to see anything of the place apart from the marina and a timberyard. What a waste of time – to come all this way only to leave the same day.

Shortly before midnight, we were ready to leave. I was very tired. The dinghy needed to be brought aboard, and I asked for someone to do this while I worked out a course. The course was plotted but the dinghy was still in the water. I hauled it aboard myself and partially deflated it. In the process, a fish hook, which had not been tidied away, sunk deep into the palm of my hand. I went down below to the light of the chart table to extract it with a pair of pliers. While I was doing this, two of the crew went out to finish deflating the dinghy. When I came out to stow it away, I noticed that three of the wooden straps, which give support to the floor, had been broken. Someone had stood on them and hadn't told me. After stowing the dinghy I said to everyone that I didn't mind gear being broken but if anybody broke anything they had to tell me about it right away. No one volunteered any more information.

We left Funchal in poor spirits. While hoisting the mainsail, the main halyard got entangled in the rigging. The only way to free it was for someone to go aloft. I had always wanted to go up the mast at night while at sea, so I climbed into the bosun's chair, stuffing a packet of cigarettes in my pocket. As Terry and Alex winched me up, I had to call out instructions. I was angry with Terry for screwing up with the rudder measurement and furious with Alex for leaving hooks lying about the deck. I called out the instructions much louder than was necessary. As I went higher up the mast, I began to feel a great sense of liberation from the troubles below and took great delight in being able to shout at the top of my voice. Since leaving Whitby, I had only raised my voice in anger once, when I thought my brother was trying to call the coastguard. But as I went up the mast it was almost as if I was no longer on the boat and could do and say what I wanted. When the main halyard was freed, Terry called out, 'Are you ready to come down now?'

I shouted in reply, 'I'll tell you when I'm good and ready to come down – now hoist me right up to the top, and when I'm up there, I want the sail raised.' They hoisted me to the masthead and started winching the sail up. I had to make sure that the main halyard didn't catch on my legs, so there was plenty of opportunity for me to shout out. From the masthead, the perfectly shaped contours of the *Warrior Queen* below looked like a boat designer's drawing. It appeared very small from high up, and the sea seemed even more expansive. I shouted down below to cut the engine. The boat was under sail in the silence of the night. I was perched on top of the mast like a fairy on top of a Christmas tree, the lights on the high volcanic island of Madeira twinkled as a thousand stars, and the full body of the sail pressed hard up against my own. I lit a cigarette and smoked it. I stayed up in the bosun's chair for about an hour, smoking the best cigarettes of my life. On coming down, I allocated the night watches before retiring to the aft cabin for a good night's sleep.

The course to the Canary Islands took us close to a group of very small, uninhabited islands known as *Isles Selvagem* – the Salvage Islands. One of these is a nature reserve with a resident warden who lives in the only building in the group, and, weather permitting, we could stop off to have a quick look. Bob and Alex spent much time discussing the time constraints that they were under, and Alex didn't want to stop off. We all discussed this amicably, and everyone was for stopping except Alex. I was on watch while the rest continued to debate the pros and cons of stopping. Terry and Bob were trying to convince Alex that it wouldn't entail a significant delay. Alex wouldn't accept any of the arguments or the consensus of opinion. The discussion was going nowhere. In exasperation, I came down below and said to him, 'Look, Alex, the majority want to stop off, and that includes the skipper, so can you give it a rest – please.' There was no more argument but, from time to time, I could see Alex counting off imaginary days with his fingers as he worked out the options.

The warden of the nature reserve on Selvagem Grande was waiting for us at the small jetty when we rowed ashore. This was as far as we got: without a permit from the Portuguese government no one was allowed to land. I tried to bullshit him with talk of the voyage being sponsored by my university but he would have none of it. Within two hours of arriving, we had left the desolate island in the middle of nowhere behind us and set a course for the island of Tenerife in the Canaries.

I stood the first watch after we left the island but was unable to sleep when I went to bed. The trip wasn't working out the way I had expected it to. I seemed to be spending all my time at sea or in port working on the boat. Since leaving Whitby, there had been no time to explore any of the places I had been to so far, and it looked as though all this was set to continue if I tried to stick to my original plan. Maybe two years wasn't long enough to sail round the world and enjoy it – that's what all the books said, but I thought I could prove them wrong. My bank balance now stood at zero, and I knew there would be big bills to pick up in the Canaries. I couldn't see how I could keep going for another month, let alone another year-and-a-half. I lay in my bunk each night, cuddling up to the pillow, wishing it was Laura. I couldn't see myself enduring this separation for much longer. Whatever way I looked at it, I was running out of time, money and love.

Terry had now been aboard for nearly ten weeks and was driving me crazy. The idea of another six months with him didn't bear thinking about. There was a strong possibility of Bob and Alex leaving in the Canaries, leaving me short-handed for the Atlantic crossing. I had been trying to meet deadlines from day one, and this was putting a big strain on me and the boat. Maybe it was time to rethink and come up with an alternative plan. One way or the other, I was determined to cross an ocean, and my fallback position was to settle for an Atlantic circuit. This could be completed in a year, at the end of which I could take up my job again and pay off my debts. That took care of the money problem. It would give me more time to have a look around some of the places I visited and avoid the need to keep putting to sea in bad weather or with suspect gear. That took care of the time problem. It would also mean that I would be back with Laura in nine months, by which time, with any luck, she would still be waiting for me. That took care of the love problem. I made up my mind that instead of going through the Panama Canal and on to Australia, I would settle for an Atlantic circuit. Sydney Opera House would be there for a long time to come – I could always fly out in my old age and go to see *Madame Butterfly* another time. It was hard to accept the dilution of my plans but there was no alternative. I dropped off to sleep with the contentment of a man who bows to the inevitable.

The wind had picked up while I was asleep. It was blowing at near gale force when I came on deck shortly before dawn, but it was coming from the north so we could run before it. It was my first day with my revised plans for the rest of the voyage, and I was a little subdued. When I went down below to cook breakfast, Bob told me that my spectacles had fallen off the chart table during the night. The left lens was smashed, but I had a spare pair and wasn't unduly bothered. After standing my dawn watch, I went back to my bunk. Everyone was now up and I didn't feel like socialising, preferring instead to stretch out and read in the privacy of the aft cabin. This was situated just behind the cockpit, and I could hear everything that was going on.

As we approached Tenerife, a dispute started between Bob and Terry. Bob felt that we should alter course slightly, to allow for the current. Terry disagreed and said, very affirmatively, that the course was 190 degrees. Bob then explained why he thought that 200 would be better. Terry once more repeated that the course was 190. I had left no firm instructions about what the exact course should be: it really didn't make that much difference, give or take ten degrees. Bob then asked Terry why he thought the course should be 190. Terry's reply made me crumple up the pages of the book I was reading. 'Because that's what I say it is.'

I wanted to leap out of my bunk and throttle him. What right did he have to lay down the law in an authoritative manner to anyone?

The golden rule on small boats is that the skipper should never take sides in disputes between the crew. I could do nothing but lie there and listen to this shit. I wouldn't mention it, but in future I would stipulate a course. This wasn't the way I wanted to run things but if they were going to start arguing among themselves about trivial details, I had no alternative.

As we neared the island there was a possibility of entering a well-defined acceleration zone where the wind increases in strength as it funnels round the landmass. These zones are at their most pronounced in the high islands of the Canary group. Tenerife, with Pico de Teide standing at over 12,000 feet, is the highest of all. I remained in my cabin until my next watch. Alex was now laying down the law about reefing the sails. There was needless shouting as he barked out the orders. Once more, I wanted to leap out of my bunk, but crumpled up a few more pages of my book instead.

It was mid-afternoon when I came out of the cabin. The summit of Pico de Teide, which seemed to be suspended in mid-air, floated above a layer of low cloud. We were heading for a small harbour called Los Gigantes, which, according to the sailing guide, had a marina and a crane. To get there we had to sail through a very tight acceleration zone. When we reached the zone the wind picked up markedly, forcing us to reduce sail quickly. The sea built at the same time, the waves crashing against the tall cliffs on the shore. Tenerife is a highly developed island with an abundance of tourists at all times of the year, but this part of the coastline was so completely desolate that it was hard to believe anyone lived on the island.

Once we were through the acceleration zone and in the lee of the tall cliffs of the Coast of Silence, the wind dropped off and the seas were relatively calm. Los Gigantes was only ten miles away. The cliffs were stark and dramatic – a solid wall of sheer rock as far as the eye could see. There was an uncanny silence. The water beneath us was as blue as ink. This deep, dark water, along with the tall, barren cliffs and the silence, lent an air of otherworldliness and imminent doom to the whole place.

Bob was the first to see it. 'Look, look – over there,' he called out anxiously. What appeared to be a giant spinning-top of grey, misty cloud with a sharp-pointed vortex was dancing over the surface of the water, heading in our direction. The wind suddenly picked up and seemed to be falling straight on top of us. Within seconds it was howling, and all we could do was crouch down low, holding on to the grab-rails with both hands. Nobody spoke a word while the wind screeched in a high-pitched tone. The spinning-top passed within 50 yards of us, darting this way and that as it went. The wind disappeared as quickly as it had come, and the grey vortex of air slowly dissolved into nothingness. Before another one appeared, we started the engine quickly and lowered all sails. If the spinning cone of air struck the boat directly, the sails would be shredded in an instant.

'What the hell was that?' Alex asked, not expecting an answer, but Bob remembered reading about this phenomenon. When there are strong winds that are interrupted by a high landmass, the wind rises over the land. If there are tall cliffs in the lee of the landmass, and a few other atmospheric conditions are right, then the deflected wind can literally fall from the sky, producing mini-tornadoes. As the wind falls from the sky, it is sucked back up in a spinning vortex at the centre. The grey, misty appearance is made by millions of droplets of seawater.

It was now completely calm but it wasn't long before we saw a patch of sea that had thousands of tiny ripples on it, and the water itself seemed to vibrate. This patch of water was darting all over the place and started to head towards us. Once again the wind fell from the sky and everyone hung on with both hands. There was no visible spinning vortex of mist this time and it wasn't quite as severe. These were the most freakish weather conditions I had ever encountered. If another spinning vortex appeared and struck the boat directly, it would most likely be lost – we might even all be sucked up into the cone of air. As these thoughts raced through my mind, Terry spotted another one. Everyone crouched down low as the whirling dervish of wind teased us with its demented dance. This one was making its way straight towards us. The wind screeched once more. At the last minute, it skipped to one side, passing behind the boat.

There were a few more patches of vibrating sea, but no more spinning vortexes, as we left the Coast of Silence behind and closed on the port of Los Gigantes. The outline of a crane on the dockside was visible from well out to sea, and the binoculars revealed that it was standing idle – a bit of luck at last! I brought the boat into the marina at dusk and looked for a spot to tie up.

Manoeuvring the boat in tight spaces was always difficult but more so now with a wheel that was practically solid. I came in very slow. The boat was virtually at a standstill in the middle of the marina when I tried to engage reverse gear to turn her round. No reverse gear! I told the others to be ready to fend off in case we bumped into anything and tried to go forward again slowly. No forward gear! I was not in the least worried because there was no wind and we would eventually drift to one side or the other of the marina. With four of us aboard, we could easily fend off and tie up without doing any damage.

When I told the other three that I had lost forward and reverse gear, everyone came up with their own ideas on what to do. I couldn't be bothered with any of the conflicting schemes or voices and let them run around the decks implementing their own separate strategies. There was shouting and general confusion. I stood by impassively. We eventually got a line ashore and secured the boat to the harbour wall. When it was tied up, I went off on my own to find the nearest bar.

18. *Falling Apart*

AS I SAT STARING AT A GLASS OF BEER, IT WAS OBVIOUS THAT the whole trip was turning out to be something of a disaster. Attending to all the jobs was not going to be easy, nor was doing something about the conflicts between the crew. Terry was the first to pass by, and I had a word with him. I told him that as from today, the ship was going to be run differently. No one would alter course without consulting me; no one would put a reef in or take one out without my permission; no one would shout needlessly at anyone else; and no one, apart from me, would give orders to anyone else. I saw Bob and Alex separately, telling each of them the same thing. None of them made any reply and they all left after the little talk. I spent the rest of the evening on my own.

First thing next morning I was waiting outside the marina owner's office. He was an elusive man. Two hours later he still hadn't shown up. When I returned to the boat, only Bob was aboard. Alex had gone for a walk and Terry had gone off with his laundry. I didn't have a clean pair of underpants to my name, and the idea of someone going off with their own personal laundry when we all had washing that needed doing, was just not acceptable. Unable to keep my exasperation to myself any longer, I expressed my dismay to Bob.

When I opened the engine hatch to examine the gear selector, I was even more dismayed. There was nothing wrong with the gearbox, but the propshaft that had come off in the Irish Sea had parted again. Ever since the repair was done in Ireland, I had worried about it. When we had forced the wheel over to try to free it, the rudder had pushed hard against the propeller, and this had probably put a tiny kink in the shaft. That kink was enough to set up vibrations, which was why it had come undone a second time.

Around lunchtime I got the OK to have the boat lifted out. We were lying on the other side of the marina with no means of propulsion – but I had a very long rope and a dinghy. This time there wasn't anyone else aboard. I rowed the rope across the harbour, securing it to a pontoon. After rowing back to the *Warrior Queen*, I cast off and began hauling on the rope to pull her across. Alex, who had seen me at work from a harbour-side café, came running round as fast as his legs would carry him, and jumped aboard. I think he had lost heart when the lift didn't happen early that morning but the prospect of hauling out restored his spirits.

When we got to the pontoon, Alex jumped off, untied the rope and walked the boat round to the small dock over which the crane was straddled. All the staff were standing by. As they pulled the boat in, one of them called out to me in Spanish, throwing a heavy rope towards me at the same time. I turned round to see the rope flying through the air just before it smacked me in the face. It knocked my only good pair of spectacles off. As they landed on the deck, one of the lenses popped out and flipped over the side – two pair of spectacles broken in less than 24 hours! The slings were slid under the keel and the boat was hauled out like some giant dead fish. The crane driver slowly inched away from the dock, parking the boat in a corner of the yard.

The owner allowed me to leave the boat in the slings for a few days while I worked on it, but he wouldn't let us stay aboard at night. I found this very unreasonable but wasn't in a position to argue. Terry and Bob had now turned up, and Terry went off to look for an apartment to rent for a few days. The rest of us got stuck into the work. I showed Bob and Alex how to dismantle the rudder from the back of the boat while I disconnected the steering gear at the inboard end. As soon as the steering linkage to the rudder was disconnected, Bob called out, 'John, this rudder's free now.' I hurried down the ladder. The rudder could be turned either way with one hand – so much for the theory about the hygroscopic nylon bush. Whatever the problem was, it lay somewhere along the steering linkage. I hadn't suspected this as there was no sign of damage when I first examined it once the wheel began to stiffen up.

Terry returned with the good news that he had found a cheap, self-catering apartment, and Bob went off with him to have a look at it. That was the last I saw of the two of them for what remained of the afternoon, but Alex stayed with me, passing spanners and hammers. He also moaned endlessly about what was keeping Bob and Terry. By nightfall the propeller and propshaft had been removed, the steering linkage had been dismantled, and the fault traced to a bearing in a small gearbox that converted a rotary motion into an angular one. The area around the boat was littered with tools and the entire steering and transmission systems. I was tired and covered in grease. Bob and Terry turned up as the tools were being put away and were visibly shocked at the state the boat was in – the giant dead fish had its guts ripped out.

Later that night, Bob told me that he was thinking of going home. Of all the people aboard, he was the one I least wanted to lose. He didn't think there was enough time to repair the boat and be across the Atlantic by Christmas, but I still thought we could do it. Although the problems with the boat were considerable, I was very pleased that we had been lifted out, and all the problem gear had been dismantled in a single day. If we found a good workshop that could machine the new bits, the boat could be back in the water in three or four days. With four of us working hard, we could be ready to go in a week. Bob was not convinced but he was happy to hang around for a few more days and was going to hire a car to look round the island. He was also willing to drive me around to try to find a machine shop.

Terry stayed behind next day, while the rest of us drove to the second largest town on the island, Los Cristianos. The car boot was loaded up with the propshaft, the faulty gearbox from the steering system, and the mainsail, which needed professional repair. Los Cristianos was once a small fishing port, but with the advent of mass tourism it has grown like topsy. There was a big boatyard, with many yachts hauled out, and the place was buzzing with activity as their crews worked to prepare them for the Atlantic crossing. We found a little shed where the local Mr Fixit hung out. He didn't have the necessary equipment to make the parts for the propshaft but he was prepared to have a go at trying to extract the seized bearing from the steering gearbox. Alex was stamping around impatiently, expecting everything to be fixed in a day, which was a prospect well beyond the limits of optimism.

There was only one sailmaker on the island. He was based in the capital of Santa Cruz, about 50 miles to the north, so I asked Bob if he would drive there to get the sail repaired. He agreed, taking Alex with him. While I was on my own, I established that there was only one machine workshop on the island capable of repairing the propshaft, and they, like the sailmaker, were based in Santa Cruz. By late afternoon Alex and Bob returned without having found the sailmaker, and Mr Fixit was unable to extract the seized bearing. He was going to soak it in penetrating oil before having another go the next day. Alex was demanding to know why he hadn't been able to do it that day, and I told him that he had to be patient. When I asked why they hadn't found the sailmaker, Alex didn't reply.

Bob was happy to drive me to Santa Cruz the next day. We set off at dawn the following morning. I left Alex behind with Terry and gave them a few small jobs to get on with. Now that Bob was leaving, I felt free to open up to him, and we talked at length about the trip. Bob's main reason for going home was that he missed his wife and kids. He also found Terry impossible to get on with when at sea and was getting fed up with Alex's impatience. He told me that the day before, when they were looking for the sailmaker in Santa Cruz, Alex just kept repeating, 'Screw the sail, let's get back and see what's happening with the other jobs.'

We arrived in Santa Cruz before the morning rush hour and by 9.0 a.m. had located the sailmaker and the machine workshop that could fix the propshaft. Things were looking up. My bank account now stood at zero, but I found a bank where I was going to draw out some cash with my credit card. After waiting in the plush lobby for about half an hour, I was told that that there was no authorisation on my credit card. Laura had agreed to pay the bills as they came in each month but she must have overlooked the last one. This was a major setback. Without cash, I couldn't pay the sailmaker, the workshop or the crane owner or buy the extra bits of gear from the local chandlers.

I knew that Bob had contempt for cheques and credit cards and worked with cash. He had some, and I needed it desperately. 'How much can you let me have, Bob?' I asked. Bob was worried. He needed his money for his fare home. His fish-and-chip shop was closed down for the winter, and the balance of his cash was for Christmas. At first he didn't want to let me have any but I pleaded with him and told him that whatever I owed him would be repaid as soon as I could get Laura to send me some cash. I had yet to talk to Laura about this but that could be sorted out later. Bob wanted to help but was uncertain what to do. He kept saying, 'I need this to buy presents for the kids at Christmas.' When that didn't work, he asked, 'Why don't you just leave the boat here and fly home? That's what I would do if I were you. You could come out next spring and sail her back.' I made no reply other than to shake my head. Bob looked at the roll of notes in his hand and looked at me, and started peeling them off.

There was enough money to pay the sailmaker and the workshop but not enough for the other bills. It was a start. We picked up some gear before heading back to Los Cristianos to see how Mr Fixit was getting on. The bearing wouldn't budge for love nor money, but the workshop in Santa Cruz had hydraulic presses, and they could extract it and make a new one. We raced back to Los Gigantes with adrenaline pumping through the two of us. On the way there, Bob said that he would love to make the trip with me but somehow he just couldn't see it happening. On arriving in Los Gigantes, we found Alex and Terry relaxing beside the swimming-pool. I was very upbeat and told them of the progress. Later that night, Alex informed me that he had decided to go home with Bob. Alex and Terry had not been getting on at all well, so I was quite relieved at the news of the departure of one of them, but it meant there would only be two of us for the Atlantic crossing.

Next day was the last opportunity to have access to the car, which Bob let me borrow to drive to Santa Cruz. When Terry expressed an interest in coming with me to see a bit of the island, I suddenly remembered that when he came up to Whitby for the first time, he had given me a lift to work before leaving. This entailed a detour of about 30 miles and he asked me to pay for the petrol. I said to Terry he could come if he wanted to but he would have to share the cost of the petrol. When this was put to him, he decided not to bother. I left on my own at sunrise next day for another dawn raid on Santa Cruz.

With the cash available to me, I was going to pick up the sail, call into the workshop to pay for the work they had done, leave the steering gearbox in to be fixed, and spend what was left over on extra gear from the chandlers. Now that the shaft was repaired, I could rebuild the transmission and get the boat back in the water. The car boot was loaded up with all the gear, and after spending my last pesetas at the chandlers, I headed back to Los Gigantes.

The road was a good dual carriageway for most of the journey but the last stretch snaked along a few narrow stretches where there was barely room for two vehicles to pass. The surface was pitted with craters, and there were sharp, steep ledges to the side. When negotiating one of these bends, a large truck forced me off the road. The two nearside wheels thumped against the ledge as they went over the edge. The car came to a juddering halt and the steering jammed. I had been driving for 20 years and had never had an accident, of any sort, in all that time – but I had had one now.

The rims of both wheels were knocked out of shape. Both tyres were flat. Traffic was hurtling past in each direction. I sweated and puffed as I pushed the car on to a dirt track that led down to a quarry. There was one spare wheel but I had two wrecked ones. All the gear was taken from the car boot along with the spare wheel, and I replaced the worst of the two. Clouds of thick dust from the dirt road to the quarry were being thrown up by the traffic. It clung to my beard and hair. The one good lens of my spectacles was covered in it. Sweat ran down my face, making clean tracks in the brown dust. I couldn't help thinking that this was probably as bad as it was ever going to get.

Some time later, a truck for the quarry came by and the driver, who didn't speak a word of English, produced an air-pressure hose to inflate the bad tyre. When everything looks bad, something good always turns up. There was a tyre centre nearby. The car bumped down the winding narrow road on the bad wheel and into the forecourt. I had no money to pay for the repairs but I told them to go ahead and fix it. When the repairs were done, I handed over the credit card nonchalantly. Shortly afterwards the manager asked me into his office. He spoke good English, explaining, very politely, that there was no authorisation on the card. I feigned a look of complete surprise, saying I couldn't understand why. Eventually he accepted my passport as security. With two new wheels on the car, one lens in my spectacles and no passport in my pocket, I screeched out of the forecourt.

When I got back to the boat, there was a note from Bob saying that he and Alex had gone home. I was sorry not to have had an opportunity to say goodbye to them. Their dream of crossing the Atlantic hadn't come true. Maybe it was partly my fault and maybe it was partly theirs: I don't think they believed in it enough to make it come true.

The apartment had been vacated that afternoon, so Terry and I had nowhere to stay. The previous night, while I was down working on the boat, the crew had met three young women from Liverpool, and we were all invited to dinner this evening. I had said that I probably wouldn't be back in time but the rest had accepted. Later that night, I saw the three of them sitting outside a bar and went over to talk with them. 'How did the dinner go? I'm sorry I wasn't able to make it,' I said, and they replied that nobody turned up. I explained that Bob and Alex had got a flight home, but they already knew that and had in fact given them a lift to the airport. 'What about Terry?' I asked, and they said that he had decided not to come.

They had planned a dinner party for seven and one of them said, 'You can have dinner if you want.' I was more than happy to accept. On the way to the apartment, I bumped into Terry and borrowed some money from him to buy a bottle of wine. He wasn't interested in coming for dinner.

They had already eaten but were quite happy to cook me a fine steak, which went well with the red wine. They fussed over me and kept trying to coax me into having more steaks – there were another three in the fridge. Terry and I were planning to sleep in the rented car that night but they had a spare sofa bed and an unused camp bed and insisted that I stay with them. They were fascinated, as most women are, by relationships and had been observing the relationship between the four of us for the last 24 hours. It was immediately apparent that they had genuine sympathy for me, and I could use all the sympathy I could get right now.

'It's not really fair on you, is it, John?' said one.

'You have all the responsibility and have to do all the work, and they spend the day sitting around the pool,' said another. None of them could understand why Terry hadn't come for dinner, but I did. They were three working-class lasses from Liverpool and two of them were considerably overweight. They were not beautiful in a glossy-magazine sense, and Terry would have regarded them as a bit common. He wasn't able to face the prospect of having dinner with the three of them on his own. I lapped it up.

All three were in their mid-twenties and they always went on holiday together. Veronica, the most talkative of the three, carried a bottle of vodka in her handbag wherever she went. Deborah was the mother-like figure, who made all the big decisions, and Susan was somewhat quiet and withdrawn.

After dinner we all went out for a drink. Veronica wouldn't dream of letting me get her a vodka and asked for orange juice, which the other two were having. After the barman left, Veronica had a good look around, leaned forward towards me, and whispered, 'John, move up a bit closer to me.' As I did so, I saw her hand move under the table in the general direction of my leg. She slipped it into her handbag. I breathed a sigh of relief. Then she deftly unscrewed the top from the vodka bottle, before topping up her glass of orange juice. 'You don't want to be paying the prices in here, John,' she said, placing the full glass neatly on the table.

Deborah shook her head disapprovingly and said, 'Our Veronica drinks far too much of that stuff.'

Later that night, Deborah made up my bed on the sofa. Veronica was sleeping in the same room, and she had a few more vodkas. I was very tired but she was talking to me non-stop. Every sentence started or ended with the word John. Deborah and Susan were in the main bedroom sharing a big double bed. They chuckled to themselves as Veronica bent my ear. Deborah called out, 'Our Veronica never stops talking, John,' and Veronica told her where to go. It got to the stage where I was unable to reply coherently and, in an attempt not to be rude, kept saying yes, no, maybe, or uhmm, but it didn't matter what order I used these words. Just as I was about to drop off to sleep, I heard Terry's voice. He was in the garden, and when I came out to the balcony to ask what he wanted, he said that he couldn't sleep in the car and would like to come in. Veronica made up the camp bed for him. She left Terry in peace but kept talking to me as I fell asleep.

For the next week, I worked on the boat in between travelling back and forth on the bus to Los Cristianos and Santa Cruz. Laura sent me £1,000. It was hard to ask her, and she did her best not to say, 'I told you so', but didn't quite manage it. Every extra day the boat stayed in the slings cost more money, and I was rushing about like a man possessed to get it back in the water as soon as possible. The marina owner was giving me a hard time about tying up the crane, and I assured him that I would be finished in a few days. After each day's work, I came back to the girls' apartment for a bath and they usually cooked me supper. I entertained them by singing from the balcony as they came up the street with the shopping under their arms. In the evenings, we went to the local karaoke bar and Terry usually came with us.

The work was going well but we were still tying up the crane. Eventually the marina owner lost his patience and gave me an ultimatum. We had one more day. All the parts were ready and everything was going well, when I hit a snag. A bolt that secured the propshaft in place had been made heavier than before and went into the shaft deeper than before. I didn't want it to come off again. It was unlikely to now that the shaft was straightened but I was taking no chances. The bolt was very stiff, and I tried to work it backwards and forwards. It sheared! It was a Saturday morning and nothing could be done about it till Monday, when the machine workshop opened in Santa Cruz.

The crane was needed for other boats. The marina owner called his men together and told them to build a cradle around the *Warrior Queen*. It was a disappointment but at the same time a relief. Although I hadn't managed to get the boat back in the water, I no longer had him breathing down my neck. Up until that point, I had been determined to get across the Atlantic for Christmas. But I knew I wasn't going to make it now. The men got to work quickly, driving nails into the timbers of the wooden frame, and the sound of hammering echoed around the yard. It was a miserable noise. I turned to Terry and said, 'They're building a coffin around her.' I had a broken boat and a broken dream.

I told Terry that now that the boat was in a cradle, I had had enough of rushing about and was going to stay in Tenerife until Christmas. He said he would leave, as he didn't like hanging around. I shrugged my shoulders and said it was his choice.

There was a day-and-a-half in which I had absolutely nothing to do. It was a wonderful feeling. On Sunday I walked along the cliffs of the Coast of Silence, pondering the options. I had made a lot of mistakes and had always rushed everything but I was sure I could sort the boat out once and for all, now that I had six weeks to do it in. The problems so far had been a combination of rushed preparations, bad luck and bad weather. Whatever I did now, it was important not to rush anything. Luck was in the lap of the Gods but maybe they would smile on me for a change. I was now in sub-tropical latitudes where the weather was warm and settled. The tradewind belt that would take the boat across the Atlantic was only about 300 miles further south. Finding crew might be a problem but there were lots of people hanging around Los Cristianos looking for a passage.

Sitting on the cliff-top looking out to the west, I could almost imagine that I could see the Americas, and I thought to myself what's the big deal? I'm going to fix this boat on my own, and after that I'm going to sail the ocean on my own. The thought electrified me. I wasn't going to make Sydney Opera House but I was going to sail the Atlantic single handed. No more crew worries! I jumped up and down with joy, laughing out loud. I was on the verge of mania and in danger of falling off the cliff, so I settled myself down on a rock and rolled a cigarette. I had never sailed anywhere on my own before, but the trip would only take about 30 days and many others had done it. Getting Laura to agree to it would be my only problem.

Terry came with me to Santa Cruz after the weekend and went off to try to find another boat going west. He asked me to write him a reference, which is customary. I gave him one that told no lies but only some of the truth. We travelled back separately, and on the way to the girls' apartment I called into the boatyard in Los Cristianos to look at the noticeboard to see if anyone wanted to crew. The idea of doing the passage single handed always seemed a great one late at night, when I had a few drinks in me, but it never looked the same when I woke up in the morning. There were about four notices on the board for *Crew Available*. One of them looked very promising. It read:

> Passage to Caribbean sought by easy-going 26-year-old male. RYA qualified to day-skipper level but more experience needed. Can participate in all aspects of sailing and knows how to *take* orders. Sailed here from Iceland but boat laid up with mechanical problems. Reference from skipper available.

While having a coffee in one of the cafés nearby, Terry came along and stopped for a moment. He was in a hurry. He had no luck in finding a passage from Santa Cruz, and was on his way to check the noticeboard. Terry was a 26-year-old male. Although he hadn't sailed from Iceland, he had sailed from Ireland – and his handwriting wasn't the best! That was the last time I looked at the noticeboard.

When I returned to Los Gigantes, Terry was already there. The girls had gone out for the night to a club. We were on our own. He had decided to leave Tenerife in two days' time for the island of Las Palmas, where there was a better chance of picking up a westbound yacht. We didn't say much for the rest of that night.

There were more bits of gear to pick up in Santa Cruz, so I set off early next morning to catch the bus. Terry and I said goodbye, as I wasn't sure if I would be back before he left. In truth, I couldn't endure the prospect of another night. To avoid coming back to Los Gigantes, I booked into a cheap hotel in Santa Cruz. Lying on the bed, smoking a cigarette and watching a solitary mosquito buzzing about, my mind went back through the last 11 weeks. Things hadn't worked out for either of us. Terry could have reasonably expected a boat in better order and a schedule that went according to plan. We hadn't known each other at the outset and had been through a lot – we could have died together in the Bay of Biscay. Even after all this, maybe even because of it, I now wanted to spend this last night on my own. When we had problems, and we had plenty of these, Terry would always say, 'What a nightmare.' Nightmare, bizarre and pretty were his three favourite words – they could always be relied upon to describe any situation. As I lay there, I thought that with Terry aboard, it had been, for both of us, a pretty bizarre nightmare.

Terry was gone when I got back to Los Gigantes next day, and I got stuck into the work. I repaired the damage to the keel caused by running aground in Berwick and fixed the leaking rudder gland that had been with me since setting sail from Whitby. The propshaft was reassembled and the steering system rebuilt. There was a multitude of other jobs to do, and one by one the most important of these were tackled and finished.

The night before the girls left I took them out to dinner to their favourite restaurant. It was in a small village just outside the town and was named after its owner, Pedro. We got the best table in the house, overlooking the ocean, and Pedro flirted with the girls. There was a small band playing and Pedro, the three girls and I danced around the tables. Pedro sang a few Spanish love songs. Veronica kept replenishing her glass with the bottle of vodka in her handbag but Pedro turned a blind eye. He served us up with a complimentary glass of the local liqueur, which none of the girls could drink. To avoid causing Pedro embarrassment, they emptied their glasses into the pot plants when they thought he wasn't looking.

There was a big argument when I insisted on paying the bill, which was only resolved by me allowing them to pay for the taxi home. The taxi driver wanted to know if we were having a party but there wasn't much vodka left and we had to say no. Veronica talked for hours while I lay on the sofa bed, trying to drink the last drop of vodka, while Deborah and Susan chuckled away in the big double bed in the adjoining bedroom. I saw them off early next morning and waved the taxi goodbye as it climbed up the hill and out of town. They leaned out the window and yelled, 'See you in Liverpool,' and were gone.

Once again I had nowhere to stay. The money was running low, and I didn't want to fork out for an apartment on my own. Maybe there would be new angels coming to town. I hung around the bars on the first night but didn't find any. Male angels would have done fine but I didn't find any of these either. I thought of breaking into one of the empty apartments, but figured it would be much easier and less risky to break into my own boat.

The night watchman's movements were predictable. When he went into the office for his cup of tea at midnight, I climbed the security fence and crawled along the ground to get to my boat. I sneaked aboard without making a sound or showing any light. The next morning, I appeared at about 9.0 a.m., with overalls on and tools in hand – to give the impression that I had been working on the boat for some hours. At dusk, I made an elaborate show of locking up the boat and broke in again the same night. This fiasco went on for three days before the boat was finally ready to be relaunched.

The giant dead fish went back in the water and once more became a beautiful ocean-going yacht. She was as tight as a drum. I stayed aboard legitimately that night and got tight myself. The next day I was ready to leave the marina to head east about ten miles to the port of Los Cristianos, where I could anchor free of charge. As the boat cleared the harbour entrance there was a young couple standing on the pier end. They looked at me wistfully and probably thought wouldn't it be nice to sail off like that without a care in the world? If only they knew.

19. *New Friends*

LOS CRISTIANOS WAS GOING TO BE MY BACKYARD FOR THE next five or six weeks, so I picked a spot carefully to lay two anchors – one from the bow and one from the stern. My immediate neighbour was a 40-foot ketch called *Potlatch – Make it Happen*, but there didn't seem to be anyone aboard. A bit further away there was a big catamaran that was obviously a party boat. The decks were strewn with half-naked women and a few men. Maybe they'll invite me aboard for a drink if I play my cards right, I thought, as I checked the anchors to ensure that they were both well dug in.

There was still a long list of jobs to attend to, but as this was my first day in my new home I inflated the dinghy to go ashore. Rowing between the boats lying at anchor, I felt like a new resident in a new neighbourhood. There were about 60 boats lying at anchor. They all had a lived-in feel to them: washing hung from the rigging of most of them; some had home-made barbecues mounted on the back; others had rusty bicycles lashed to the guard-rails. It was a bit like a gypsy camp-site, and I felt very much at home.

On nearing the jetty, a young man with long, lank hair rowed past in the opposite direction in a beaten-up wooden skiff. 'Where's the best place to tie up round here?' I asked. He kept rowing but, speaking out of the corner of his cigarette-filled mouth, directed me to the far side of the jetty. 'Is that a Dublin accent?' I called out after him.

He stopped rowing and took the cigarette out of his mouth. 'Sure is.'

'What boat are you on,' I asked.

'That little white cat over there.'

'I'm on *Warrior Queen*, you can just see her.'

'I'll call over and see you tomorrow,' he said.

'What's your name by the way?'

'Peter.'

'Mine's John, and I have a Belfast accent.'

Peter's piercing blue eyes and broad, wicked smile made an instant impression on me. I had made my first friend. Later that evening, while

133

rowing in again, I started up another conversation, this time with an Englishman called Michael. He was going ashore for a drink and invited me to join him. Michael was the genuine article as far as sailing goes. He was 60 years of age and had 45 years' sailing experience. He had sailed his boat, *Glaisbrooke Springs*, single handed to Tenerife and was planning to sail round the world. He had already sailed the Atlantic on six previous occasions but had never done it on his own before. Here was a man worth getting to know.

Within an hour we knew a lot about each other. Michael would lean over the table towards me before making a point and usually begin by saying, 'We single handers . . .' I felt an absolute fraud. But when I first introduced myself to him, he asked how many were aboard my boat. When I said I was on my own he beamed broadly and shook my hand, saying, 'Great, it's always good to meet another single hander.' After that, it would have been too embarrassing to explain that I had yet to sail anywhere on my own.

The way I was making friends made me feel like a kid who had just spent his first day at school. How easy it was then to make friends. Everyone had so much in common, and there were no barriers to striking up conversations. Somehow, as we get older, we lose this gift and become more circumspect. But here in this harbour, I felt I could talk to anyone about anything without any need for the usual formalities. These rambling drunken thoughts stayed with me as I rowed out to the boat late that night.

Next morning Peter turned up in his old skiff, and I welcomed him aboard. The sun was shining brightly. Peter smiled and said, 'Well, John, another day in paradise.' I made him some breakfast, before he filled me in on the local gossip. He knew every boat in the harbour and everybody aboard and wanted to know if I was looking for crew. Once again, I was in the awkward situation of saying I was single handed without ever having been so. Although he wasn't looking for a passage, he knew two German girls that were. He offered to bring them over later in the day to have a look at the boat.

Peter was a wandering Irish minstrel. He played guitar and worked the local bars, with a regular spot in a pub called the Flying Haggis. He lived aboard an old catamaran in the harbour, which he shared with a man called Ralph. This was much cheaper than an apartment and more to his taste. There was a fish-trap tied up alongside the boat, and he usually caught two or three small fish a day. His routine was much the same every day – lie in late to recover from the night before, sunbathe on deck for a few hours, row round the bay for a bit of social chit-chat, go ashore for some shopping and a few drinks, get ready for the night's work, play guitar in the bars, and row back out to the boat. Sometimes, when Ralph was away, he rowed back with a friend.

Before leaving, he asked me if I had met Tony yet. I didn't even know who Tony was, but he explained he was my neighbour on *Potlatch*. He urged me to get to know him and said that, if I could, I should help him out from time to time. Tony was down on his luck apparently. He had sailed nearly all the way round the world but his boat was out of action with engine failure and he had no money. Peter told me that he had very little to eat and that if I had any food left over I should give it to him. As I was getting more details, Tony stuck his head up through the main hatch of his boat and Peter called out, 'Hey, Tony, this is John, your new neighbour.'

Tony spoke with a slow Yankee drawl and said, 'Hi, John.'

I replied, 'Good to meet you, Tony.' I was somewhat disturbed by Tony's situation. The idea of a man starving next to me was not a comforting one, and I hoped that Peter was exaggerating a bit. Tony certainly looked very thin but maybe he had always been like that.

Peter left after breakfast. Later in the day, while I was working down below, I heard him call out. He was in the skiff with the two German girls, and I asked them all to come aboard. They had left Germany about three months ago. After hitching to Spain, they travelled to the Canary Islands by ferry and were now hoping to hitch a lift across the Atlantic to the Caribbean. Neither of them had done any sailing, and they had been hanging around Los Cristianos for about a month. The main reason why they had been unsuccessful so far was that one of them had a Spanish boyfriend – they were trying to get a boat to take all three of them. The boyfriend was kept in the background, in much the same way as he would be if they were standing at a roadside trying to hitch a lift from a passing car.

Helga had the boyfriend and Gerta was unattached. Gerta had the blondest hair I had ever seen. Her eyebrows were almost white. The rest of her face was freckled and suntanned. Peter had his eye on her. In fact, he told me earlier that he loved her, but, as I was to learn later, Peter fell in and out of love every week. They came to the point quickly, asking if I would take them to the Caribbean. I think Laura would have been happier for me to go on my own – in a bathtub – than take these two with me. I knew it was a non-starter.

We talked about their various options and the problem for any skipper taking on three inexperienced crew for such a long trip. They had already been round all the other boats in the harbour and visited each new one that came in. Gerta said that it did look, at one stage, as if they had found a boat but it didn't work out. I asked why not and she said in a matter-of-fact way, 'The captain, he want to have both of us to fuck.' Peter gulped his tea. I coughed to conceal what threatened to turn into a nervous laugh. She pointed the boat out, with some contempt, and I made it clear that I had work to be getting on with. Peter took them ashore in his skiff, where they no doubt hung around and waited for another boat.

Tony had seen the goings on and drawled out, 'Hey, John, did those German girls ask you to take them to the Carib?'

I told him what he already knew, and he replied, 'Well, you know the old saying – screw to crew. But you can do without that, man.' Peter had dropped off some fish for Tony, and he was now busy scaling these on the aft deck of his boat. Tony said that there was too much for him and invited me to supper that night, 'It's nothing fancy, mind, just these scrawny fish and some rice.'

I had discovered since Terry's departure that a carton of wine in the supermarket was cheaper than a carton of fruit juice, and I never bought one without buying the other. When I rowed over to Tony's boat I made sure to bring some wine. Beacuse of his engine problems, Tony had no way of charging his batteries, so at night he lived by candlelight. There was enough light from the candle to illuminate a large-scale chart of the entire Atlantic Ocean, north and south, that hung above his bunk. A red line on the chart indicated his sailing route from Cape Town, up through the South Atlantic and across the Equator before finishing at the Canary Islands.

Tony was a little lethargic and apologised once more for the simple food, but the wine went down well and he began to open up. He had once worked as an economist in the US but decided to pack it in and sail the world. He was married at the time and his wife was all for the idea, as long as it was an idea. When the idea started to become a reality, she backed off. Tony found other crew and set sail without her. The plan was for her to join him from time to time in various exotic locations. This worked out well at the start, but after 18 months she divorced him and claimed her half of the boat. Tony kept going. Within another 18 months he had a second wife, whom he met in Australia and married in Mauritius. Things were working out well with the second wife when a posse of attorneys and federal officers boarded the boat in an island in the Indian Ocean and disabled the engine and removed the steering wheel. His first wife had done him.

The boat was impounded while lawyers dealt with the title to the vessel. The second wife now found herself without a home and entangled in what Tony described as legal bullshit. She left a year later. Shortly after, a court in America released the boat to Tony on condition that he sail it to an unspecified port on the eastern seaboard of the US, where the dispute would start all over again. He made it as far as the Canary Islands when his engine packed up beyond repair and he ran out of money. Tony had now been in Tenerife for a year and spent weeks on end without ever going ashore. Going ashore was difficult because someone stole his dinghy. All he had was a big plastic bucket. He made this himself from scraps of fibreglass. There wasn't enough room to sit down in it. To go ashore he had to balance himself, standing up in the bucket, and paddle with one oar.

Up until six months ago, he had got odd jobs in the boatyard, which kept him going. But he now thought that they regarded him as crazy and he didn't get any work. He sometimes wondered himself if he was crazy and would say, 'Maybe they're right, man, maybe I am crazy,' and at the same time laugh at the absurdity of the notion. Tony was on a downward spiral. Even if he got his engine fixed and sailed to the US, the authorities would take his boat from him and he would end up bartending or living on welfare. For a man who had held responsible jobs and had sailed oceans, this was a dreadful prospect, and he knew it. Maybe he was happier sitting on his boat in the bay in Los Cristianos — at least that way he didn't have to deal with the legal bullshit.

I had work that needed doing on my boat that I knew that Tony could do, but I couldn't afford to pay him. I told him he could use my dinghy anytime he wanted to. We talked about exactly what was wrong with his engine. We didn't resolve anything or come up with any quick fixes. Tony didn't expect any and wasn't disappointed. I think he was just glad to have someone to talk to and had in any case, as he said himself, learned a lot about patience and humility. He had a brother in the States and had thought for a long time about contacting him but decided against it. His ultimate fall-back position was to leave the boat and go to the American embassy and ask to be repatriated. With each passing month, he considered this option more seriously. I listened intently as Tony told me his tale. It made me feel even more insecure about Laura. Without her help, I would be on the road that Tony had travelled for a long time. A journey into despair and hopelessness. All the problems that had beset me now seemed like nothing.

Next morning I called out to Tony as I did everyday thereafter. On rowing ashore, I usually dropped him off some fruit and vegetables with the excuse that they were about to spoil. Tony always refused but I left them on the deck of his boat anyway. Peter was usually sunbathing on the deck of his boat in the mornings. When I rowed past he would always call out, 'Another day in paradise,' and laugh to himself. A few days after he had stopped by with the two German girls, I noticed that he was sunbathing with Gerta.

The work was going well, and if I needed advice I could always talk to Tony or Michael. The batteries were sorted out once and for all. The trouble had been that, in addition to the earlier wind-generator problems, the fan belt that turned the alternator when the engine was running was worn and slipping. This was the first thing I should have looked at but the faulty wind generator threw me off the trail. I was still having difficulty obtaining some parts for the outboard engine, which had packed up in Ireland, and I also needed to find a new oil-pressure gauge for the main engine. The self-steering system would be my key piece of equipment on the Atlantic crossing and I agonised about buying a new rudder for it and shipping it out from England. The problem was expense. I had already invested a considerable sum on the solid piece of mahogany that I had bought in Madeira. This was bolted on to the shaft at present, but if I was to stick with this, it had to be fitted properly.

Los Cristianos may have been the place for a hamburger and fries, but Santa Cruz was the place for engineering workshops and oil-pressure gauges. I left the rudder at the workshop, explaining what needed doing to the one employee who spoke English. He was surprised to see me again, and I told him that I had decided to stay in Tenerife until after Christmas. He wanted to know more, so I explained that my 'wife' was coming out to visit me for the festive season. All the other men in the workshop were informed and listened to every word as he translated the conversation. 'How long since you last saw your wife?' he asked.

'Nearly four months,' I explained.

'You must be very lonely. Four months is a long time.'

'You bet!'

'You must use the right hand a lot, si.' He made a gesture with his own right hand that didn't need any translation, and the whole workshop collapsed in laughter. It was time to leave and find the oil-pressure gauge.

Three hours later I gave up looking and tried to find the outboard-engine parts instead. After another three hours I found the main agent for my make of outboard motor. They had all the outboard engines, from the smallest to the largest, on display. They did no other business other than supply and repair these engines. Success at last! I needed six parts to rebuild the ignition system and had the part number for each one. The person behind the counter spoke a little English. I decided to take it one part at a time. 'Do you have a condenser for a 2.2 HP motor, part number G34765/2?' I asked. There was a polite, 'Momento', before he went off to the storeroom for about ten minutes. When he came back he shook his head, saying, 'No, Señor.' I then asked for another component, and after the polite 'Momento', waited another ten minutes. He returned saying 'No, Señor.' I asked for the third part on the list. Before he could say 'Momento', I was already thinking it. He was back in ten minutes, saying as I expected, 'No, Señor.' This wasn't working out according to plan. I tried a different tack. 'Do you have any parts for a 2.2 HP engine?' I asked. This time there was no 'Momento.' He just smiled and said 'No, Señor.'

Laura was due to join me for a fortnight at Christmas. I phoned her and gave her the part numbers and the address of the supplier. She wasn't happy to be running my errands. She had her own life to get on with and couldn't be expected to understand how difficult it was for me to get these parts, but she reluctantly agreed. In the meantime, I kept up the work and spent most evenings in the company of Tony, Peter or Michael. Every time I cooked dinner aboard, I invited Tony over to join me and we talked and played chess. He barely knew the rules but studied every move very carefully and I found it hard to beat him.

Michael always stopped by on his way ashore to invite me to join him for a drink. I accepted on most occasions, but usually ended up with a hangover the next day, and declined once or twice. I never refused an invitation to dinner though, for Michael was a good cook. With 45 years of experience behind him, he had his boat set up perfectly. It had pieces of equipment that I had never even heard of, and his pride and joy was his shortwave radio transceiver. Each day he used this to talk to people all over the world. All I had on my boat was a VHF radio with a range of about 20 miles. It didn't work very well and I hardly ever switched it on.

Michael gave me plenty of tips: how to catch tuna fish, how to keep eggs fresh by smearing them with Vaseline, and how to avoid cockroach infestation. He warned me that it is very easy to bring cockroaches aboard in cardboard boxes and that once they started to breed it is almost impossible to get rid of them. We talked about the cockroach problem at length. He told me that even if the boat is kept meticulously clean and all food is locked away in airtight containers, the little bastards, in their search for food, eat the dead skin from the soles of your feet when you are asleep.

Michael's wife had died a few years earlier and he obviously had never got over it. He nursed her through a long illness, and now that he was on his own he saw no reason not to go to sea. There was a girlfriend back home, and he kept writing to her asking her to join him, but she never did. She didn't like the idea of the cockroaches or the pirates. I had yet to hear the horror stories about the pirates but that was the next topic of conversation.

There had been lots of blood-curdling accounts in the papers about the recent upsurge of piracy. Michael knew all the details – captains shot in the head at point-blank range or hacked to pieces with machetes, boats pillaged and left to sink after the seacocks had been opened, the crew bound and gagged as the boat went down, and drug runners who would pretend to be drifting in a life raft, only to produce a kalashnikov when you went to their aid. The mother ship would be over the horizon, and as soon as they were aboard they would call it up on the radio and transfer the drugs to the commandeered safe vessel. If you were lucky they put you in the same life raft and set you adrift; if you were unlucky they emptied their kalashnikovs into you. Some parts of the world were worse than others but no ship was safe. A yacht with one man aboard was the softest target of all. Michael took the view that if you had the slightest reason to suspect anyone encountered at sea, you should shoot first and ask no questions later. I had thought about taking a weapon with me but decided against it. Michael was of a different view, and we discussed his defence systems. Among other items, he had a combat helmet, a bullet-proof flak jacket and a bolt-action Lee Enfield 303 rifle that was standard British army issue during both world wars. He insisted I try on the combat helmet and flak jacket before unlocking the secure locker where he kept the rifle.

Guns are strangely fascinating. They are always beautifully made from the finest materials, superbly engineered, and well balanced. The fact that they are capable of delivering death in an instant draws you to them and repels you from them at the same time. I drew the bolt back with a firm click and pushed it back into place with another click. Click-click, click-click. 'Wouldn't that sound put the fear of God into you?' Michael said, while I worked the bolt back and forth. I had to agree that it would before handing it back to him. After he had locked the weapon away, I asked him to play some more Mozart and we finished off the wine.

On the evenings I wasn't dining with Michael or Tony, I usually went ashore with Peter. He seemed to know everybody in town – all the entertainers, nearly all the sailors, a lot of the female tourists, and most of the time-share sharks. Peter introduced me to all and sundry. I found the company of the musicians enjoyable but the time-share sharks were a pain in the arse. They spent the day trying to get tourists to sign up to a two-week time-share in one of the new apartment blocks, and the evening bragging about their success. The deal was a con from start to finish, and they used every high-powered sales technique in the book – free gifts, free food, free drink, free cash for attending a sales talk. Everything was free, until it came to signing the contract, and you ended up paying for your freebies for the rest of your life. They were an arrogant bunch who strutted around as if they owned the place, which I suppose they did. Peter pointed out the one who owned the big catamaran in the bay. This was the party boat with all the half-naked women aboard that I had seen on my first day. I was glad that they hadn't invited me aboard.

It was on one of these nights that Peter told me about the Lord. He was brought up as a Catholic in Dublin and had lived a life of harmless dissolution. He smoked non-stop and drank all night. He hardly ever had a decent meal and lived on potato crisps and sandwiches. Although Gerta had by now gone off with someone else, there were almost as many girlfriends as there were hot dinners. We were sitting in a corner, well away from the time-share sharks, when he leaned over the table and told me he had given himself to God. I thought he was pulling my leg at first but he was deadly serious. He was a member of a Christian Brotherhood and went to Bible class twice a week. I asked him how all this squared with his lifestyle. He assured me that his God was a God of love and wanted his children to express that love every day. The best way for him to love God was to love women. That's what the Lord wanted him to do! He asked me if I would like to come along to one of the meetings but I politely declined. He didn't press the point but said instead that he would say a prayer for me to the big man upstairs and told me that he had already prayed for Tony.

The prayers must have been answered because next day a saviour arrived for Tony. I called out to Tony in the morning but there was no answer. The big bucket was tied up alongside his boat, and I was worried that something might have happened to him. As I was beginning to think that I should row over and check things out, Tony came roaring up on a high-powered launch. The launch belonged to his friend Kenny. Kenny knew Tony from a long way back, and each time he arrived in the Canaries he came to Los Cristianos, giving Tony some work and a kick up the backside. Kenny chartered his boat from time to time to rock stars and the like, taking them wherever they wanted to go. He made a good living, and when there was work that needed doing he had plenty of money to hire help. Later in the day, I rowed past Kenny's boat. Tony introduced us. Kenny's presence was very large for his diminutive frame, and his American accent could be heard all over the bay. He was a small man with a big mouth and a big heart.

There were a couple of outstanding jobs to do and Laura was due to arrive in two days' time. I wanted everything finished before she came. I still had the problem of the improvised self-steering rudder. Tony thought it was too heavy and would put excessive strain on the stern of the boat. It had worried me for weeks, because if he was right and it broke off, I would be in serious trouble on my own in mid-ocean. The only way to obtain one quickly was to ask Laura to get it from the supplier in England and bring it out with her. I had been asking a lot from her and was worried that this might be the final straw, but decided to do it. She wasn't pleased and made no promises, but said she would do what she could.

I didn't go ashore on the morning of the day that Laura was due to arrive and spent the time tidying up myself and the boat. I had been keeping my best white trousers and light-blue denim shirt for the occasion. I also found a matching silk tie. The tie was a big mistake. As I rowed towards the shore, Kenny spotted me and called everyone up on deck to have a look. They had never seen a man row across the bay wearing a tie. They all knew where I was going. The wolf-whistles started and the cat-calls followed. These alerted the next boat and everyone aboard that boat came on deck to repeat the performance. I had to row past 20 or 30 boats. As I approached each one, the humiliation continued. Even people I didn't know joined in the fun, and the women also had a go, which I thought was very unsporting. By the time I reached the jetty, there was steam coming off the back of my neck.

Laura's flight was on time. I waited outside the glass doors of the luggage-collection area, pacing up and down. As the passengers began to gather to collect their luggage, I could see Laura's blonde hair in the middle of the crowd. When she came into full view she was wearing a black-and-white polka-dot dress. Under her arm, in a cardboard box that was almost as big as herself, was the new rudder.

20. Christmas and New Year

LAURA HAD A FULL TWO WEEKS AND WAS STAYING FOR Christmas and New Year. We arrived in Los Cristianos under cover of darkness. The taxi drove us right down to the beach where I had left the dinghy. This was the first time that she had joined me when I was lying at anchor. I could tell she was slightly worried at the prospect of rowing out across the bay in the middle of the night but the novelty of it all overcame her anxieties. On the way out to the boat, I gave her a running commentary on all the other yachts at anchor:

'That's the laundry ship, they do washing for you '

'There's two young kids on that boat.'

'This one's for sale.'

'Don't you think it's a good idea to have bicycles aboard?'

'They've come all the way from Australia.'

'He's been here for years.'

'There's an old man of 75 who's skipper of that boat.'

'My friend Peter lives on this one.'

Laura was taking it all in, only interrupting me occasionally to ask where my boat was. She kept looking over the side at the deep water below us. Suddenly she exclaimed, 'There she is, I can see her, there's the *Warrior Queen*.' The last time Laura had seen her was in Scotland, and she reacted as if meeting an old friend. I was very pleased. It looked as though we were going to make it without being seen, when I heard Peter call out. He was rowing ashore and came over to meet Laura. This was a real stroke of luck. The Irish are a mildly chauvinistic people and love meeting their own kind overseas. When Peter spoke his first word, Laura instantly recognised his Dublin accent. Peter himself had heard much about Laura and was dying to meet her. We exchanged a few pleasantries before I dispatched him on his way.

On rowing past Tony's boat, I lowered my voice, saying that another friend lived aboard this one and I would tell her all about him later. I don't know whether Tony saw us but he didn't come on deck. After tying up at the stern of my boat, we went down below and lit some candles. The boat was spotless and everything was in its place. I was happier than I had been at any time on the trip so far.

Next morning we invited Tony over for breakfast. He paddled across in his big bucket without a hint of embarrassment. I took a back seat in the galley while the two of them chatted away in their easy-going manner. Laura was greatly taken by his self-deprecating sense of humour and laconic way with words. Michael also knew that Laura was arriving. He stopped by as we were finishing off our coffee and came aboard for a cup himself. Peter was next. I put another pot of coffee on.

Laura's idea of Tenerife was apartment blocks and package holidays but this little impromptu breakfast party in the middle of the bay, with its assortment of strange characters, soon dispelled these notions. Peter was playing that lunchtime at the Razzmatazz Jazz Bar and invited us along. Laura loved jazz and was mad about jazz bars, so we accepted without hesitation. I had often telephoned her from this bar in the evening but up until now she had only heard the music over the telephone line. That was enough to make her want to visit the spot without delay.

The lunchtime jam session went on to late in the afternoon and didn't disappoint her. Later that evening she bought me dinner in one of the town's best restaurants. I had *paella*, a favourite dish of mine. I had looked at the restaurant and the *paella* longingly for the previous five weeks but decided to wait until Laura arrived. The wait was well worth it. As we were finishing off, Peter rolled by, saying to me, 'Now you really have had a day in paradise, John.'

Before Laura came out, I had written to her to tell her of my plans to make the trip on my own. She very diplomatically didn't discuss it for the first few days. She accepted it reluctantly but was liable to bring the subject up at any time with remarks such as, 'You can't possibly go on your own,' or, 'You don't need to prove anything to me, you know.' My standard response was that plenty of people had made the crossing on their own in the past and that getting the right crew was very diffi-cult. When I told her about Terry's note on the *Crew Available* board and the two German girls this usually pacified her for a while.

I was now borrowing money from Laura but had a scheme to get some money of my own. Before leaving from England, I had researched the entire route to Sydney and had bought a full set of charts and pilot books. Most of these weren't needed now. Michael was making more or less the same trip that I had planned. He only had charts as far as the Caribbean and was going to buy the rest as he went along. We agreed half price of face value and I handed my set of 32 over. In return, he gave me a big roll of pesetas. It was a good deal and I had no basis for complaint, but somehow I felt short-changed to be handing over

Approaches to the Panama Canal, Plans in the Iles Marquises, Tonga to Archipel des Tuamotu, Kadava to Suvu Harbour, and many more, for mere money. I was selling my dreams.

Laura hired a car, and it was good to get away from the sea for a few hours to see Pico de Teide close up. The scent from the pine forests was sweet when we drove up through the hills. Laura asked me to stop while she took the top off one of the young trees. Later that evening she placed the tree in the cockpit and hung Christmas decorations from it. She cut out the most attractive patterns from Christmas wrapping paper and stuck these to the walls of the main cabin. The boat had never looked so good. When people rowed past, they all stopped to remark that they had never seen a boat with a Christmas tree.

On Christmas Eve, Kenny had a cocktail party aboard his boat, serving up rum punch with ice. It was an international gathering and Kenny was the perfect host, making sure no one's glass ran dry. Tony, who Kenny now described as his boatboy, helped in the galley. Laura enjoyed meeting the people from the other boats and Kenny's attention. I enjoyed the rum punch. She was seeing one of the best sides of sailing, and I made the point to her, over and over again, that if we pooled our resources we could have a boat just like Kenny's.

The sun was shining brightly on Christmas morning. I insisted on Laura putting her swimming-costume on, and we climbed into the dinghy to test the water. It was a bit nippy. Laura decided against it after dipping her big toe in – but I had her in a vulnerable position, sitting in the dinghy in her swimsuit. I soaked her with scoopfuls of water from the bailer – all she could do was scream. The sound of a woman screaming on Christmas morning echoed across the bay, bringing people on deck. None of the men had any sympathy with her and shouted out to her to get in the water. When Laura told me to stop being a bully, I splashed her with more cold water. I eventually took pity on her before helping her back aboard.

Shortly after, Peter rowed over to ask if he could bring a friend to Christmas lunch. I had half-expected this and told him there was no problem. Laura sat out in the cockpit in her Christmas dress. I served her with gin and tonics while preparing the lunch in the galley. I had decided to do smoked salmon as a starter and roast turkey for the main course. Everything was going well. The smell from the turkey wafted up through the hatches and hung over the boat. Michael turned up dressed like a proper English gentleman, and Tony rowed over in his big bucket, wearing his best clothes. Peter was next, along with a friend, a woman whom I didn't know. I had been keeping my favourite jacket for the occasion — a patchwork, multicoloured, light-cotton affair, which Laura disparagingly described as my attention-seeking jacket. The tie that had caused so much embarrassment a week earlier was now worn with defiance.

Everyone sat in the warm sunshine in the cockpit. I cracked open a bottle of champagne to accompany the smoked salmon. The smell from the turkey had got everyone going, and I timed it so that the bird, the roast potatoes and the vegetables were all served up together. The cockpit table had already been set with Laura's dinner service. When everything was placed on the table, it made such a fabulous sight that for a while all we could do was look at it. Tony was overwhelmed. He said that he had forgotten that food could smell, look and taste so good. Everyone else was equally impressed. They complimented the chef — which was me — for preparing such a meal aboard. Laura told them all to go easy on the praise and get stuck in. We had an abundance of good wine, and the empty bottles started to pile up on the deck. We all had seconds, and I made sure that nobody did any tidying up. When no one could eat any more turkey, Laura gave us all a little present. Tony produced an envelope which he gave to me. Inside was a hand-painted watercolour of a sailboat at sea. The boat could have been any sloop and the blue water could have been any sea, but as I looked at it I saw the *Warrior Queen* in mid-Atlantic, where I knew I would be in a week's time.

After the debris from the main course was cleared away, I set the table again, this time with small plates. For the last six months I had been keeping something especially for this day. Before leaving Whitby, a good friend had come up to visit. I think she never expected to see me again. She arrived carrying a heavy object. It was wrapped in tinfoil, decorated with great attention to detail and had been injected with brandy using a hypodermic needle. It was a Christmas cake; one of the finest I had ever seen. Since leaving Whitby, it had lived in a large, airtight box and hadn't been touched. When the cake appeared in front of me, as I came up the companionway, the disbelief was total. Up until this moment nobody thought they could eat any more but everyone was now smacking their lips in anticipation. The cake tasted even better than it looked, and the men overdid it, while the women nibbled. Somehow I had managed to clear away everything as I went along, and the galley was spotless when Laura went down below to make Irish coffees. It was a great meal.

Peter had to play later that night. He and his friend nearly fell in the water while getting into the skiff. Once he was out of earshot, Tony gave us the low-down on his new friend. She had been living in Los Cristianos for more than a year and was the steady girlfriend of a man called Ralph. Ralph, who owned the catamaran that Peter and he lived on, had gone to Germany for Christmas. He was in for a surprise when he came back. By sundown we were still sitting in the cockpit, and Tony had to undo the belt of his pants by at least two notches. We all rowed ashore later that night, singing songs on the way in, and spent the rest of the evening visiting the bars in town. It was the best Christmas I had ever had.

Laura did her best to come to terms with me setting out on my own, and we spent the next few days provisioning the boat. As we went round the supermarket, she selected expensive items of food and put them in the trolley. I protested, putting them back on the shelf, but by the time I had gone off to another shelf, they had reappeared in the trolley. This ritual went on every day, and Laura fussed about my provisions the way a mother does about the contents of a child's lunchbox. There were certain items which were so outrageously expensive that I kept taking them out of the trolley over and over again. Laura's response was to get a small basket of her own, fill this with these items, and pay for them separately.

As well as food and drink, I also needed books and music. None of the music shops in town had tapes that interested me enough to buy, and the books stocked by the local newsagents tended to be modern fiction that overdid it with sex and violence. Fortunately, Terry had brought a good selection of books with him when he joined me in Ireland, and he left most of these aboard to lighten his backpack. These would keep me going for most of the trip. There was also a secondhand bookshop that had a book-exchange service for visiting yachtsmen, which I was hoping to check out before leaving. One night, I bumped into the skipper of another boat who had just returned from this shop. He had a big smile on his face and a large pile of books tied together with string under his arm. 'What are you grinning about?' I asked.

'I've just got all my reading material for the Atlantic crossing,' he replied.

'What kind of stuff do you read?' I inquired.

'Westerns, nothing but westerns,' was his reply. 'You can't beat a good western at sea,' he elaborated. I glanced at the covers of the books. Each one that still had the dust-jacket intact had a picture of a cowboy on a horse. Yip, sure enough, every one was a western.

As it came nearer to the time Laura was due to go home, the tensions between us began to mount. I did my best to defuse these and was reasonably successful. A beach barbecue was planned for New Year's Eve. Laura and I were intending to go to this, before finishing the night off at the jazz bar. We had a few pre-dinner drinks aboard and started talking about our future and past. Laura was engaging in her withdrawal strategy and began to give me a hard time. I didn't try to defuse it. Things started to get out of hand. The insults and recriminations began to fly on both sides, and it went from bad to worse. I knew this was going to happen at some stage but couldn't accept it on New Year's Eve, so I sulked. This was a tactic that I used very rarely – it was normally very effective, but it wasn't working now. Once you start sulking it's hard to back off and easy to convince yourself that you are the injured party. Sulking begets more sulking, as the imagined injustice wells up inside you. It's also a form of emotional blackmail. If it doesn't work you have to step up the pressure and turn the screw.

I took the sulking to its limit, retiring to the aft cabin alone, where I locked the hatches. Laura was also sulking. We both heard the barbecue get underway on the beach. By 11.0 p.m., the party was going strong. We were still sulking. At 11.45, Laura came and knocked on the aft cabin hatch. I was now so deeply enveloped in my own foolish pride that I refused to answer her. At midnight on New Year's Eve, bells rung out and fireworks went off, everyone was singing 'Auld Lang Syne'. Laura had already made her gesture, and it was too late for me to make mine. The music from the clubs and the sound of happy people drifted across the bay till dawn, but I stayed in my cabin. It was the worst New Year's Eve of my life.

Laura was due to leave in two days' time. Next morning, after an awkward breakfast, we made up. We both knew that we had missed a great party and were desperately unhappy. Later in the morning, while walking round the town, we bumped into Peter and Kenny, who had not been to bed yet. Kenny had the last traces of his make-up on – he had celebrated New Year in fancy dress, dancing around the streets as a pirate – and was still flying. They told us what a great night they had and asked, 'Where the hell were you guys?' We made some lame excuse about being too tired to come out but I think they both knew the truth.

There was no more quarrelling or sulking before Laura left. We got up at about 5.0 a.m. on the day of her flight home. It was still dark when I lowered her bags into the dinghy. I had difficulty in finding a taxi so early in the morning but we made it to the airport on time. We were still barely awake when we said goodbye. I watched her go through the security gate. She turned and gave me one last wave. I was very sad to see her go, but there was work to do and I wanted to get going in a day or two. On the way back to town in the airport bus, I saw the plane take off from the runway and knew that she would be home in three or four hours. The sun had just risen. It was blood red. I was angry with myself for allowing things to get out of hand on New Year's Eve, but happy that Christmas Day had gone so well. When I got to the beach, the attendants were starting to put out the deckchairs for the day. I took my shoes off and pushed the dinghy out. As I rowed out to the *Warrior Queen*, I passed all the other boats that I had talked to Laura about on the night she arrived. Everyone aboard was fast asleep. The lower lip was beginning to tremble but I was still in control. I tied up at the stern and went below to make strong coffee. As I sat rolling a cigarette, waiting for the kettle to boil, my eye passed over the Christmas decorations on the cabin wall. The sight of them was too much for me.

21. *The Wide Blue Yonder*

MICHAEL HAD SUGGESTED THAT INSTEAD OF SAILING direct for the West Indies, I should make a southerly course to roughly latitude 20 degrees north, before heading west. The winds in the North Atlantic follow a broadly clockwise rotation. In the high latitudes, above about 40 degrees north, they tend to come in from the west. Along the coast of the Iberian peninsula and North Africa they swing round and start coming down from the north. Further south, they begin to blow from the east, and in the tradewind belt, which is north of the Equator, they are almost guaranteed to come from this quarter. The tradewinds then swing to the south and blow up the eastern seaboard of North America, before becoming westerly again and completing the circulation. There is considerable seasonal variation to this pattern but, by and large, the wind does behave according to this grand scheme. In oceans south of the Equator, the circulation of air is reversed and the wind blows in an anticlockwise direction – in the same way as the rotation of water going down a plug hole is reversed. Straddling the Equator, and moving north and south with the seasons, is what is known as the doldrums, or to give it its technical term, the inter-tropical convergence zone, where there is virtually no wind at all apart from that which accompanies rain squalls.

My plan was to sail south until I was certain that I was in the tradewind belt and then head due west. The dog-leg involved meant that the passage would be about 3,000 miles. If I assumed a rate of 100 miles a day, it would take me approximately 30 days. Michael also suggested that I should select the island of St Lucia as a destination, because the customs-and-immigration formalities are not as onerous as elsewhere. He also recommended that I go to Rodney Bay on the north-west corner of the island, as this had all the facilities I would need after a long passage. Finally, Michael thought it a good idea for us to set sail on the same day. He didn't expect us to keep in visual or even radio contact for long but said it was good for morale to head out with someone. Michael would not be making a solo crossing after all – an old friend of Michael's had joined him from England. They were planning to stop off in the Cape Verde islands about 800 miles south of the Canaries, but if all was well, I would keep going.

On the night before I was due to leave, I spent the evening ashore in Halleys drinking club. On the way there I met Tony, who was making a long-distance telephone call from a phone box. He was calling his only brother in the States and was trying his best to sort himself out. We had a brief word. He took me to one side and said, 'John, thanks very much for everything. You've been a good friend, and I don't have too many of those right now.' I was too embarrassed to say all I wanted to say. He told me to take care and keep in touch. Peter was in Halleys when I got there, and he tried to talk me out of going. When that didn't work, he suggested coming with me himself. Being on the run from a credit-card company that had been chasing him round Europe for the last five years, he saw the trip as a way of finally giving them the shake. He was also in hiding from Ralph, who had returned from Germany – things were beginning to cool between Peter and Ralph's ex-girlfriend. When I refused his offer, he shoved his hand into his inside pocket, producing a copy of the *New Testament and Psalms,* which he gave to me. Inside the cover were the words:

To John,
May the Lord keep you
and guide you on
a safe passage. ·
Peter Nolan

He told me that he had said a prayer for me at the Christian Brotherhood. After accepting a last glass of Irish whiskey from him, I took my leave. It was about 4.0 a.m. and the wind was blowing hard as I struggled against it to row the dinghy out to the boat, which I had moved earlier in the day to the edge of the bay.

Next morning I awoke with a thumping headache. The whole idea of leaving seemed a very stupid one, but I knew it was now or never. I stumbled around the deck, only just managing to haul up the anchor chain. When the anchor was stowed securely on deck, I headed out of the bay. The sails were hoisted as I passed Michael's boat and yelled out to him, 'What's keeping you?' Within ten minutes, Los Cristianos was already beginning to fade. The Atlantic Ocean lay before me.

With the wind blowing very fresh from the east, the seas began to mount once the shelter of Tenerife was left behind. As I watched the island get smaller, I thought of all the friends I had made there, knowing that I was unlikely ever to see any of them again. Michael was about a mile behind me when I left but he was falling back all the time and the gap between us was widening. It wasn't long before I couldn't see him with the naked eye, although I could still pick him up with the binoculars. After a few hours out, he called me up on the VHF radio, enthusing about the conditions, which were perfect for making a fast southerly passage. I gave him a bit of lip about his progress, asking him once more what was keeping him. The signal was poor. It was clear that we would be out of radio contact very soon.

The island of Gomera, where Columbus had sailed from in 1492, was on the starboard beam by mid-afternoon. It was well astern by dusk. My hangover was long gone. I rigged up the self-steering gear and settled down for my first night alone at sea. Being too excited to cook a full dinner, I warmed up a tin of soup, which I had with heaps of bread and butter. I had stocked up with plenty of bread before leaving and knew that it wouldn't last long, so I could have as much as I wanted. Once night settled around me, I realised for the first time in my life what it is to be truly alone. Michael's navigation light wasn't visible. There was no other shipping. The lighthouse on the southern tip of Gomera was already fading: by midnight it had disappeared. There was no artificial light but the stars shone bright. The wind kept blowing fresh from the east. Tenerife was now 50 miles behind me.

Colliding with something in the darkness would almost certainly mean the loss of the ship and death. The best way to avoid a collision was to keep a constant watch but this wasn't feasible on my own; I would have to sleep sometime. Maybe I could catnap in the cockpit and wake every 15 minutes to have a good look around. After a last cup of tea, I stretched out under a blanket. The boat was taking the seas on the beam, riding most of them well, but every now and then an extra-large wave broke over the decks, soaking the cockpit. It also soaked my blanket and me. Sleeping outside wasn't going to work. The next plan involved getting into my bunk in the aft cabin and keeping all the hatches open so that I could pop my head up at a moment's notice. Most seas that broke in the cockpit didn't dump any water in the aft cabin, but about every half hour or so an exceptionally large sea soaked not only the cockpit but also flooded this cabin. Sleeping in the aft cabin with the hatches open wasn't going to work either.

It was now about 3.0 a.m. and I was getting tired and needed to sleep. There was a hammock aboard, which I had brought with me for warm tropical nights lying at anchor. I rigged this up in the cockpit, suspending it between the mast and the backstay, well above any breaking seas. If I could sleep in it, I only had to open one eye to keep a good lookout. This seemed like the perfect solution. It was difficult to climb into but I eventually made it. The hammock started to swing freely. The first swing had my backside knocking against the steering wheel; the second had me suspended out over the edge of the boat, looking straight down into the dark ocean. So much for the hammock!

There was likely to be another 30 nights like this. I had to find somewhere to sleep. The obvious place was the main cabin. It was dry, comfortable and safe, but it would involve me sleeping in the bowels of the ship while the boat surged ahead through the night without a lookout. I resisted the temptation and stayed up until dawn. Daybreak revealed an empty sea. I had come through my first night at sea alone. All the islands had gone, Michael's boat had long since vanished, and there was no other shipping. I tried calling Michael up on the radio but he must have been out of range. I got no reply.

The chance of a collision in daylight was much less than at night, so after putting a third reef in the main, I crawled into my sleeping-bag in the main cabin and fell fast asleep. It was near midday when I awoke. I could feel the boat ploughing through the waves. When someone wakes from sleep, it is usually in a bed and all is still. Aboard a small boat at sea, the sensation of movement is ever-present. The oceans are always restless. Even when there is no wind they are in a continual state of flux. The boat not only makes headway towards its destination but is buffeted by each wave. Weightless from the buoyancy of the water displaced by its hull, it responds to every disturbance of the sea's surface. Alarming as this may sound, there is a natural oneness between a boat and the sea that bears her up. I wasn't disturbed by the perpetual movement and began to feel as though the boat was slowly becoming part of my own body, and the harmony that existed between her and the sea began to suffuse itself through me. The boat was alive and the movement was usually soft and gentle – she lifted and fell with grace and style. Stillness is death's constant bedfellow – I liked the idea of perpetual movement.

Everything seemed to be under control and the self-steering gear had worked well while I was asleep. When I came up on deck, there was still no sign of any other shipping – I was alone in the centre of my own solitary world. The sky was slightly overcast but there didn't seem to be any clouds as such – more of a haze. The sun was barely visible and there was a brownish-red hue to it. The whole sky was tinged with the same colour. The haze puzzled me. But I had a fair wind straight out of the east, blowing about force 7. This was good news, because the last thing I wanted was fitful winds at the start of the crossing.

I was still technically in the Horse Latitudes, where the wind is un-reliable and can often desert you for days on end. These latitudes form a belt of flukey wind, between the westerlies to the north and the tradewinds to the south. They are so called because sailors in days gone by were often becalmed while crossing this area and had to put their horses overboard to conserve water supplies. Horses are creatures of the wide open plains which evolved to gallop over dry land. The idea of putting one over the side seemed particularly gruesome. The poor animals would have survived for some time before drowning and I could imagine them swallowing seawater – what does seawater taste like to a horse? But worse still were the slave ships that threw their human cargo over the side, all manacled together, when pursued by a man o' war, enforcing the law after the vile trade was outlawed. These wretched men, women and children were dumped overboard and dragged down to the ocean floor by the weight of their chains so that the slavers would not be caught red-handed.

I didn't want to join the bones of the horses and slaves and was terri-fied at the thought of falling overboard. One slip and I could be over the side. By the time I would come up, the boat would be at least 50 yards in front of me and there would be no chance of swimming after it. Within ten minutes, only the sails would be visible. In less than half an hour, everything would be gone from sight. The idea of finding myself all alone in the water, with the boat gone, nothing around for hundreds of miles, and knowing that the end had come, was something that I didn't like to think about but couldn't help dwelling on. With the water temperature about 25 degrees centigrade, I would probably survive for up to 24 hours. The body, no matter how desperate the mind, would not allow itself to drown. I could imagine no worse way to die.

A life-jacket would be useless and only serve to prolong the agony, but a life-line attached to a firm harness and clipped on every time I left the cockpit would give me a fighting chance. It would be very difficult to struggle back aboard against the speed of the water rushing past but at least there was a chance. I kept the harness draped over the steering wheel in the cockpit and never went on deck without fastening it to me and clipping in. This rule was enforced without exception. No matter how calm or settled the weather was, I resolved not to leave the cockpit without a life-line.

It was also important for me to establish a series of routines. These quickly suggested themselves. There was plenty of booze aboard but I made a rule that I would not have a drink before noon. At the same time, I would write up the ship's log and check the distance run during the last 24 hours, as measured by the trailing log. After these tasks were complete, I would tune into the ham-radio mobile-maritime network and try to pick up conversations from other yachts with transmitting shortwave radios. I had a little domestic shortwave set that could receive but not transmit. If I fiddled patiently with the fine-tuning knob, I could usually get snatches of the conversations. The fishing line would be trailed 24 hours a day, and I would pump out the bilges twice a day.

Food was going to be crucial for my morale, so I would make a cooked breakfast in the morning, have an uncooked snack for lunch and prepare a good meal each evening. There was enough wine aboard to allow me half a litre with my evening meal and enough cigarettes for me to smoke my head off. Freshwater would need to be rationed, so I would use saltwater for washing dishes and clothes as well as for cooking potatoes and other root vegetables. Books would also have to be rationed but I had plenty of writing paper. Before leaving Tenerife, I had copied some tapes from Tony and Peter and now had an extra Ry Cooder cassette as well as a country-and-western collection of Meryle Haggard songs. That, together with a Leonard Cohen tape and what I already had aboard, was my lot.

On putting the routines into action, I discovered that in the first 24 hours I made good 135 miles. This was the best I had done since leaving England. I was overjoyed. I had had my first drink, which was a small one. My spirits were high when I stood at the wheel, glass in hand, preparing to sing my favourite song. It was a negro spiritual and particularly appropriate to the circumstances I found myself in. I cleared my throat, flicked the cigarette over the side and sang it loud and in as deep a register as I was able to. The first three lines repeat themselves in the manner of many songs about the sea. The words are about hope, faith and the defiance of the human spirit.

It takes a long pull to get there.
It takes a long pull to get there.
It takes a long pull to get there.
But, I'll anchor in the promised land.
In the promised land.

And if I meet Mr Hurricane,
and Hurricane tell me no.
Then I'll take ole Mr Hurricane by the pants,
and I'll throw him in the jailhouse row.

I sang the chorus again, and after each 'long pull to get there' made the noise of men pulling on rope.

I only just remembered to tune the knobs on the radio set at 1.0 p.m. and picked up Trudy on the airwaves for the first time at sea. Trudy, who lived in Barbados, was a radio ham. Every day, without fail, she ran the maritime mobile network. This was something she did for no financial reward, and she was usually on the air for about an hour-and-a-half. She began by welcoming everyone to the network, before talking about the propagation of the radio signal. After her introduction, other stations came up and gave her a report. Each station was usually a small boat at sea. They gave their position, their day's run, the sea state, the current weather they were experiencing and the barometric pressure. She gave them kind words of encouragement and issued a weather forecast for the various regions of the southern part of the North Atlantic. Michael came up and gave his position, which I jotted down. I was delighted to discover that I was over 20 miles ahead of him after the first day.

After listening to the ham-radio network, I stretched out in the cockpit to read my first book of the crossing – *Empire of the Sun* by J.G. Ballard. Laura had selected this for me before my departure, and I was enjoying having all the time in the world to read. The wind persisted from the east, the sky grew redder and became more overcast, and the boat kept driving on. Sometime in the afternoon, I dozed off to sleep.

22. *A Desert in the Sky*

ON MY SECOND DAY AT SEA, I SAT OUT IN THE COCKPIT AT dusk, watching the sun set in the west. It wasn't very bright. There were no vivid colours as it slowly dropped below the horizon, sinking into the sea. Darkness followed quickly. The stars were only just visible.

With no shipping of any kind, I reasoned that the chances of a collision were very small. What's more, if there was a crisis, I wouldn't be able to deal with it if I was exhausted through lack of sleep, and I had noticed that while dozing in the afternoon I remained tuned into every movement of the boat. I felt confident that I would wake as soon as anything went wrong. With these thoughts in mind, I checked all the sails and gear, set the self-steering gear, and turned in for a full night's sleep.

The main cabin only had one berth, which was on the wrong side given the way the boat was leaned over. It was impossible to remain in it without some support. To prevent me falling out I rigged up the lee cloths. These stout pieces of canvas are pulled out from under the bunk, where one edge is already attached, and the other end is tied to the ceiling of the cabin. I now had a cosy little cot which was stuffed with cushions for extra comfort. Before going to bed, I made a cup of cocoa and cut a slice of Christmas cake, half of which had been saved for the crossing. The brandy in the cake helped me sleep.

Despite the brandy, my first sleep on my own at sea at night was a restless one. My bladder never seemed to be empty. I kept getting up to have a pee. Everybody hates getting up in the middle of the night to have a pee but doing it aboard a small boat is a real test of character. With the boat bouncing around, it's almost impossible to use the lavatory bowl. With whatever spare arms and legs at my disposal, I braced my body in the toilet compartment and aimed for the bowl. But I had so little success that I shouldn't have bothered aiming. The sea toilet itself is not like any on dry land. It has a valve which allows effluent to be pumped out to sea. If this valve fails, seawater is siphoned back aboard and the ship sinks – a lavatory bowl that can kill you while you sleep! Fortunately, I didn't have to use the sea toilet all the time and had the biggest urinal in the world over the side of the boat. I had to make sure to hold on with my free hand, taking care not to end up becoming an FOA – the term used by coastguards when they pick up the body of a sailor who has fallen overboard while relieving himself – Flys Open on Arrival. After the pee over the side, I had a quick look around – blackness everywhere. Not even the stars were visible. With no shipping in sight, I climbed back into my cot and fell asleep once more.

Next morning the sky was completely overcast and the sun was hidden from sight. The haze was thicker than any cloud and the decks of the boat were covered in a very fine red dust. It clung to the ropes and rigging. The sails, which were covered in it, were no longer white. I wrote my name in the dust on the roof of the cabin, only to find that within three or four hours it was covered in dust again. The strong easterly winds persisted. I consulted the British Admiralty sailing directions to try to solve the mystery. The wind that was hurtling me down the coast of West Africa was blowing straight off the Sahara Desert. It was a seasonal wind known as the *Harmattan* that carried with it billions upon billions of tiny particles of sand held in suspension. Even though I was about 400 miles from the landmass of Africa, the sand from the desert carried all this way out to sea. As I touched the fine dust and made contact with the world of dry land, the sand of the Sahara Desert became lodged under my fingernails. The ridiculous sight of it and the sheer incongruity of it all made me smile.

The routine I had established served me well – on the second day I had covered another 135 miles. I was now well rested and intended to go to bed every night for a good sleep. Michael's position was again picked up on the maritime ham-radio network – I was now more than 50 miles in front of him. The Canaries were more than 250 miles behind me. I had nearly finished *Empire of the Sun* but it was ironic that while reading the book I didn't see the sun once. The fishing line with its lure, a ridiculous-looking bright-green-and-yellow plastic squid, skipped out of the water as the boat continued to forge ahead. Nothing had taken it yet and I couldn't see how any fish could catch it. Never having caught a fish in my life, I wasn't bothered about not catching fish now and was content to sit in the cockpit and read.

As well as reading, I also listened to the tapes from Tony and Peter. I enjoyed all those corny country-and-western songs about broken hearts and unrequited love. The best of them told a simple tale about ordinary folk and embodied a set of old-fashioned values – even the worst of them were amusing for their absurdity. There was one that surely had the best title of any song ever written: 'Dropkick Me, Jesus, Through the Goalposts of Life'. It wasn't Jesus who was dropkicking me but I certainly felt like a football as my spirits soared up into the sky and flew through the goalposts in my own life.

Later that night I finished my first book and saw my first cockroach. It darted into the corner of a locker before squeezing its dirty body in behind the panelling. I emptied the locker and unscrewed the panelling. The cockroach cowered in the corner. I squashed it firmly with a piece of tissue paper, wiping up all the mess so as not to spread any eggs. If the eggs are left behind, then for each cockroach killed a hundred turn up to the funeral. It unsettled me to find the cockroach because I knew there would be more. The little bastards would already be breeding and colonising the whole boat. It was warm, and there was food and water everywhere. With no natural cockroach predators aboard, the boat would no doubt seem like a holiday camp to the filthy things – I think I would have preferred pirates!

I was so nauseated by the sight of the single cockroach and the thought of more that I had to retire to the cockpit. The wind was still blowing hard and the boat was racing along through the night. I could hear the sound of the water rushing by the hull but the visibility was very poor. Standing in the cockpit, I strained my eyes to look forward and realised I couldn't see the bow of the boat. I looked over the side, only to realise that I couldn't see the sea. The red desert dust was blocking out all natural light from the night sky. The only thing I could see by was the light from the masthead and the reading lamp over the chart table.

I went down below and switched everything off before groping my way back into the cockpit. The boat was bowling along at a ferocious pace. There was complete and utter blackness all around me. I slowly raised my hand in front of my face with the five fingers outstretched. I could not see any of them! Everything was black. I touched my nose with each finger in turn to reassure me that they were still there. If I fell overboard now, I wouldn't even see the boat. The thought of being in the water in the total blackness was the ultimate in desolation and loss. I don't believe in God, but even if there was one, I couldn't imagine him being able to see anyone this night. I was alone on the ocean; the Sahara Desert was in the sky; the boat was infested with cockroaches; it was hurtling through total blackness; I couldn't see my own fingers; and the sea toilet might at any minute spring a leak and suck the boat down the plughole. This was a world and a state of mind I had never known or even dreamed of – I was exhilarated and terrified at the same time.

I switched the lights back on before making some cocoa and pampered myself with another slice of Christmas cake. Not wanting to dwell any further on the blackness, I played a little Mozart and started reading *Love on the Dole* by Walter Greenwood. It was set in a north-of-England industrial town and reminded me of my own childhood in Belfast – the small terraced houses, the mill girls, the moneylenders, the tickmen, the bookies, and the ever-present scourge of unemployment. My father was once on the dole, after having been laid off from Harland and Wolff shipbuilders, and I remembered him coming home from work with his toolbox the day he collected his cards. He came in by the back door to avoid being seen by the neighbours. The toolbox sat on the kitchen floor and everyone in the house was dejected – I had never seen my father so unhappy. I opened the toolbox and looked in. All the tools seemed very big and heavy to the small boy that I was then. When he died, I asked my mother if I could have his tools. They were now in the locker beside me, and I never took any of them on deck to do a job without tying a line to them. *Love on the Dole* was my life as a boy, and here I was all alone on a dark, empty ocean living the dream that I dreamt while delivering newspapers in the backstreets of Belfast. The characters were with me on the boat, and I forgot about the all-enveloping blackness outside. My childhood memories kept at bay the reality of my dream, just as my childhood dreams had once kept at bay the reality of my childhood. After the first six chapters, I snuggled into my cot bed and slept like a baby.

The haze persisted for a few more days but diminished each day. The wind continued to blow from the east. Progress was good, and in less than a week I was about 100 miles north of the Cape Verde islands, ready to alter course to the west. Once this decision was made, there was no turning back. With the tradewinds behind me and the North Equatorial Current running in my favour there was no alternative but to keep heading west. It was a big decision to alter course to the west and I could have put into the Cape Verde islands. But everything was going so well that I found the decision easy and big decisions are always the best ones to make. St Lucia was over 2,000 miles away, with nothing in between except the sea and the sky.

Having seen no evidence that the planet was inhabited by human beings since leaving Tenerife, I was now quite happy about going to bed each night. With the wind dead astern the boat was sailing upright. As there was no counterbalance from the keel, she rolled from side to side as she ran before the wind. I found it impossible to sleep on the first night on this tack as the pots and pans and tins and dishes clattered in the lockers. The noise reminded me of the dustbin-lid protests in Belfast. I kept getting out of my bunk to jam cushions, towels and jumpers in the lockers to try to stop the racket, but every time I thought it was under control, something else started banging about.

Next day I rearranged the contents of all the lockers, ensuring that everything was wedged firmly in place. The clattering stopped and I started to get used to the rolling from side to side. The seas followed me as the boat ran before them. I was surprised at how big they were. The stern of the boat lifted gently with the approach of each wave and the body of water passed under the ship as she settled back down again. Up and down, side to side, on and on she rolled, with the fishing line trailing astern skipping out of the water.

One morning I awoke to find the haze completely gone. There were brilliant blue skies and a few puffy white cauliflower clouds on the horizon. I checked the fishing line as I did every morning but this time, for the first time ever, it was tight. I began to haul the line in by hand. Every now and then it went slack, only to tighten up again a moment later. With about 30 feet to go, something broke the surface of the water. The line then went deep down below the boat. I kept hauling in and was now talking to myself non-stop. With 15 feet to go, a streamlined silver shape darted under the boat. It was a big fish. The brightly coloured plastic squid was hanging out of its mouth, like one of those paper whistles at a kids' party. I dragged it in close to the hull. With one mighty yank, I pulled the fish out of the water, swinging it through the air and landing it in the cockpit. It was a tuna fish of about 20 lb – the most beautiful fish I had ever seen. It had a perfectly streamlined body and a smooth, silvery skin. Its big, black, bulging eye was looking straight at me as I smacked it over the head with the winch handle.

There was dark-red cold blood and inner organs everywhere as I cut its head off and disembowelled it before slicing off a middle section. I filled a pan with butter and onions and washed the steak in seawater before frying it. In ten minutes it was served up with the last of my fresh bread and a big mug of tea. As I sat savouring every morsel of the firm, dark flesh, I could see the remains of the fish in the cockpit twitch with the nerves that were still alive in its body – this gave a whole new meaning to the term fresh fish. Later that night, I prepared another steak with a white sauce and boiled up some potatoes to have with it, along with a can of peas. There was plenty of white wine, which provided the perfect accompaniment. The remains of the beautiful fish went overboard after dinner. I had no compunction about the waste because it was going straight into the food chain, where it would no doubt find its way through that chain and into the belly of another tuna.

The fish was the first living creature, apart from the cockroaches,

From Boston to the Caribbean – Bill soon after arriving (Bill Stanhope)

En route to a coral reef with Tim (Bill Stanhope)

Going crazy at the carnival (Bill Stanhope)

First encounter with Waroa Indians (Bill Stanhope)

Indian settlement on the Rio Orinoco (Bill Stanhope)

that I had come into close contact with since leaving the Canaries. I had been a little feverish in dispatching it with the winch handle but that was probably less cruel than leaving it to drown in fresh air. Anyway, it thought nothing about eating other fish so I shouldn't be too upset about eating it – at least I wasn't a cannibal. There was another one on the line next morning. This was catapulted through the air and into the cockpit just like the one the day before. It was even bigger and just as beautiful, and it gave me the same bulging-eye treatment. I had heard from someone in Tenerife of a kind way to kill fish and decided to give it a go. A fish uses its gills to extract oxygen from water in much the same way as a human lung extracts oxygen from air. I fetched a bottle of whisky and poured a small amount on to its bright red gills. The results were dramatic! The fish quivered and died very peacefully in less than ten seconds – no blood or guts. Although I can't be sure, I think that fish died as happy as any fish can.

There were plenty of other fish dying aboard but they met their deaths in a manner which was the nautical equivalent of a car crash. I came across the first one lying in the scuppers of the port deck. It was about six inches long, with pectoral fins that were nearly the full length of its body. The fins emerged just behind the gills and reached all the way back to the elongated tail. They had the appearance of an insect's wing. I had seen strange things flying over the top of the waves and now realised they were flying fish. The tuna that I had just dispatched with my best whisky was probably chasing one before taking my lure by mistake. A quick inspection of the deck revealed about six flying fish – they had taken flight from a predatory tuna, only to crash-land on my boat. Some fish don't have any luck. Now that I had my marinated tuna, I had no need to cook these but I could try them another day.

The flying fish were a pathetic sight on my decks but a joy to behold in their natural element. Sometimes, and always without warning, a dozen or more of them would break free from the side of a wave. The fins were held out rigid once they became airborne. They then glided for up to 50 yards as they caught the wind. The flying fish were chased by the tuna, and the tuna were chased by the dolphins. You could always tell when there was a large shoal of fish around because a whole school of dolphins would appear and go charging across the bow of the boat without paying me the slightest attention. It must be an exhausting life being a fish, I thought, as I sat watching the flying fish for hours on end.

The food and supplies of water were holding up well but I was now out of fresh salad and bread and would miss them both. I had forgotten to buy yeast in Tenerife so I couldn't have a go at trying to bake my own bread. Still, the fresh fish was a welcome addition to my diet and I was living very well. The next book on my list was *Zorba the Greek*. I couldn't help thinking that Zorba would have been great company on a boat. He would have driven me mad, though, with his endless talk of women, and the supplies of wine would have been quickly depleted. But then again, he would be a good man to have in a real crisis. I liked Zorba and pondered on him for a long time in between reading the chapters of the book and watching the flying fish.

The sun had been in the sky all day, and what little clouds there were always seemed to stay on the horizon. The ocean was deep blue from the sunlight. The crests that blew off the top of the big following seas were the most brilliant white I had ever seen – I felt like diving into them. The breaking crests made rhythmic, comforting noises, and small rainbows flashed when the sunlight caught the spray. Sometimes the spray from a wave soaked me, but the water was warm and invigorating. Every now and then there was a breaking white crest, a flashing rainbow and half-a-dozen flying fish all together. I never touched the wheel once or adjusted the sails. With each passing hour I felt more at ease with myself and was getting closer to my destination. The boat was heading west across the ocean, and I was travelling through the uncharted seas of my mind.

23. *Rapture of the Deep*

ZORBA KEPT ME COMPANY FOR A FEW MORE DAYS AS THE tradewinds continued to blow. I listened to the ham-radio network every day and picked up the weather forecast. For a sailor, the weather is one thing and one thing only – wind. All other aspects of the weather are incidental and only of interest insofar as they might herald a change in the wind. I was obsessed with the wind: the direction it came from and its strength; how long would it keep coming from the same direction and blow at the same strength; would it veer or back; if so, when and for how long; was it going to increase or decrease; if so, when and to what force; were line squalls likely with sudden increases in wind strength; was the wind going to die completely and becalm me; or would it play tricks with me and go against all the rules by swinging round to the west? I studied the barometer for any sign of a likely wind change and scanned the skies for cloud formations that could foretell the wind.

The wind was as the breath of angels and had the power to transform the world. When it was light, the sea was subdued, apart from the heavy ocean swell which heaved up and down like the chest of a sleeping giant. When it was strong, it whipped the sea up into boiling froth like a cauldron in hell. It transformed the materials on the boat itself. It filled the sails, making them full and firm and perfectly smooth. When the moonlight reflected off the polished, white canvas surface, it looked as though they were sculpted in marble. The soft, supple ropes that held the sails in place became iron bars with the power of the wind. My own mind was manipulated by the changing moods of the wind – it could depress me or make me sing with joy.

Two worlds came together on the surface of the sea – the worlds of the water below and the air above. The two worlds fought and quarrelled with each other like lovers attracted by their differences, but for all the restless turmoil of their union they never parted company. There were long periods when they lived in relative harmony and other times when they left each other in peace, but the mood could change in an instant. The world of air always made the first move, and the sea responded slowly. Her gentle breath raised ripples on the skin of the sea. As she whistled her siren call, the sea began to answer. The wind blew harder and the sea started to rise. He swelled up more as she persisted. His response was rhythmic and powerful and it built steadily, gathering its own momentum. Nothing could calm the sea now. When the wind blew harder still, the sea reached up and threw itself into the air. In the final fury of the storm, the sea was out of control and the air screamed. Tears ran down her cheeks, and the water and air mixed and became one . . . Always, after the passion of the storm, they rested as if exhausted. The air slept on top of the sea without moving her body, and the chest of the sleeping giant that was the sea heaved even heavier than before. I was but a flea in the bed of timeless lovers.

Most days the wind came from the east but some days it backed to the north-east and on other days it veered to the south-east. Since leaving Tenerife, there had always been wind with an easterly component. This meant that I was making good progress. I began to think that I could make the passage in three weeks. When the wind was strong and I made a great day's run of over 140 miles, I divided the remaining distance by 140 to work out how many more days it would take – not many. When the wind dropped off and I made a poor run of less than

100 miles, I did the arithmetic all over again to work out how many days to go – a lot. This was the mathematics of the madhouse, because it would all average out in the end, but the crazy calculus reflected my deranged obsession with the wind, and each day I struggled with the rationality of my own mind and the compelling simplicity and immediacy of the current arithmetic. It became a point of pride to take the best advantage of the wind: whenever I had a day's run that exceeded the best so far I danced around the cockpit like a child at a birthday party. If I was making good progress during the day and there was a chance to set a new record for a day's run, I left all the sails up at night as I slept and the boat charged along through the dark, empty ocean.

I had never known real solitude before: the longest I had gone without talking to another human being was less than a day. The longest time without seeing another person was probably no more than three or four hours. Now I found myself completely alone on a vast ocean. I had read about lone sailors hallucinating, waking one day to find a shipmate, and I awoke every morning just before dawn hoping to find one. Maybe Sir Walter Raleigh would be hiding in the forepeak or Marilyn Monroe would be tucked up in the aft cabin. None of them materialised but I had plenty of companionship. The flying fish were with me all the time and a lone frigate bird followed the boat for days on end. As I watched the frigate bird soar above, I almost felt it was my own spirit, getting so carried away that I penned a little poem:

> Oh that I could fly like a bird
> Oh that I could fly
> If I could fly as a bird can fly
> Then a bird could fly like I

I also had the characters in the books I was devouring to keep me company, as well as Mozart, Verdi and Puccini. Mozart entertained and delighted me with his *Little Night Music*, while Verdi inspired me with his grand operas and Puccini played on the heartstrings. Gary Kasparov, the world chess champion, was with me in the form of a computerised chess board – he gave me some very good games. I played chess for six hours at a stretch, setting the level to suit my play. When I left Tenerife, I was on level three, but I was now beating Gary regularly at level five.

Sometimes I sat in the cockpit, gazing out upon the ocean until time itself seemed to melt away. Once, five years earlier, I had looked upon the wide Sahara stretching out to the west beyond the pyramids at Ghiza, but that was nothing compared to the vast expanse of water all around me. The oceans may have been over-fished and polluted but they have never been tamed; in this regard they are the same now as they were long before any pharoah even thought of building a pyramid. I was alone in this domain and was the captain and the king. The sea that surrounded the boat, holding her gently in its hand, encircled the globe. Its hegemony over dry land was beyond dispute. This was the last wilderness on earth, and it would remain so whatever man's endeavours. The land had been colonised and fought over, and it was running with the blood of a thousand generations. Ancient forests had been cleared for agriculture, and deserts had been irrigated and made into gardens. The wild animals of the land had been tamed and put in harness for human use or bred for human consumption. Temples had been built from the finest materials, to all the Gods. Terraces had been carved by the toil of man's labour into the sides of mountains, and bridges had been built by the ingenuity of his mind to span the widest rivers. Swamps were drained and rivers dammed. Cities had grown up in every continent, and roads and railway tracks had been laid for commerce and communication. All this and more – but the oceans remained unchanged.

No one owned the sea on which I sailed; no one could ever control it. It was beyond morality and had no right or wrong. It just was. It was allowing me a safe passage so far but it could claim me, or any sailor, at any time it felt like it. Many men and women before me had been taken by the sea. The little double crosses on the charts for coastal waterways bore sad witness to that, but out here in the ocean no one knew where a ship went down, and with its rotten hull lying at over 4,000 metres it didn't matter where it was. Those that were claimed came from every race and every age: fighting seamen in warships, shipwrecked sailors in lifeboats, passengers on luxury cruise liners, honest fishermen on trawlers trying to make a living, young boys on square-riggers whose only crime was to love the sea, oarsmen on Viking longboats, day sailors out for a race round the bay, children playing on rubber ducks, explorers searching for unknown lands, harpoonists hunting the great whales, press-ganged landlubbers on passages to distant shores, refugees fleeing from persecution, officers murdered by their mutinous crews, merchantmen overrun by pirates, slaves – who had lost everything – in the foul holds of evil ships, yachtsmen who had gone missing without trace, and local fishermen swept out to sea in small open boats. Most of them drowned, others died of disease or injury, some died of hunger, countless thousands froze to death in the high latitudes, and many died of thirst and were burned by the hot tropical sun. The same sun that was shining on me.

As I sat in the sunlight, sailing over the ocean, my thoughts often turned to what lay beneath me. There must have been all kinds of strange creatures lurking on the ocean floor. That's where I would end up if I sprung a serious leak and sank – right at the bottom of the deep ocean. What was it like down there? It would be even blacker than the night the dust from the Sahara hung thick above me, and there would be no noise. Perfectly still and black and silent. It would be icy cold, and the pressure from all the water above would be crushing. If I did end up down there, what would happen to me with all that pressure? I didn't know for sure but that didn't stop me speculating. My lungs would be compressed to the size of a grain of sand, and the blood in my veins and arteries would be squeezed out. My eyeballs would collapse in their sockets, and the marrow in the bones would become as hard as the bones themselves. My whole body would be crushed beyond recognition before the strange creatures devoured it. How long would it take me to reach the bottom? If the boat had a big hole, from an impact with a container washed off the deck of a cargo ship, it would fill with water very quickly. I dropped an old bolt over the side, trying to judge how fast it went down – about two metres per second. That would mean I could be on the bottom in 2,000 seconds, or about half an hour. It would only take me about a minute before I became unconscious, so I would be well dead before the sides of my veins started to collapse in upon themselves.

When these idle and macabre thoughts filled my mind I was quite happy to let them run their course until I felt the need to eat. They quickly vanished once the stove was lit and the smell of food and the sound of a little soft music filled the cabin. After dinner, I would again sit in the cockpit and gaze out upon the sea, remembering some long-forgotten experience from my childhood. It always made me feel sad to think of my father, whom I loved more than any man, and I often wondered what he would make of my trip. I had given him a lot of heartache with some of my antics as a boy, but I think he could accept this trip as a way of channelling the reckless side of my nature. He was always worried that I was going to get into big trouble; I would have loved to be able to tell him that everything worked out fine in the end. If I was going to hallucinate and have a stowaway of the mind aboard, I would gladly trade Sir Walter Raleigh and Marilyn Monroe for him.

Each night I'd get into the cot with a mug of cocoa, a slice of Christmas cake and a book, and the milkmaid smiled benignly upon me. She was on the front of a packet of powdered milk hanging in a net above the galley. She had light blonde curly hair, red rosy cheeks and she carried two pails of milk. Her teeth were pearly white, her lips were soft and pink. There was a green meadow behind her with a few dairy cattle munching the grass. She smiled down at me while I sipped the cocoa and ate the Christmas cake and was the last thing I looked at each night before turning the cabin light out. She was still smiling first thing in the morning when I opened my eyes. The powdered-milk packet was made of aluminium foil, and I made sure not to wrinkle the milkmaid each time I took a spoonful. I always placed the packet carefully back in the net so that nothing stood between me and her smile. After saying 'Good morning' to the milk-maid, I would get up and check to see if there was any shipping – nothing. I would brew a cup of tea and find something to eat before getting back into my bunk. I had always found lying in bed one of life's least complicated pleasures and enjoyed indulging myself by dozing off and reading until mid-morning.

The pump in the sea toilet wasn't very efficient, and I soon discovered the joy of sitting and shitting in a bucket. It was really comfortable to squat out in the cockpit in the sunshine with my backside squeezed down in the plastic rim. I felt like a two-year-old and took all the time in the world over it. There was only one bucket aboard but it was easy to clean out by trailing over the side. I watched the turds float in the water and fall astern. It was strange to see part of me consumed by the sea. No doubt a fish would come along and eat it. Then I would catch a fish and it would go in the cleaned-out bucket, before being eaten by me, whereupon it would end up becoming a turd in the bucket again. There was a wonderful circularity and completeness about it all.

Most nights I wore an Egyptian *djellaba* as a nightshirt, and sometimes I kept this on all through the day, tying a cord around the waist to stop the hem getting in the way. It kept me cool in the hot tropical sunshine and stopped my skin from burning. I must have looked like something to frighten a child and had a distinct biblical appearance, what with my long hair and shaggy beard and the *djellaba* blowing in the wind. In fact, I felt like one of those crazy Old Testament prophets who every now and then would take off into the wilderness for 30 or 40 days. If I didn't have a book in my hand, it was because I had a blood-stained knife instead, and there was hardly a moment when I wasn't singing to myself.

The solitude was soothing though, and with each passing day I felt more contented and had an overwhelming sense of goodwill towards my fellow man. To find an outlet for this, I would often spend five or six

THE BREATH OF ANGELS

hours writing letters. Each letter was addressed with the name of the boat and my current latitude and longitude. I wrote to my mother, telling her I loved her, which I did, but had never had the sense to say so before. A letter was penned to Shelagh, thanking her for the Christmas cake which I was rationing carefully, and I wrote to Bob in Whitby about what a wonderful trip I was having and how he would have loved it. Peter, who gave me the New Testament, got one, care of the Christian Brotherhood, as did Tony on *Potlatch*. I had already written Laura three letters and wrote her a fourth, sealing it with a big kiss. Strangely enough, I missed Laura less now that I was on my own. I also wrote to Tim, who had joined me for the weekend trip across the Irish Sea, asking him to come out to join me for a fortnight in the Caribbean. I felt the circumstances entitled me to a certain poetic licence. Most of the letters ended with variations along the lines:

> You would love it. The glorious sunsets and the flying fish and the frigate birds and the warm steady winds that drive the boat relentlessly westwards. The sheer beauty, truth and simplicity of it all.

> Happy New Year

> John

The pile of letters waiting to be posted from St Lucia got bigger every day.

I was now approaching the halfway mark, which I was going to celebrate with a bottle of champagne and a good lunch. For some reason, the tuna fish were no longer taking the lure so I had to settle for boiled potatoes, corned beef and cabbage. The cabbage had kept well but this was the last of it. I finished the champagne off with a box of fancy chocolate biscuits that Laura had bought and wrapped especially for the halfway celebration lunch. The champagne went straight to my head, as I played music and danced around the cabin. I could swing and spin around on the stainless-steel pole down the middle of the cabin that John Walko fell in love with in Scotland. The pole was quite a nifty dance-partner and really knew how to jive. After the fast numbers wore me out, I played a Mills Brothers tape with sentimental old slow sets. There was one in particular that I liked – it always made me think of Laura. I played it over and over again, waltzing round the cabin with a pillow. It was almost as if it had been written especially for us and was called 'Till Then'. It went:

Till then,
My darling please wait for me.
Till then,
No matter when it will be.
Till then,
When I will hold you again.
Please wait for me.

Although there are oceans we must cross,
and mountains that we must climb.
I know every game must have a loss,
so pray that our loss is nothing but time.
Till then . . .

After dozing off for the afternoon, I awoke before dusk with a headache and a hangover. I hope to hell it doesn't blow tonight, I thought, as I tried to sober up by splashing cold water over my face. It didn't blow that night, and in fact the wind began, very slowly at first, to drop. My next day's run was a miserable 29 miles. It didn't take long to do the arithmetic – with another 1,400 miles to go, it would take me a further 48 days.

After a few days of little wind, I started the engine for the first time on the passage, running it for six hours before the wind picked up again from the east. I was angry with myself for not having the patience to wait for the wind, because, as every sailor should know, it would return, and I wanted to make the entire trip under sail. But at least it topped up the batteries and I now had hot water for a shower: my first hot shower in 16 days. With clean clothes and a clean body and a mind that had been purged of all the accumulated waste and trivia of a lifetime, I felt as though I had been reborn. The world I was born into was as unspoiled as the Garden of Eden, and, being alone, I was without sin. The sun was on its way down, and it shone for me – 93 million miles away it blazed in the blackness of space, its warm, bright light bathing me and the boat as if in a ritual of daily baptism. I looked at it every day with the sextant: it spoke to me, telling me where I was and where I was going. The source of all life on earth, it now guided me across the ocean. It sung me a visual lullaby each night before setting, and, like an innocent child with a loving parent, I was comforted by its benign presence and knew it would never let me down. It painted pictures of flaming red and orange in the sky, and the paint from its palette spilled off the edge, flooding the sea with fire.

When the lullaby was over and the lights went out, I was ready for bed. Even though I could pick up the world service of the BBC, I didn't bother tuning in. World affairs seemed remote and unimportant to me. Up until now, I had spent a good proportion of my sentient life listening to the news and reading newspapers, without having the slightest influence over any of the events – it now seemed utterly pointless to acquaint myself with what was going on. I knew that there were wars and injustices and famine all over the world, but it made me miserable to think of them, and I didn't see the need for details. I did listen to the ham-radio network every day though, and there was endless talk about a single-handed woman who was last seen by another yacht about nine days ago, roughly 400 miles east of the island of Dominica. There was visual contact at the time and the yacht that reported the incident came within hailing distance after being called on the radio. Her VHF radio was giving her problems and she was worried that it might pack up altogther. Her self-steering gear wasn't working either. No one seemed to know what happened to her; so far she had failed to turn up in Dominica. With only 400 miles to go, Dominica should have been no more than four days away. This worried me a great deal because it could just as easily be me.

I now had less than 1,000 miles to go. If the ship went down, as long as I got in the life raft, I would probably be alright. The currents and wind would take the life raft west before it fetched up somewhere or other. With the wind and current, I would probably make about 30 miles a day, so even if I had to abandon ship right now, I would only have to spend 30 days in the life raft. For each 100 miles sailed, it would be three days less in the life raft. This was a very comforting thought as the boat pressed on.

24. Sailing Towards Venus

ONCE I WAS ON LATITUDE 14 DEGREES NORTH, THE COURSE to St Lucia was due west. For each 15 degrees of longitude I sailed, which was about 850 miles, I set the clock back one hour. All the time, the little impeller on the trailing log, which was towed astern, spun in the water, turning the piece of line to which it was attached. The line was hooked on to a mechanical instrument with a clock face of sorts, the single hand of which registered the miles the boat travelled through the water. I studied this clock face every day. It measured not only distance travelled but also my growing confidence in my own ability as a sailor. I had to add another 18 miles for the current, which I estimated to be running at three-quarters of a knot. As long as a westerly course was maintained, I would reach St Lucia.

The navigation was simplicity itself, and I hardly needed to look at the compass. To stay on course all I had to do was look at the sun during the day and the stars at night. As long as the sun came up slightly to the port side of the stern and set slightly to the port side of the bow, I was on course. At midday, the sun was due south – dead centre on the port beam. I soon learned to spot any deviation to the course by looking heavenward. Just before the sun set, I could already see Venus, which was bearing due west. The bow pointed straight towards it. When the sun set, darkness fell quickly, as it does in the tropics, and Venus, being a planet close to the earth, stood out from all the distant stars. Even though it was low in the evening sky, it stayed with me for a few hours before setting. I always spent these hours in the cockpit.

Venus was like a small moon. When the sea was relatively calm, the surface of the water glistened with the reflected light from this heavenly body. Its reflection formed a shimmering line of silver that stretched from the bow of boat to the horizon, and I stayed on that line as if it were a railway track. On the nights when there was no moon, Venus reigned supreme, and when it finally set, the other stars took on an added brilliance the way the chorus line does when the *prima donna* goes off stage. The Milky Way stretched right across the night sky like a flowing river of stars. I looked up at it with the binoculars to see millions of worlds clustered within. The constellations of the Great Bear, the Little Bear and Cassiopeia loomed above me, and with the departure of Venus Sirius was now the brightest star. To find out if I was on course, all I had to do was look towards Polaris, the North Star. As I was close to the Equator, it was low in the northern sky and relatively indistinct, but once you knew where to look it could be picked out easily. All the other stars rotated around Polaris, which never moved and was always due north. If Polaris was dead centre on the starboard beam, I was on course.

Sometimes a shooting star streaked across the heavens – it always took my breath away. With no background artificial light or pollution in the atmosphere, I saw the stars as primitive man must have seen them, and I began to understand the wonder of their captivating power. Unlike primitive man, I had some idea how far away they were, and I now had a better understanding of distance, having sailed day and night for nearly 20 days. When I thought about how vast the ocean was and set this against the vastness of the cosmos, I could only laugh out loud in disbelief. Viewed from up there, this ocean was not even a teardrop. My boat was too insignificant to mention. As for me, I was as important to the grand scheme of things as the cockroaches that were multiplying down below. The little bastards were everywhere, and I often found them in my sleeping-bag at night. I hated the cockroaches aboard the *Warrior Queen* almost as much as Humphrey Bogart hated the leeches aboard the *African Queen*.

The *African Queen* set me off on another long train of thought about what I would do for the rest of the voyage. From what I had read about the Caribbean, it seemed to be a good place for a sailing holiday, but I didn't want to come all this way just to hang around a few islands. I knew there was a big street carnival in Trinidad that was believed by Trinidadians to be the best in the world. I would probably take that in and then sail on to Venezuela. Since I was a boy, I had been intrigued by the Rio Orinoco, which flows out to sea in Venezuela, and I had read an article in a sailing magazine about a boat sailing up this river. Taking a sailboat up a jungle river and into the rainforest would be something worth doing, I thought, as long as I don't have to go over the side to haul it through the swamps with the leeches. Humphrey Bogart had Katherine Hepburn with him, but Laura was not going to be with me.

Whatever I was going to do, there would be plenty of time but I had to make sure that I was reasonably close to an international airport by Easter, when Laura was planning to join me for ten days. I was pleased with the way the boat was standing up and was looking forward to being able to enjoy the sailing without having to spend all my free time in overalls. Everything that I fixed in Tenerife was working well and I hadn't had a single piece of trouble with gear since leaving. The outboard motor still needed fixing but I had managed without it for a long time and got good exercise from all the rowing when at anchor. I was getting fitter every day, with the continual movement about the boat, which honed my muscles to a state they had never been in before.

I was also fit mentally, apart from the mathematical lapses, and exercised my brain with literature and thought. *Dubliners* by James Joyce was my current book, which somehow, although Joyce was one of my favourite authors, I had never got round to in the past. The book is a series of semi-autobiographical stories about growing up in Dublin. Even though Dublin had changed, I could still identify with most of it. The last story, 'The Dead', is about the loss of love that death brings and contains the lines that I often thought summed up my own feelings about death:

Better to go bravely into that other world, in the full glory of some passion,
than fade and wither dismally with age.

It ends with the snow softly falling, and falling softly, on the grave where
Michael Furey lay buried somewhere in rural Ireland. As I read it in the
cockpit, alone on the ocean under a warm, star-clustered tropical night
sky, Ireland seemed like another world. But it was late January now;
maybe the snow would be falling softly this moment in that very grave-
yard.

The nights were so magical that I was reluctant to go to bed, but
there would be more of them, and the stars in the powdery Milky Way
would come out again. The milkmaid bag of powdered milk was now
empty but I kept the packet in the net above the galley and made my
cocoa with tinned milk. Shelagh's Christmas cake was holding out well; I
wasted not a single crumb each time I cut a slice from it. My books were
nearly finished though, and there was only one good one left – *The Last
Grain Race* by Eric Newby. I allowed myself two chapters before saying,
'Goodnight' to the milkmaid and turning the lights out.

The closer I got to the Caribbean, the more unsettled the weather
became. The wind still had an easterly component to it but it was starting to blow hard. Every now and then a violent rain squall would hit me
without much warning. The skies darkened and the rain came down like
a cataract. As each squall was accompanied by very strong winds, I
needed to reef the sails in an instant. When they occurred during the
day, the sun came out as soon as they passed, raising clouds of steam
from the decks. When they occurred at night, I leaped from my bunk
and rushed out to get some canvas down. With the strong winds, I was
cracking along faster than ever before. It wasn't long before I broke the
150-mile barrier with a day's run of 153 miles. Now that I had broken
this barrier, I was determined to push the boat to the limit and try to
beat 160 miles. Two days later, I clocked up 158 miles in 24 hours.

The talk on the ham-radio network each day was about the single-
handed woman who had gone missing. I was now in the general area
where she was last seen. The chances of coming across her were negligible but that was no reason for not looking, so I kept a keen lookout just
in case. *The Last Grain Race* was nearly finished – the *Moshulu* was home-
ward-bound from Australia with its cargo of grain. Newby had joined
the ship in Belfast, signing up for a return trip to Australia as a deck-
hand when he was 18, on what turned out to be one of the last working
sailships without power. The captain and the crew raced the boat home
in 91 days. Newby was as obsessed as I was with the challenge of

making a fast passage.

Each night before climbing into my cot, I looked at the twin head-sails poled out on either side and the deep-reefed mainsail sheeted hard in the centre to counteract the rolling. The rig was perfect for sailing downwind. Provided the self-steering gear held her on course, all would be well, but if she was knocked sideways to the wind and the following seas, the rig would become a liability and the boat could capsize. The self-steering gear had never let me down – I trusted it. As I looked at the sails, debating with myself whether it would be prudent to take some canvas down, I could feel the driving energy of the wind in them. The 160-mile day's run had not been made yet, so I left everything up and was ready to spring into action in the middle of the night when the squalls hit me.

It was on one such night that I had a strange dream. There was a large gathering of well-dressed people all attending a somewhat formal party in what appeared to be a hotel. Waitresses in black-and-white uniforms floated among the gathering with trays of drinks and light snacks. The one thing that everyone had in common was that I knew them all, but nobody was paying any attention to me. I couldn't under-stand what was going on, so I took one of the waitresses aside and asked her who the party was for. She looked at me with genuine surprise and said, 'Don't you know?' I assured her I didn't have the slightest idea and asked her again. 'It's for you,' she said.

I still couldn't understand it – the formal dress, the subdued atmos-phere, the drinks and the food. 'What kind of party is it?' I asked.

She was now getting irritated with me. 'Are you sure you don't know?' she asked. I was getting exasperated by this stage and asked her again. She paused for a moment, before saying, 'It's a funeral.'

I woke up instantly. Every detail of the dream was vivid and the logic of it was simple – everybody knowing me, but not all knowing each other, and no one paying any attention to me because I wasn't really there.

I got out of my bunk and went over to kiss the milkmaid through the net before making some strong tea. I drank the tea out in the cock-pit as the boat charged along. The wind vane on the self-steering gear was making small deflections to each side. I knew the rudder in the water would be responding to these movements. It was holding the course well. I was sure I would do 160 miles before noon next day. With about three hours to go till dawn, I climbed back into my bunk, satisfied that the dream was but a dream.

The next thing I was aware of were drops of water on my face. I could taste them on my lips. Fresh sweet rain was being driven in through the open companionway by the following wind. It was already all over the chart table. I climbed out of my cot to do something about it. It was another squall. The rain was heavier than it had been for any previous squall but the wind wasn't as severe. The best way to keep the rain out was to put in the three wooden washboards that are used for locking up the boat, but I didn't like the idea of restricting my access to the cockpit. I settled for the first two washboards and jammed my waterproofs in the space where the third one goes at the top. The rain continued to pour in. There was nothing else for it but to put the third washboard in, which I locked from the inside. The rain was kept at bay.

This was the first time that I was down below in the boat while under sail with all the washboards locked in place. I felt like Jonah in the belly of the whale. I was just about to dry myself off and sort out the wet bedding and charts when the wind came. It hit hard. The bow shuddered as it was forced down into the water by the power of the wind in the twin headsails. I heard the sails flap as the boat was knocked off course. She lurched over to one side. I nearly lost my balance before grabbing hold of the pole in the cabin. The boat was no longer upright and sailing downwind. She had been knocked beam to the wind, and the big following seas were crashing on to her side. I could see nothing but water out through the port window, nothing but sky out through the starboard one. The sail on the starboard side had backed, and the one on the port side was in the water. The end of the pole that held the port-side sail out was deep in the sea, and the mast was panting.

If I didn't get to the cockpit quick and get the boat back on course it would capsize or be dismasted. I tried to undo the lock on the top washboard. It was jammed! The flesh was torn off my knuckles as I tried to force it free. It refused to budge. Digging through the toolbag for a hammer to smash it, I saw the skylight in the main cabin. It was firmly battened down but I quickly released it, climbed up on the stove and started to pull my body through its narrow opening. When my head and shoulders were out, there was water everywhere. The driving rain was mixed with spray blown off the tops of the endless grey crests on all the waves. The mast was right beside me, straining with the water and wind in the sails. The boat was leaning over at an angle I had never known before. The harness was in the cockpit! My hands reached out and grabbed the rail on the high side of the boat. I pulled the rest of my body free. It was the first time I had been on deck on my own without a harness and life-line. If I let go of the grab-rail, I would slide over the port side of the boat and die. I held on vice-like with bleeding knuckles and inched along the rail. Inch by inch, the cockpit came closer. The wind vane had been driven over to one side and the self-steering rudder (which had served me well for 2,500 miles) was useless. The need to hang on and get to the cockpit was all I could think of. I got my right leg over the edge of the coachroof, my left followed – I knew I was going to make it. With both hands on the wheel, I forced it hard over and yelled, 'Come on, come on, COME ON!'

Nothing happened. I yelled some more. She started to come round. 'That's it, come on, keep coming.' The port-side sail began to lift clear of the sea. The panting of the mast stopped. The starboard side head-sail, which was backed, caught the wind with a whiplash crack and filled. Blood flowed from my knuckles, which stood out like white pieces of bone, as my hands clutched the wheel. I was wearing nothing but my underpants. The driving spray and rain lashed my back. It rolled down between my shoulder-blades and funnelled into the gap between the cheeks of my buttocks.

The boat was under control, but there was far too much sail up for the conditions. I rolled up all of the big headsail, leaving only the storm jib in place. I strapped the harness over my bare chest and clipped in, before going forward to remove the boom poles and going aft to set the self-steering gear. It took an exhausting 30 minutes to attend to these jobs, during which the rain and the wind never stopped. But the boat was now sailing comfortably with reduced sail. She was back on course and upright.

When I opened up the washboards from the outside and went down below, I was shaking uncontrollably from head to toe. It took me a full 15 minutes before I could stop shaking. I put a heavy towelling bathrobe over my naked body and a woollen hat on my head. My hands trembled like an alcoholic's when I poured myself a small whisky, and my fingers fumbled with the cigarette paper as I rolled a smoke. There was debris all over the place. The wet paperback of *The Last Grain Race* was lying on the floor of the cabin. I kicked it to one side, pointed my finger at it and said, 'It's all your bloody fault, Newby,' but I knew it was my own and deserved everything I got. There were less than 400 miles to go, and I had nearly come unstuck, all because I wanted to make a day's run of 160 miles. I had been severely punished for my vanity and pride. The sea had shown me that it was not to be taken lightly. From now on I would pay it the respect it demanded and sail with minimal canvas and be satisfied with 100 miles a day.

I finished my book off with little enthusiasm later that day and tuned in to the ham-radio network. They were predicting more rain squalls and still talking about the single-handed woman who had not yet turned up. She was now giving real cause for concern. With the reduced canvas, the boat dealt with each squall well, and I had a lazy day playing chess and listening to *La Bohème* and *Rigoletto*. After dark, I went through the books for something to read but there were only two left, neither of which appealed to me in the mood I was in. One was *Collected Horror Stories* and the other was *Survive the Savage Sea*. What I needed right now was a good western.

I sailed under reduced canvas for the rest of the passage. Traces of vanity remained, and to try to prove to myself that the squalls didn't bother me, I stripped off in the cockpit and showered with a bottle of shampoo during the height of one of them. After the shower, the sun came out. I went and sat on the aft deck and trimmed my beard, which hadn't been touched for 21 days. I wanted to make sure that I arrived looking my best, so I used a bull's-eye mirror and took a long time over it. I could see all of the boat in the mirror's convex contours, so I took a picture of myself with the boat behind me.

Tidied up and ready for shore leave, I knew that land was close. On my 23rd night at sea, at 1.30 a.m., I picked up city lights on the southern part of the French island of Martinique. It was something of an anticlimax, because I knew that the ocean would be left behind and that I might never again sail it on my own. For 23 days I had escaped from the world I had lived in for 41 years. I had mixed feelings about going back to it.

Now that I had sighted dim lights in the distance, my main worry was fetching up on a coral reef or smashing into a rock. After more than three weeks of seeing no land, the sight of it was somewhat intimidating. With the wind from the east, Martinique is a lee shore, so I put the boat on a southerly course to find the passage between the south of this island and the north of St Lucia. After I assured myself that there was no possibility of reaching land before dawn, I turned in for my last sleep of the voyage and let the boat sail itself once more, as it had done for the last three weeks.

At dawn the outline of St Lucia and the passage to the north of the island was just visible. A landfall is a slow, subtle experience that beats the pants off flying into a new place in an aeroplane. At first all that could be seen of the island was a vague, grey outline above the horizon. After a couple of hours and a good breakfast of pancakes and strong coffee, the grey outline gave way to shades of green and the skyline became more distinct. An hour later, I could pick out cliffs on the coastline with the binoculars. By mid-morning, I could see settlements with the naked eye. With the sun now high in the sky, the island revealed itself to be covered in lush, tropical vegetation. Before noon, I was close to the northern shore and palm trees stood out along the white sandy beaches.

There was a multitude of sailboats: big yachts mostly and some reproduction square-riggers with towering masts and acres of canvas. I knew this was a popular cruising ground but the number of sailboats far exceeded my expectations. They were everywhere but I didn't get close enough to any of them to see the people aboard. Even close inshore, the sea is a big place, and none of them passed within a mile of me. From the course they were sailing, it was clear that they were all making passages between the various islands of the Windward Island chain – St Lucia, Martinique, Dominica, Guadaloupe, St Kitts, Antigua, the list is endless.

After rounding the north-west corner of St Lucia, I could see the wide, sheltered bay and more yachts lying at anchor. To clear customs, I needed to go into the marina, the entrance to which was about two miles away. It was time to start the engine. With the batteries fully charged, it fired up straight away. The small town of Cros Islet, with its brightly painted houses straggling along the sandy beach, stood out against the palm trees. There were a few small fishing boats lying to a bow anchor, their sterns tied to swaying palms. I couldn't help congratulating myself, when I suddenly smelled something burning. Oh no, not a fire with less than two miles to go! The engine's burning, I thought, as I opened the inspection hatch, expecting to be engulfed in flames. No sign of any fire. The stove must be on fire, I thought, as I ran down below to the galley. No sign of any fire there, but I could still smell it, and I knew something was burning. The ashtray must have tipped up and dropped a butt in my sleeping-bag, I thought, rushing down below again to shake it out. The sleeping-bag was fine, but I could still smell the burning. It was then that I saw the smoke. It was drifting upwards from a small fire on the beach. My sense of smell was so heightened after my time at sea that I could pick it up over a mile away.

'Don't congratulate yourself until you're tied up,' I murmured aloud as I continued to steer towards the marina. On the way in through the narrow entrance, an open boat with a pointed bow came up behind and overtook me. I was shocked when I looked down at it. There were two men aboard, the first human beings I had seen since leaving Tenerife. But what gave me the biggest surprise of all was that they were black. One of them had Rastafarian dreadlocks, and the other had short-cropped hair. For some reason that must have had something to do with an unknown but very deep-seated racial prejudice, I had never thought that the first person I would see would be black. They both smiled and waved at me. I gave them a thumbs-up sign and returned the smile. Welcome to the Caribbean.

Five minutes later, I was passing my lines to a bystander on one of the pontoons. He secured them to the cleats. I stood in the cockpit and grinned. It was 1.17 p.m. local time, and I had sailed over 3,000 miles on my own in 23 days and three hours. The boat was in good shape. I was in even better shape. Having lost the little paunch that had been getting bigger each year since I turned 30, I now had the figure of a 21-year-old. The bystander asked me where I had come from, and I told him. Before he had a chance to congratulate me, I already had the bottle of whisky in my hand with two glasses under my arm. I poured both of us a large one.

PART THREE

Tropical Waters

Ships that pass in the night, and speak each other in passing,
Only a signal shown and a distant voice in the darkness;
So on the ocean of life, we pass and speak one another,
Only a look and a voice, then darkness again and a silence.

HENRY LONGFELLOW

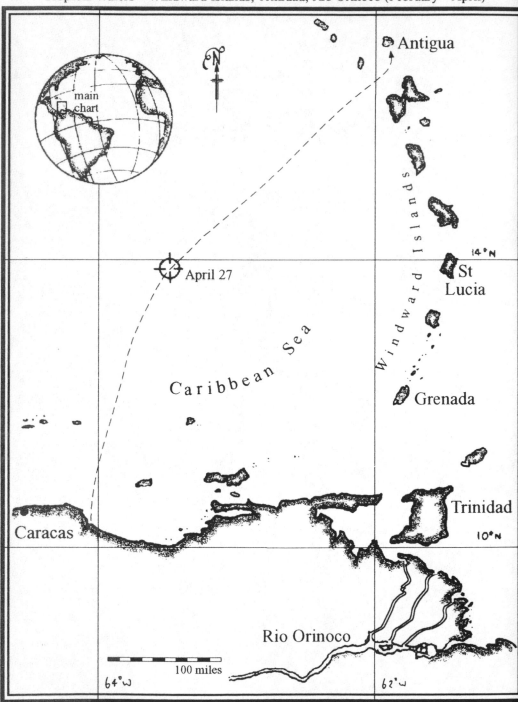

25. *Boatboys and Lost Sailors*

I HAD NEVER SEEN SO MANY BOATS IN A MARINA AS THERE were in Rodney Bay, most of which were significantly larger than my boat. There was big money tied up in these boats, the majority of which were foreign registered in the US or Canada, the UK, France or Germany. I had no idea what to do now that I had arrived, but as there was a water pipe on the pontoon I thought I may as well fill the tanks. No water came out when I fiddled with the faucet, and another passerby told me that all the water was metered and had to be paid for. He pointed out the marina office, where I could arrange to have the water turned on, but I couldn't be bothered with any paperwork. The customs-and-immigration office was nearby but I was even less interested in dealing with their paperwork. I set off to find a bar instead. On the way there, I realised I had no currency. For the last three weeks, banknotes were just useless scraps of paper to me but now I couldn't get a cup of tea without them. There was no alternative to queuing up in the bank and filling out forms to draw some cash on my credit card. Queues, impatient people, forms, personal identification, officials, bureaucracy, banknotes – less than an hour after sailing the ocean, where none of this counted for anything, I had the whole lot in one go.

I felt like getting back on the boat and putting out to sea but visited the clubhouse bar instead and ordered the local speciality – rum punch. It's a strong cocktail because in the Caribbean the rum is cheaper than the fruit juice; instead of topping the fruit juice up with rum they top the rum up with fruit juice. The social order of things was immediately apparent. All the staff were black and all the customers were white. This made me feel a little uncomfortable but the rum punch soon put me at my ease.

On the way to the clubhouse, I had spotted a boat called *Comus*, which was registered in Belfast. After finishing my drink, I decided to go down and check them out. The skipper was doing an oil change, and I asked him, in my broadest Belfast accent, 'What part of town are you from then?' When someone from Belfast asks another person from Belfast what part of town they're from, it usually gives rise to immediate suspicion. But we were both a long way from home, and the troubles of our native land now seemed remote. He invited me aboard for a beer. David had made the passage from the Canary Islands with three friends from Ireland. This was his third time across the Atlantic, and he asked me about my trip. When I said that I had arrived less than an hour ago, he asked where my mates were. I explained that I had come on my own. He became very excited, asking, 'How many days?' I told him, and he said approvingly, 'That's a very fast passage. Well done.' We talked at length about our crossings and shared a few more beers and cigarettes. I could see that David was going to adopt me.

I was enjoying David's company but was anxious to get out of the marina. He gave me directions for catching a bus into the capital town of Castries, and we arranged to meet later that night. I boarded the minibus just outside the marina compound, squeezed in tight, and headed into town. It had a high-powered sound system that blasted out reggae music. All along the road on the way in, there were small, clapboard houses with children playing outside. Tropical fruits hung from big-leaved trees. The windows of the bus were wide open, and the warm, soft air kept blowing my long, untidy hair into my eyes. The sea shimmered in the afternoon sun.

I disembarked in the centre of town and headed straight for the market. There was a distinct colonial feel to the town, with its narrow streets, wooden buildings, overhanging balconies, and rough-looking rum houses. The streets were thronged with people, but there was hardly a white face in sight. The young women wore bright, tightly fitting clothes which looked good on them, and the superbly built young men wore T-shirts and jeans. The older people all seemed to be very fat or very thin, but most of them looked healthy, and everyone certainly knew how to smile.

The market-place bowled me over. Little old ladies in floral dresses and straw hats tried to persuade me to buy some of their produce. Everyone spoke English, but it was heavily stamped with their own native patois, and they had quite a few words that I didn't understand. My time at sea had sharpened my senses, and I took nothing for granted: the sound of people talking echoed round my brain; the sweet, sugary smell of rum, which was on sale everywhere, filled my nostrils; the sight of strange vegetables and fruits that I had never seen before, along with big barrels of flying fish, had my eyes popping; the rough texture of the flour-bag shirts felt good when I ran my hand over them; and the smoke from the local brand of cigarettes, which I sucked deep into my lungs, tasted strong and pungent.

On the way back to the marina, I shared the minibus with a gang of school kids. They were all wearing smart uniforms. The girls were dressed in green pinafores with white blouses, and the boys wore long pants with a white shirt and tie. They capered about the bus, the way school kids do everywhere, and the driver had to stop at one point to tell them off. I was dying to have a look at their schoolbooks but decided against asking. I would have been quite happy to keep driving round the island in the bus but it was now late evening in the UK and I needed to ring Laura.

When she answered the phone, I simply said, 'Hello Laura.'

I already knew what her reply was going to be, but was looking forward to it nonetheless. 'John, John, where are you?' she asked. I had given her an over-estimate of the time for the crossing, telling her not to worry if she didn't hear from me for 40 days. She knew this was an over-estimate and had thought 30 days was more realistic, so she was still surprised to hear from me. She wasn't very coherent and kept saying things like, 'St Lucia, St Lucia, I can't believe it,' and, 'I wish I could fly out right now,' and, 'You must be exhausted, totally exhausted.' I managed to convince her that I was where I said I was but she didn't believe me when I said I had never felt so rested in my life. She agreed to phone my friends and relatives to tell them I was fine. We lingered on the phone for a long time.

I met David in the clubhouse bar later that night, and he introduced me to all his friends. David had a certain charm that made him equally attractive to men and women. There were lots of introductions. I was very flattered because he always began the same way: 'This is my friend, John, just arrived from the Canaries, single handed, 23 days.' After that I didn't have to say anything. As we were heading off to another bar, he took me to one side and said, 'Listen, I'm going to be introducing you to some other friends of mine – a man and a woman. The woman was attempting to make the passage on her own, but she abandoned her boat at sea, so I'm just putting you in the picture.' These words stopped me dead in my tracks. I asked if this was the woman that was heading for Dominica. David asked how the hell did I know that, and I explained about all the traffic on the ham-radio network, and that I had spent days keeping a lookout for her. It was the same woman! She had radioed a passing cargo ship bound for Trinidad and asked to be lifted off her boat. They took her aboard, leaving her boat drifting at sea.

I met Julia and her boyfriend, Barry, later that night. I talked briefly with Julia about what happened, but she didn't want to go into too many details. I told her about all the traffic on the ham radio, which she didn't know about, and suggested she get on the air on someone's shortwave radio to clear things up. Barry had made the passage in his own boat with two other men, and he and Julia had now got together as more than friends.

David, who had been in the islands about a month, gave me plenty of advice. Most of this centred around how to deal with the customs-and-immigration authorities and the boatboys. When I pointed out that I hadn't bothered to clear customs yet, David was taken aback. 'You could get yourself in big trouble, John.'

'I don't see why, I don't have any contraband or guns aboard.'

'That's not how they see it. If you don't clear as soon as you arrive, they can impose a very heavy fine or even impound your boat.' Up until now, I had been sailing in European waters, where nobody paid much attention to these formalities, but it seemed that each island was a separate state unto itself and enforced the law to the letter. David insisted I get down to the office first thing in the morning and tell them that I had not been ashore since arriving. It was no good lying and saying that I had just arrived, because they would probably already know the boat was there. He also told me to make sure to keep saying 'Sir'.

'What about the boatboys then?' I asked.

'Don't worry, you'll find out about them soon enough.'

'But who the hell are they?'

'Well, let's put it like this. They're not boys for a start but they do have boats – open boats with outboard motors on the back. Everywhere you go, you're likely to meet them. If you're going into port they might approach you about a mile or two offshore and offer to help you anchor. Sometimes they have fresh fish and vegetables, and they'll want to sell you these. When you take your dinghy ashore, they'll offer to look after it for you. If you need anything special, they know where to get it. Most of them are OK but if you're on your own you need to be careful. Always agree a price before doing a deal. I usually buy stuff off them. Once they've got a few ECs, they leave you in peace.'

'What's an EC?' I asked.

'These bloody things we're buying drink with – Eastern Caribbean Dollars.'

I stayed up until 3.0 a.m. and was too excited to go to sleep when I climbed back aboard my boat. Although I had only been here for just over 12 hours, I had already made half-a-dozen new friends. It was very quiet now, and the boat seemed strangely still. It was hard to believe that I had been out in the ocean the previous night, surging ahead with the sails straining and the yacht rolling from side to side. I finished off the last of the whisky and the Christmas cake before tidying up the net above the galley. The milkmaid went in the rubbish bag.

Next morning, I was receiving a stern lecture from the officials in the Customs House. 'You are the captain, and it is your duty to report to this office as soon as you arrive.'

'I realise that, Sir, but I was on my own and totally exhausted when I arrived and have been fast asleep ever since I came in.' They finally stamped my passport, gave me official clearance and told me that I was now free to go ashore. Before leaving, I asked them if they would be kind enough to direct me to the bank.

I hung around Rodney Bay for a day or two before sailing down the west coast to the small town of Soufrière. David was taking his boat there, and Barry and Julia were also going. Sailing on the western side of the island, sheltered from the ocean seas, was a new experience for me. There was plenty of wind but the sea was very calm, and it was an effortless trip. Soufrière was surrounded by a large sheltered bay. The skyline was dominated by two mountains that were shaped like ice cream cones – the Little Piton, which was anything but little, and the Grande Piton, which lived up to its name. The steep sides of these ice-cream cones were covered with lush, tropical vegetation all the way to the summits. It was the classic image of a tropical island, and the bay itself was fringed with golden sands and palm trees. With about two miles to go, I had my first encounter with a boatboy. Like me, he was on his own. He brought his boat close up to my stern, asking if I needed any help with anchoring in the bay. 'I can show you where to go and take your line for you.'

'I'm used to anchoring on my own. I don't need any help.'

'Hey, man, we gotta earn a living.'

'How much do you want?'

'Just give me a few EC.'

'How much is a few?'

'Give me eight EC.'

'I'll give you five.'

Five EC is about two US dollars. If I had to pay this everytime I anchored, I would soon run out of money, but he no doubt thought that most yachtsmen were rich, and quite a few are, and he was right about the need to earn a living. It was a precarious way to go about it. If his outboard engine broke down, he would be swept out to sea by the west-setting Antilles current. I wouldn't have come out this far in an open boat, with no backup to an outboard engine, for five EC, at least half of which would have been needed for fuel.

Barry and Julia on *Red Shift* and David and his friends on *Comus* were already at anchor, and I selected a spot close to them. The beach shelved very steeply, and with less than 50 yards to the shore there was over 50 feet of water. The only way to moor was to go in very close and drop a bow anchor. The man in the boat who had met me at sea then took a long line from the stern and tied this to a palm tree that stood at the edge of the beach. He then came back to the yacht for his five EC, telling me he would come to see me tomorrow in case I needed anything. I said that I didn't need anything but he said he would come anyway with some fresh fruit and fish.

It was now near dusk. The sky was soft pink. My old friend Venus was already visible, and I could hear the rhythmic sound of the waves breaking on the beach and a thousand palm leaves rustling in the wind. Children from the town were swimming all around the boat, splashing about in the water and laughing. There was a big hand-painted sign on the beach advertising the Humming Bird bar and restaurant, and the majestic Pitons stood in the background. Soufrière was a beautiful anchorage.

You lose new-found friends at sea as quickly as you find them. Next morning everyone was pulling out. I was staying in St Lucia for a few more days, awaiting the arrival of a friend from Boston. Laura and I had met Bill and his son Adam in India about five years earlier and had kept in touch ever since. We were on a three-week holiday at the same time as Bill and his son were travelling round the world in four months with one of those special airline deals. When he heard about my trip he was mad keen to join me, and I had arranged to meet him in Tahiti for the passage through the south-sea islands to Australia. Things had changed since the plan was hatched, and he was now going to join me for a few months in the Caribbean. It was a strange turn of events because Laura and I first saw Bill aboard a boat. We were sitting on silk cushions under the canopy of a *shakara* being rowed across Dal Lake in Kashmir, and Bill and his son were sitting drinking tea on the verandah of the house-boat we were going to stay on – *The Omar Khayam*.

While waiting for Bill, a few other boats came and went. I was beginning to slot them into categories. All the boats were sailboats – there were no cabin cruisers. The social pecking order was like a microcosm of society itself. There was a surprisingly large number of well-appointed big luxury yachts, mostly from the US, but quite a few from the UK. They tended to have a semi-professional crew of young men and women. The owners were getting on a bit and not always aboard. They kept themselves very much to themselves and had an offhand, business-like manner with the local population. These were the very rich.

Next there were charter boats. They were all very similar in appearance, each one belonging to two or three large charter companies that operated out of the islands. They tended to have a few couples aboard, who only had the boat for a week or two. They rarely stayed more than one night in any one place. They were having a sailing holiday and wanted to see as much as they could in a short time. There was always high jinks going on at night, and I never got much opportunity to meet the people aboard. These were mostly middle-class sailors on holiday.

After that came the 'liveaboards'. Most of these were from the US, and they often stayed in the same spot for months on end. They had usually sailed here by hopping down the eastern seaboard of the US as far as Florida, and then sailed from island to island through the Bahamas, the US Virgin Islands, the British Virgin Islands and the Leeward Islands, before arriving in the Windward Islands. Their boats had everything aboard: televisions, videos, microwave ovens and water-makers. They never took any chances and didn't like strange boats anchoring too close to them. The people aboard tended to be well turned out and never seemed to be short of clean clothes. These were the settled and respectable suburban sailors.

Then there were the cruising boats. These were the smallest boats and usually had self-steering gear and wind generators. They came from Europe mostly but there were some from the US and Canada. Some of them were built by their owners in steel or ferro-cement, others were mass-production fibreglass boats. The younger the people aboard, the smaller the boat was likely to be. Many had couples aboard, and some even had young children. Others had a crew of two or three friends. They moved about a lot but never seemed to be in any great hurry. I gravitated to the people aboard the cruising boats, finding them all very friendly and outgoing. Most of them had to scrape together their money to get the boat in the first place, and they lived the life of gypsies afloat. These people were the bohemians of the sea.

Finally, there were the boatboys. The boatboys were the working men of the sea.

26. New Crew

THE TRIP TO THE AIRPORT TOOK ME OVER THE TOP OF THE island, through banana, coco and grapefruit plantations. Bill stepped out of the airport building in the clothes he had been wearing to protect him from the snow in Boston eight hours earlier. He looked a bit pale and had a cold but was in good spirits. The layers of clothes were shed on the journey back to Soufrière. As we walked along the beach to the boat, I could sense his mounting excitement.

'There she is, Bill,' I said, pointing to the *Warrior Queen*. She didn't look anything special and was dwarfed by some of the big yachts in the bay. It was the first time Bill had seen her. She was going to be his home for the next couple of months. His cold was already beginning to clear up. He looked at me, smiled and said, 'She looks beautiful, John.' The dinghy was on the beach being 'looked after' by a young boy. I gave him his one EC for 'taking care' of it. There was no need to row out. We pulled the dinghy up to the boat using the long line from the stern secured to the palm tree. I had spent most of the morning cleaning out the forepeak cabin, which was his living space, and killing cockroaches, which were in every locker and under every canopy. I thought it best to mention these to Bill but he didn't seem to be concerned.

I knew there would now be a new supply of books and tapes aboard and was anxious to inspect these. Bill had a good selection of swing music from the Thirties and Forties and plenty of reading material. He also had a couple of harmonicas, so now there would be live music aboard. Bill had a few friends in Massachusetts who owned their own boats, and from what I had seen of American boats so far, it was more than likely that they would have been much fancier than mine. He had also spent a life accustomed to a limitless supply of ice and was disappointed to learn that I didn't have any. Up until this point, ice had never crossed my mind.

Later that day, after Bill had gone ashore to have a look around town, he called out to me from the beach on his way back. His two hands were stretched up above his head. In each hand he held a bag of ice. He was now a completely happy man. Bread may be the staff of life for most of us, but in America no one seems to be able to manage without ice.

We spent the next few weeks cruising south down the chain of Windward Islands. Each time we left an island, we had to go through the rigmarole of clearing customs and immigration and then clear in at the next island. In one place where we stopped, there was a long questionnaire which asked all the usual questions about illegal substances and firearms but finished off with two questions that had me rolling on the floor of the office: 'Do you have any stowaways aboard? If so, how many?'

Each night Bill played the harmonica while sitting at the bow, and the strains of 'Red River Valley' carried out across our anchorage – how I loved that tune. As well as the big luxury yachts, there were a few reproduction square-riggers complete with white-uniformed crew. The owners sat on the aft decks, drinking cocktails while the young crew scampered about the rigging. I got to know the first officer on one of these square riggers during an island stopover. When we weren't sailing during the day we found a coral reef and rowed out in the dinghy to go snorkelling.

We kept heading south, stopping off at the island of Canouan where we anchored close inshore. The square-rigger on which I knew the first officer was anchored about a mile away. It was late in the afternoon when we arrived, and after rowing ashore Bill and I found a restaurant for dinner. It was about a mile up the beach from the boat. During dinner the wind began to get up and I was a little concerned about the boat, so, instead of lingering for a few beers as we usually did, we headed back along the beach. As it was dark, Bill led the way with a flashlight. We were having difficulty finding the dinghy, which had been pulled up the beach and tied to a palm tree. We knew it wasn't far away when the beam from the flashlight lit up the face of an old man running down the shoreline towards us. 'Do you know who owns the small white yacht anchored down there?' he asked breathlessly, pointing in the direction of where the *Warrior Queen* was.

'Yes, I do.'

'You had better get aboard quick. She's going ashore!'

We ran down the beach, shining the flashlight out to where the boat should have been. It wasn't there! The light from the beam bounced over the waves before flashing on the white hull of the boat. She was already beginning to lie over on her side, less than 20 yards from where the waves were breaking. The anchor was dragging and she was going ashore fast. We found the dinghy nearby, rowed out as quickly as we could and leaped aboard. I started the engine immediately and slammed her into forward gear. She didn't move by an inch. The only hope was to row another anchor well out into deep water and try to haul her off. With every incoming wave she was bouncing closer to the shore and rolling from side to side with her keel on the bottom. I switched every deck and navigation light on, and Bill and I worked frenetically to prepare the spare anchor and long line.

The next thing I knew there was a strange man in the dinghy. He called out for the anchor. Before we could pass it to him there was another man in the dinghy with the oars ready. As I worked to uncoil the long rope, another man appeared on deck beside me. I left Bill and this man to sort out the anchor and rushed back to the cockpit, only to find two more men trying to use the engine to help get her off. The lights illuminated the shallow water around us: other men were wading out from the beach. Some were trying to push the boat off with nothing but their bare hands and muscle.

The spare anchor was set by the two men in the dinghy. The line now needed hauling in. Before I knew what was happening, there were six men holding the end of the line on the seaward deck of my boat. As the boat rolled one way towards the shore, they were all nearly pulled through the rails. When it rolled the other way, this was their chance. They hauled up the slack and jammed the rope. The white-suited first officer from the square-rigger had seen the masthead lights rolling from side to side and raced up in his high-powered launch. He put another line on us. We now had ten strong men on a rope attached to a well-set anchor, a powerful motor boat and my own engine. She started to move. Everyone yelled out with joy as if it was their own boat. When it was clear that she was coming off, one of the men in the cockpit turned to me and said, 'She's going to be OK, man.' I was completely disorientated in relation to where the shoreline was, but he guided me out to safe water when she came free. Two more helped Bill set the main anchor after the man in the cockpit had scanned the lights ashore and picked the spot with the best holding ground. 'You'll be safe here,' he said, as I cut the engine.

There were 12 men aboard my boat. I didn't know any of them and I didn't know where they came from. They had seen the boat rolling from side to side in the surf once the decklights had been switched on and rushed down to the beach to help. It was a Saturday evening and most of them were having a night out. Some of them waded out in their best clothes. Others stripped off to their underpants and swam out, leaving their clothes on the beach. Two of them didn't have a stitch on. Everyone sat in the cockpit, smiling now that the danger was past. Their white teeth stood out against their black faces in the darkness. The boatboys had saved my boat.

I didn't know what to do to express my thanks or repay the men, but I made a start by passing the cigarettes round. We had plenty of beer aboard and everybody had one. I knew I only had a small amount of cash and asked Bill what he had. Between us we had some US and EC dollars, and we gave all of this to the oldest man and asked him to divide it up. He didn't want to accept it but Bill and I insisted, pointing out it was only a small amount. The first officer ferried them back to the beach. It had been a close call but I now understood what the words 'brotherhood of the sea' really meant.

After our narrow escape, we made sure to anchor further offshore and, if possible, seek local advice about good holding ground. I was reluctant to leave the boat if the wind looked as though it would get up and always liked to be able to see her lying at anchor as we worked our way further south through the Grenadines and cleared into Union Island before visiting Tobago Keys. This is a group of four or five small, uninhabited islands, protected from the open ocean by a horseshoe-shaped coral reef. In the middle of the horseshoe, the water is flat calm whatever the weather. The bottom is covered in sand as white as snow. The water itself is a brilliant shade of swimming-pool light blue, and the visibility through the mask of the snorkel seemed endless. The bottom was alive with conch – big, desert-island, convoluted shells with a rough white exterior and a smooth, psychedelic pink interior that housed the animal within – the kind of shells that Polynesians use as trumpets to sound a war cry. They could be picked up by diving down 10 or 12 feet. The easy way down was to swim along the anchor chain. From the bottom looking up, the boat appeared to be floating on air. I felt like one of the many fishes that must have looked up at her as she sailed across the ocean. The firm flesh of the conch, when seasoned with a little salt and pepper and onions, made a tasty stew even if the meat was a bit chewy. Tobago Keys was the picture-book image of a coral-island paradise with one drawback – there were almost as many sailboats as there were conch shells. Everyone was looking for paradise, but in finding it, they destroyed it. Twenty years ago you would have been lucky to find another boat, and in ten years' time visitors will probably need to reserve a space months in advance. Large cruise liners anchored in the deep water nearby, bringing passengers to the horseshoe reef in powerboats. Some of the luxury liners had been fitted with absurd masts that were capable of carrying sail, even if they hardly ever did. For thousands of years, before the advent of steam, boats had sails which caught the wind. Now, with the advent of tourism, they once again have sails which are used to catch the punters – what a travesty.

Next stop Grenada, where my friend Tim was due to join us for a sailing holiday. I had arranged to meet him outside the police station in the capital, St Georges. We anchored in the main harbour in the centre of the town, which was reserved for the big liners, and were several hours late. I fully expected to find Tim sitting on the harbour wall but there was no sign of him. The police station drew a blank when I rowed ashore, and it looked as though he wasn't going to turn up. We knew that we couldn't stay long in the main harbour, but when the anchor was being hauled up I heard a voice call out, just as it had in Scotland six months earlier, 'Well then, Johnnie Boy.' Tim was rolling along the quayside with a friend in tow. The two of them were smashed out of their skulls. I rowed ashore and picked them both up. Tim's pal was a local man called Patrick, whom he had befriended four or five hours earlier. They had both been imbibing various liquids and substances in the meantime. We took the boat round to the spot for anchoring yachts while Tim sat in the cockpit grinning uncontrollably as a result of what he had been taking and the sheer exoticism of the location he found himself in.

After the formal introductions, he struggled to get his act together enough to fetch his gear and a few items I was expecting from England. He had managed to get hold of a big box of cigarette papers that would keep me going for the next six months, and he also had a bottle of whisky. He was a little hesitant about producing the whisky because half of it had already been drunk.

Tim had got the low-down from Patrick on the American invasion of the island in 1983 and filled us in on the details as he saw them. The fort of St Georges, where the popular socialist leader Maurice Bishop had been shot by firing squad, stood on a cliff at the entrance to the harbour. It had been built by the French in the seventeenth century. On another hill, on the other side of the bay, stood the jail. Most of the surviving leaders of the coup were now locked up in this jail, from where they had a clear view of the fort they once controlled. The role of the US and the CIA in promoting the coup to dislodge Bishop has never been fully established but a large number of the local population believe that they were the key players. After the coup, the US had a ready-made pretext for invasion in the form of American medical students studying at a local hospital college. The invasion was launched, the Queen was miffed, and the people of Grenada fought bravely to resist the invaders but lost. Reagan had a victory and the US had its national pride restored after the débâcle in Iran. Not only was the whole affair in flagrant contravention of international law but Grenada was no more of a threat to the legitimate security interests of the US than a butterfly is to an eagle. No one knows how many died, and no one has been told the story that the plotters in the jail keep a secret to this day.

Bill was an old-fashioned American liberal and he made no excuses for anything Reagan did in his name, but he felt uneasy about his country being run down. To make matters worse, Tim kept trying to explore the psyche of the American people and would usually end up by saying, 'Nothing personal, Bill, but the Americans are really screwed up.' All I wanted was a happy crew, and I knew Tim would be with us for a fortnight, so I changed the subject reluctantly and we planned our sailing route.

Bill and Tim were both keen to get to the carnival in Trinidad but we agreed to spend a day or two sailing around Grenada. We found a peaceful anchorage in the south-west corner of the island, which was reputed to have good coral reefs. Tim had never swum in tropical waters before and had never looked down upon a coral reef through a face-mask. I knew it was going to be a big headtrip for him and was keen to rediscover my own delight through the newness of his experience. Before setting out for the reef in the dinghy, he smoked a little ganja and was very relaxed about the prospect. When we got to the reef, I positioned the dinghy on the edge and threw the small anchor overboard.

From the dinghy it didn't look anything special. You could see the brown and grey coral heads below but they looked just like any other lumps of rock. Once over the side with the face-mask on, the world was transformed. The dull-coloured lumps of rock became intricate and chaotic patterns of living tissue: great mushroom heads of brain coral with a surface that bore an uncanny resemblance to the human cortex; fields of staghead coral with long pointed antlers; and soft coral fans that flowed backwards and forwards with the undertow. There were fish everywhere: trumpet fish with long snouts and pencil-thin bodies swayed with the water between the antlers, while brightly coloured parrot fish caressed the cortex surface of the giant mushroom heads. Angel fish, with false eyes in their tails, came up to the mask to look at you with their real eyes, and sometimes a shoal of jewel fish enveloped you as they swam past, without any touching your skin. On the bottom, the vague outline of a ray could be seen lying half buried in the sand, and you always felt that unseen creatures were watching you.

Tim came up breathless with disbelief at the beauty of it all and somewhat alarmed by the sight of a large ray that gently flapped its wide body as it swam past. The ray freaked him out, and he hauled himself into the dinghy to get his wits back. He was unable to get the words out to express his sense of amazement. Shaking his head and laughing out loud, he kept repeating the words, 'I can't believe it, I just can't believe it, it's unbelievable.'

There was more to come. I persuaded him to get back in the water as I hauled up the anchor and passed him a short line. 'Hold on to this and you'll feel what it's like to fly,' I said, starting the outboard engine and pulling him, face down, through the water along the edge of the reef. Another ray had him clambering aboard, repeating the only words he was capable of saying. It was my turn next. Tim pulled me along the edge of the reef. The coral floated past in an ever-changing world of phantasmagoria while the brightly coloured exotic fish darted about. With one hand straight out in front holding on to the rope, the other by my side and with my legs together, I glided through the water effortlessly and felt like Superman flying over the surface of a strange planet.

Later that night we decided to go for a moonlight swim. Tim was first over the side and came up in seconds, screaming and yelling. Bill and I helped him aboard and struggled to get some sense out of him. We kept asking him what the fuss was about, but he kept saying, 'Just dive over, go on – dive over, see for yourself.' Neither of us was prepared to give it a go without knowing more, and Tim eventually told us that the sea was full of tiny green lights. I knew this was phosphorescence and dived over to have a look. As I was going in, I heard Tim tell me to keep my eyes open. I had seen dolphins in a phosphorescent sea and knew how spectacular they looked but even this didn't prepare me for the underwater sight of my own body. The full length of my arms in front of me was covered in thousands of green lights: tiny, brilliant, glowing specks. The fingers on the end of each hand appeared to have been dipped in green luminous paint. As I pulled my arms back through the water, the wide arc of dancing light that trailed behind them made me feel like a wizard waving a magic wand. I could stand no more than three or four seconds of it and was hauled out by Bill and Tim, my heart pounding.

27. Carnival

THE WARM WATERS, WITH THEIR CORAL REEFS AND PALM-fringed golden beaches, were fine for a couple of weeks, but I wasn't sorry to leave them behind as we headed south to Trinidad. Here we were less likely to find the thousands of sailboats that cruise up and down the island chain, and the capital city of Port of Spain would be more than big enough to accommodate those that were there, without the whole economy being distorted by nautical tourism.

We set sail from Grenada before sunset. The passage south was easy and pleasant. Bill and Tim sat out in the cockpit for most of the night, marvelling at the stars. By early afternoon of the next day, we were negotiating the Dragon's Mouth, a narrow strait that separates the north of Trinidad from the mainland of Venezuela. Columbus had a difficult passage through here, hence the name. If he had encountered it in the conditions that we did, it would probably have been known thereafter as Serenity Passage. The Dragon's Mouth opens up into the Gulf of Paria, and at the south end of Trinidad there is another strait known as the Serpent's Mouth.

The island of Trinidad has a population of over one-and-a-half million, and its economy is based on oil and asphalt. There are plenty of rich people on the island, which was obvious from seaward as we passed elegant villas built on rocky ledges overlooking the sea. Port of Spain, with its high-rise commercial buildings, was visible from a long way off. On approaching the bay in front of the Trinidad and Tobago yacht club, the sound of calypso music could be heard clearly. There were quite a few yachts lying at anchor but there were no charter boats and none of the really luxurious yachts. On the way down to Trinidad, I had heard horror stories about crime in the city, and this had obviously prevented the 'liveaboards' from turning up.

We dropped anchor and rowed ashore to check the place out. The yacht club was a real club, rather than a marina, and the clubhouse was friendly and lively. The waitress who brought us our beers literally danced over to the table with the tray in her hand. Trinidad is the home of calypso and the steel band, and the carnival was winding up to its climax. Everyone was in the party mood. As far as I could gather, the carnival lasted for about two weeks, reaching its high point in the last three days. We had timed our arrival to perfection: the last three full days were just starting. There was an official programme of activities that took place in various sports stadiums but the real action was on the streets. There is something inherently democratic about street activities, and I couldn't wait to get into town.

The three of us caught the minibus into the centre about six miles away. The volume of the music in the back was deafening – the base notes pumped out of the speakers, their diaphragms pulsating like human hearts. As we neared downtown Port of Spain, the crowds became more congested. The energy of the streets was palpable when we stepped off the bus. Heavy bass notes blasted out from sound trucks parked on every street corner, reverberating in our ears even louder than in the bus. We made our way towards a road junction where there was a throng of people that would have put any football crowd to shame. Everyone was moving to the music. We found ourselves beginning to move with them. Most of the time the movement was hardly a dance in the conventional sense. In athletic terms it was more of a jog than a sprint. If this party was going to last three more days, energy had to be conserved.

There were particular tunes and songs that seemed to get the crowd going more than others. One called 'Jump Up' had everyone bouncing around like jack-in-the-boxes. All along the streets, hawkers had big barrels of ice filled with bottled beer, and everyone seemed to have a drink in their hands at all times. After a few hours, and to save our energy for the night, we decided to go back to the club for a rest and a break from the noise, before coming back into town later on. People were gearing themselves up for the *Mas*, or masquerade, which wasn't due to get under way until about two o'clock next morning.

When we got back to the club, the barman told me there was a message for *Warrior Queen*. Two women had been in looking for the boat an hour or so earlier. They had given my name. I couldn't think who they could be and discussed it with Bill and Tim. Tim knew all about them. Before catching a local flight to Grenada, he had flown out to Barbados from London and had met them on the plane. They were going to Barbados for a two-week holiday. Tim had told them about the carnival in Trinidad and our plans to be there. He didn't expect to hear from them again but it looked as though they had been talked into it. While eating dinner, I saw Tim rise from his chair and smile. On turning round, I saw his two friends coming towards us. Now we were five.

There was an air of great expectation about the forthcoming

evening. People who lived on the island told us not to go into town too early. The *Mas* was an all-night affair that lasted until well after dawn. We sat in the club, which was buzzing, and tried to go easy on the beers. Later that night, the five of us headed back into town. The sound trucks were still blasting away, and everyone was jumping up and down to 'Jump Up'. We joined in, dancing through the streets with the crowds. Trinidad is a racially mixed island – most of the population is Afro-Caribbean or Indian, but there are also quite a few Chinese and some Europeans. There aren't many tourists, and the whole spectacle that was beginning to unfold before us was a home-grown event for home consumption. The police had a low-key presence. Those that were visible danced on the street corners. The two girls with us were a big hit with the local men, who came up behind them, grinding their pelvises up against their backsides. The girls responded by gyrating their hips and stretching their arms up above their heads. Sometimes two men made a sandwich of one of them, with one man grinding at the back and another grinding away at the front.

As well as the sound trucks, the steel bands were now out in force. Some of these had as many as a hundred pieces, with everyone beating out the synchronised rhythm. The sound was hypnotic. We sat down on the roadside in front of the big oil-can bass drums, the vibrations running through our bodies. It was only a few weeks earlier that I had been on my own in the Atlantic feeling like the only person in the world. At that time I had been picked up and swept along by the elemental forces of nature. Now I was surrounded by a sea of people, and the energy that they created was, in its own way, just as overwhelming. It was a world as far removed from the solitude of the ocean as it was possible to imagine, and I was glad to be part of it.

Every hour or so we escaped from the noise and mayhem of the streets to find a bar in a side alley where there was relative quiet. At about 1.0 a.m., the streets began to clear. Within an hour some semblance of sanity and order returned for a brief while. The *Mas* was about to start. The first sign that we had was a tall, thin man with a grotesque mask. He approached the girls from behind. The gargoyle-like mask, with its lewd, phallic-shaped nose, leered at them as he writhed his half-naked body, which was covered in thick brown mud. More men appeared. All of them were stripped to the waist and covered in the same mud. Women appeared, plastered in mud. They wore small tops over their breasts and danced through the streets with the men: fat women, thin women, young women, old women, black women, white women – all covered in mud. Everyone formed up in large groups, as if obeying some field commander, and followed the steel bands as they made their way through the city. It seemed as though every person in Trinidad was on the streets performing a strange, bacchanalian mass-fertility rite.

We joined in somewhat self-consciously, not being properly dressed for the occasion. No one seemed to mind, and we danced until 4.0 a.m., by which time we were flagging, even if everyone else in Trinidad looked as though they could go on forever. We tried to find a taxi back to the club but there weren't any. All the minibuses had vanished, and it looked as though we would have to walk. As we tried to motivate ourselves to get going, I spotted a solitary minibus and ran out in front of it to get the driver to stop. The Indian driver's bright white eyes and teeth smiled out from a face caked in mud. He agreed to take us and we piled in.

The minibus weaved its way through the side streets to avoid the crowds but by the time we reached the residential suburbs our progress was halted. Wave upon wave of people of all ages, classes and races were making their way through these normally sedate streets. Each wave crashed against the small bus, and masked faces pressed hard up against the windscreen. Tongues were stuck out and fingers wiggled on the end of noses as the crowds began to rock the bus from side to side. The two girls were frightened and closed all the windows. Mud was being plastered over the bus. People were jeering at us as they passed. Why wouldn't they? Here we were going home in a minibus and here they were celebrating life. I opened the windows wide and stuck my head and shoulders out into the oncoming crowd. Every man patted me on the back, and the women kissed me on the cheek. They began to cover me in the mud. Tim and Bill opened their windows to receive the same treatment. The girls were next. Before long the five of us were hanging out of the windows as the sea of people poured over us. The small bus inched forward, making its way through one crowd before coming upon another. Crowd after crowd, in a sea of elemental humanity, just like squalls in the ocean. I had tried to lock myself away from these squalls once before and had nearly come unstuck. I wasn't going to make the same mistake again.

It was already daylight when Bill, Tim and I rowed out to the boat. We slept until early afternoon. Bill went into town to take some pictures of the kids' parades, and Tim and I met the girls in the club. Later on we found a small house down by the beach where beer was sold on its verandah – Tim had no problem getting more ganja. Everyone in Trinidad smoked it but it was strictly illegal. The penalty for possession was imprisonment. Tim handed the money over and was given a bundle of stuff wrapped in cellophane. The two girls bought some fresh fish to cook for dinner aboard that evening.

When we got back to the boat, Tim opened up his package and was amazed at how much he had got for so little money. I myself had never bought the stuff, but if someone offered me a joint I would usually smoke it. Bill was pleased with the pictures he got in town, and the three of us sat in the cockpit puffing away on the ganja while the two girls busied themselves in the galley. There is something wonderful about lying at anchor with women aboard cooking in the galley. It is not so much being waited on by them but more their very presence. They lend an air of refinement and civility to the boat and bring out the best in the men. Sometimes they also know how to cook.

It was my 42nd birthday next day, and I wanted to celebrate it at midnight on the streets of Port of Spain. We headed into town, fortified with the food and wine and ganja, for the next instalment. The mudders had changed into their best gear, and the streets were once again packed. If anything, there were more steel bands than the night before. All the bars were doing a roaring trade. The rougher establishments sold the drink from behind a wire grill, and they didn't give you any glasses. The usual order was a half-bottle of rum and a big bottle of Coke with five plastic cups to go. We sat on the pavement outside and drank it. Tim had befriended a man from London. He was of Afro-Caribbean descent but was born in England and was in Trinidad on holiday. I felt a little sorry for him because he didn't really belong anywhere. Many people in England didn't accept him because he was black, and the Trinidadians saw him as English. Tim told him about my trip across the Atlantic, to which his response was, 'Respect, man, respect.' He then gave me a complicated handshake which involved about four movements and ended with two fists being pressed hard against each other and the mutual words 'respect'. He took his red beret off and gave it to me as a present on the stroke of midnight as everyone sang 'Happy Birthday'.

The steel bands were making their way through town. We all fell in behind one. With the beret on my head, a half-bottle of rum in my hip pocket, a bloodstream full of alcohol and ganja, and good companions by my side, I let the music do its work. Each pure, clear note from the steel drums lodged in my brain and bounced around inside. The rhythm from the percussion pieces animated my body, which began to feel weightless. The notes poured out like fantastic geometric shapes, forming and reforming themselves in my mind into ever more complicated patterns.

Time itself became elastic and was measured not by any objective standard but by the beat of the drums. The musicians fused with their instruments, which became an extension of their bodies, and then everyone in the band fused with each other and became one complete being. This being reached out and took hold of me. I happily surrendered to it.

The girls left next day to fly back to Barbados, and we saw them off after a late lunch in the clubhouse. As this was the last day of the carnival, they were worried that they wouldn't be able to get a flight after it all finished. Bill had booked a place in the main stand in the centre of town to get good pictures of the final parades, and Tim and I were going to do the streets. Before leaving, I noticed Barry and Julia sitting in the clubhouse. It was the first time I had seen them since St Lucia. They, like me, had sailed down for the carnival and were enjoying it as much as I was. They had gone to a lot of trouble to enter into the spirit of things on the last day and were both wearing fancy dress. Their black-and-orange costumes were identical. Julia, who was very slim, was a wasp, and Barry, who was not slim, was a bumble-bee. We had a brief chat about our plans, and I mentioned that I was thinking of going up the Rio Orinoco. They were interested in the idea, and we arranged to talk about it later.

I was dead tired from the previous night's partying but it was the last day and I didn't want to miss it. With all the main roads closed, the bus dropped us a long way from the centre of town. As we walked the remaining few miles, it was clear that this extraordinary event still had one or two surprises for us. There was going to be nothing but parades through the streets all day – virtually everyone was in fancy dress. On one street corner, there was a crowd of Zulu warriors complete with assegais and shields. On the next corner, there were fairy queens and pixies. After that, we had the cowboys and Indians followed by the ancient Egyptians, and next to them we had the wasps and bumblebees. Some of the costumes were outrageous in their design, with one that looked vaguely Chinese and was topped off with a pagoda hat. Capes and spears and hats and jewellery made from golden foil were everywhere. A Zulu warrior asked me to hold his spear, while he went off for a leak, but he never came back.

At the head of each band, there was a special exhibit, which was usually about 20 or 30 feet high. Sometimes it was a dragon; at other times it was a giant spider or a massive butterfly. There were a few extra-terrestrial creatures that could have graced the set of any Hollywood movie. The costumes were strapped on to the back of one person but were usually supported by two or three others. The dragons, spiders, butterflies and extra-terrestrials made their way through the streets, causing major disruption when they encountered the Trojan Horse. Tim and I climbed on to the top of a float that doubled up as a mobile bar and saw the whole show from roof-top level. When we felt like a beer, the man who was selling them to the people below passed us one up and we passed him the money down. There was a middle-aged woman on the float beside us who was in fancy dress and drinking neat rum. She kept sticking her big bum in my face and wiggling it.

All along the pavements, couples stood grinding away. The women seemed to be unattached. When one man left, another came up behind her and grinded some more. This activity wasn't confined to the young or body beautiful. No one seemed to be concerned about the shape of their bodies. The bars were empty as everyone drank outside. From the top of the float I could see the television sets inside: they were showing pictures of the carnival as it happened. No one was watching TV, but then someone would probably televise the end of the world, even if there was no one left to watch it.

We climbed off the float in late afternoon and found a park to lie down and rest. There was hardly any space available, and it was clear that people were beginning to flag. The parades went on for a few more hours, but by 10.0 p.m. things were breaking up and the streets were beginning to clear. Everyone had burned up their reserves – the carnival was coming to an end. The streets were littered with debris and bits of costumes. People were wandering about aimlessly. The spears were either lying on the ground or carried listlessly by their bearers, and the whole scene began to take on the appearance of an army in retreat. At midnight, with the beginning of Lent, the pounding of the drums fell silent and peace was declared. The carnival was over.

28. *Winning and Losing*

EVERYONE HAD ENJOYED THE CARNIVAL BUT LIFE IN PORT of Spain seemed very ordinary now that it was finished. Bill was uneasy about going up the Rio Orinoco and was worried about not having a gun aboard. Guns are as much a part of life in American households as cups and saucers, and I could understand his concern. I had met one American who had a whole armoury. He had guns for long-range work, guns for short-range work, and he even shot the fish he caught before landing them. But guns afford little protection against determined pirates, and it is much better to do without them and sail with another boat. Pirates will think twice about hitting two boats at the same time. With these thoughts in mind, I put the word out that we were thinking of going up the river. Everyone in an anchorage soon hears about what's going on, and the next day I had a visit from Bob who sailed aboard his own boat, *On The Way*. Bob's standard line, which he never tired of repeating, and which I never tired of hearing, was, 'I don't know who I am or where I'm going but I'm *On The Way*'.

It turned out that several other boats were thinking of the same trip, and we arranged to meet later that night aboard a Canadian-registered ketch. Barry and Julia were also interested. The first thing I noticed about *Chancy* was that she was registered in Whitby, Ontario. Anybody who called their boat *Chancy* and was a member of Whitby Yacht Club, even if it was the Whitby in Ontario, was worth meeting. Before we got there, I could hear loud laughter coming from down below, and Bob was already waiting to take our line when we came alongside. *Chancy* was a solid 40-footer built of concrete. Gordon, her skipper, welcomed us aboard and offered us all some rum. There were about 15 at the meeting, which Bob chaired, and it seemed that as many as four or five boats were interested in going. We talked about who had what charts or other information, allocated jobs to various people and arranged another meeting. Before leaving, Gordon asked if anyone played chess. Rather fancying myself now that I had been getting plenty of practice and had been hammering Tim ever since he arrived, I blurted out that I played. Gordon just smiled and said, 'Good.'

On the way back to the club, Barry and Julia asked if they could come aboard *Warrior Queen* for the trip. I saw no reason why not and agreed. The boat would need to be steered all the way upstream and back down again, so the more aboard, the less work for each. Tim flew home next day. The first time I had said goodbye to him on the voyage was after he had joined the boat for the crossing of the Irish Sea. That passage had been a very hard one, but his time in the Caribbean had been two weeks of pure rapture. Before he went through the security gates, he slipped me the remainder of the ganja.

After obtaining our visas for entering Venezuela we contacted a shipping agent in the port of La Güiria who would deal with all the paperwork for us on arrival. Three boats were going: *Warrior Queen* with four aboard; *Chancy* with three; and *Borne Free*, also with three. Bob's boat was in need of repair, so he was going aboard *Borne Free*, which belonged to an American called Paul. We had one more meeting, where we finalised the details and presented all the information. It was agreed that no guns would be taken, and it was obvious that we had very little navigational information for the river itself.

After messing about for a whole day with the customs-and-immigration officials in Port of Spain, we eventually got our clearance papers and set off early the next morning. It was the first time I had ever sailed with other boats. *Borne Free* was well out in front, which wasn't surprising, seeing that she always sailed with her engine running. *Chancy*, who got away before us, was about two miles in front, and we had some 40 miles to go to cross the Gulf of Paria to the mainland of Venezuela.

By the time we were halfway across, *Chancy* was only a mile in front and it was beginning to turn into a race. With less than ten miles to go, she was half a mile in front and it was touch and go if we could catch her. I had never raced before and couldn't understand what the attraction was. But now the most important thing in the world was catching *Chancy* — nothing else mattered. The sheets were being adjusted every second and we helmed the boat to take advantage of every wind shift. By the time the harbour entrance was in sight, *Chancy* was less than a quarter of a mile in front of us. With the binoculars, I could see Gordon looking over his shoulder every few minutes. His crew were on deck adjusting the sails. With the harbour wall coming up fast, we were on her tail. It looked as though she was just going to hold us off. We had been closing on her for eight hours, and at times it had looked hopeless, but now that we were snapping at her stern the slight difference in speed was more pronounced. With only 100 yards to go to the harbour entrance, we sailed past on the windward side and stole her wind. *Chancy*'s sails flapped pathetically, and she stalled as we came abreast and flew past. Everyone was outwardly very polite. The four of us stood in the cockpit of the *Warrior Queen* as we hurtled past. I waved at Gordon and smiled and simply said, 'Hello.' His two crew had gone down below to avoid the embarrassment. Gordon was on the wheel. He gritted his teeth and smiled back without saying a word. We narrowly avoided hitting the harbour wall before cutting in front of him. It was my first race and I had won it!

Everyone aboard was ecstatic. All we could say was, 'Did you see his face?' It would have spoiled the victory to be seen gloating so we did all the laughing below decks. *Chancy* anchored nearby. When I managed to get my breath back after all the hysterical laughter, I came on deck and couldn't resist calling out, 'Did you enjoy the race then?'

'What race?'

'The race that you've just lost.'

'I didn't know we were racing.'

'Of course we were.'

He had seen us on his tail for eight hours, we both kept full sail up until the last minute, we passed him with yards to go to the harbour wall, and he didn't know we were racing?

No one could go ashore until our shipping agent had cleared us in. We spent our first night in Venezuela aboard. Bill and I were getting to know Barry and Julia well. After dinner we sat in the cockpit and talked. Barry had been an undercover drugs agent with British Customs and Excise and had been involved in a couple of big busts. Julia had been a probation officer before setting out on her abortive trip. I rolled a joint from the stuff Tim gave me and passed it round. Barry declined but Julia accepted. Before she could put it to her lips, Barry interjected with, 'What are you doing? You don't need that.'

She made it clear, without getting huffy, that she knew she didn't need it but liked a puff from time to time.

This started a long conversation about drugs. Barry, not surprisingly, had a very negative attitude. Bill thought that marijuana was a lot less harmful than alcohol, which he hardly ever touched, and presented a very compelling argument. He concluded by pointing out that it was unreasonable for Barry to take the view he did without trying it for himself. Barry pondered on this. He then asked for the joint. He had spent a professional lifetime stopping other people smoking it, and now he was about to take his first drag. I could see him waiting for an effect like a kid who takes their first drink. After a short while, he exclaimed, 'What a load of rubbish, this has no effect at all. Absolutely no effect whatsoever – complete rubbish!'

Bill explained that its effect was subtle and advised him to take some more. Barry finished off the joint, still maintaining it was having no effect on him. It was certainly having an effect on the rest of us. Barry insisted on me rolling another one, and he smoked most of it himself. He had now boxed himself into a corner and had to keep saying that it was having no effect on him.

'I've been doing a very important job all these years, stopping people wasting their money on this rubbish,' he said, before finishing the joint off. This idea appealed to him and he kept repeating it. In fact, he wasn't able to say much else. Bill, Julia and I were now giggling quietly away as Barry, the undercover drugs agent, began to fall into a deep, contemplative silence. A silence that was punctuated every now and then with the words, 'Rubbish, absolute rubbish.'

Eventually Bill said, 'It isn't rubbish, Barry, it's shit.'

A grin began to creep over Barry's face. He tried to suppress it but failed. He eventually replied, 'What's the difference? The shit is rubbish and the rubbish is shit.'

Our shipping agent, Julio, could be contacted on the VHF radio. Bob was doing the negotiations, which he was very good at. Julio was doing his best, which he was very bad at. He did give us advance warning, though, that the boats were likely to be searched by the National Guard. I threw the remainder of the ganja overboard. I was indifferent to its loss but Barry looked a bit peeved and suggested ways that we could hide it. It would have meant jail and the impounding of the boat had we been caught with it and I wasn't interested. All three boats rafted up along the harbour wall and a stream of officials came aboard, checking passports, visas, ships' papers and lockers. We were cleared in and given permission to go ashore.

La Güiria was like something out of a spaghetti western, with armed guards outside and inside the banks and public buildings. Hardly anyone spoke any English, and the population was of mixed Spanish and native-Indian descent. The further down the social ladder you went, the greater the concentration of Indian blood. They didn't have many visiting yachts, so we were something of a novelty as we walked round the dusty streets. The Venezuelan men were laid back and easy going. The women were beautiful. Everyone, including the two women in our group, agreed that the women were the most beautiful they had ever seen. Many yachtsmen are divorced or separated, partly because their original partners had no interest in sailing, and they tend to be lonely and in search of love. They have an abiding fantasy of finding a beautiful young native girl to sail away with. Venezuela was fantasy land. We all found a bar in the town square and engaged in that most ancient of pastimes – people-watching. After a few beers, which were dirt cheap, I gave all these love-sick sailors a little song.

> I met her in Venezuela,
> with a basket on her head.
> She was a picture, plain to see.
> I loved her and she loved me,
> in Venezuela.

Bob finally got to meet Julio and was negotiating with him to get fuel. Venezuela is a major oil producer, and diesel oil costs next to nothing. It may have been cheap to buy but finding somewhere to buy it in the harbour was another story. There were pumps everywhere but no one was allowed to sell us any without advance permission. Julio kept promising that we would get fuel soon but we knew we were in for a three or four-day wait.

While Bob kept up the pressure on the shipping agent, Gordon invited me over to his boat for a game of chess. All the boats were now back at anchor, and I rowed across full of expectation. Gordon was already waiting for me with the chess board and rum. I drew white. Gordon won the first game in about 40 minutes and we played a second. He won this in 20 minutes and the one after that in less than ten. With each game it became easier for him and harder for me, and I was making blunder after blunder. All the hours of playing my computerised board in the middle of the ocean were to no avail. By late afternoon the score was 8–0. I had been totally outclassed and was thrashed comprehensively.

I stayed aboard *Chancy* for the rest of the evening. Bob joined us later, along with the other crew member from *Borne Free* – a New Zealander in his late twenties called Hamish Scott. Hamish had a quiet manner without a hint of shyness and had been sailing for about six months, jumping from boat to boat all the way from Europe. He had the perfect temperament for a good sailor and never got ruffled. He was the youngest of the group and the most likely to find a native girl to run away with – he told me that he had seen one with a basket on her head on the outskirts of town. In addition to Bob and Hamish, we also had Gordon's two crew. They were a Canadian couple called Steve and Christine. Steve was a long-standing friend of Gordon's, and they had both built their own boats together about 15 years ago. Christine was a semi-retired nurse and was spending three or four months with Steve.

Gordon had spent most of his life employed by General Motors. He was a jack of all trades. While working for GM, he was on standby in case the production line broke down. When this happened, senior management would get Gordon to get the line running again. He had made a fair amount of money from the GM suggestions box, coming up with new schemes to improve production. His boat had been built from the suggestions-box money and equipped with anything of practical use from the GM factory. 'Un-negotiated fringe benefits' was how he described these pieces of equipment. Gordon was interested in big ideas and moral dilemmas. He loved an argument and would always try to steer the conversation to topics such as God, altruism, love and lust, and the nature of the universe. Gordon took nothing for granted – the world for him was 'one big, mind-boggling ball of wax'.

Steve had heard all his views a hundred times before and only participated when the conversation went off on an unexpected tangent. I was hearing them for the first time and was happy to argue any point. Bob enjoyed listening to me and Gordon argue. He interjected with his booming voice from time to time, with something like, 'God damn it, Gordon, you are one crazy son of a gun.' Hamish sat on the aft deck smiling and would seek clarification about a point that Gordon or I raised. Whenever there was a momentary pause in the debates, Gordon fetched the rum and topped up everybody's glass and picked up the argument again. We all enjoyed ourselves.

We spent four days waiting for the fuel, which in the end was negotiated through a third party. We ended up paying him more than we did for the fuel itself but it still worked out very cheap. I managed to get through to Laura from a telephone in Julio's office, after trying for two days, and told her that I was setting off for the river and that she shouldn't expect to hear from me for maybe three or four weeks. As it was now late February and she was planning to join me in mid-April, we talked about where she should fly to. It was a bad line, which threatened to go dead at any moment, and we had to make our minds up quickly. I thought of suggesting one of the Windward Islands but didn't like the idea of retracing my steps. Laura had never been to Latin America, and she could fly direct to the Venezuelan capital, Caracas. It would mean a difficult beat for me across the open Caribbean on the way home, but we agreed it anyway. Unknown to me at the time, this decision, hurriedly made in a run-down shipping office over a crackling telephone line, was to have far-reaching implications.

29. *The Serpent's Mouth*

WITH OUR *ZARPA*, OR CRUISING PERMIT, STAMPED BY EVERY official in the port of La Güiria, we set sail. The Rio Orinoco, the eighth largest river in the world, is one of the three great rivers of South America. It drains the landmass bordered by the Andes to the east and the Parima mountain range along the Venezuela–Brazil border to the south. Before flowing out to sea just north of the Equator, it begins to deposit the silt and mud carried downstream from these mountain ranges, forming a large web-foot delta. The main river, which is buoyed all the way upstream to the city of Ciudad Bolivar, is in the centre of this delta, and the channel is kept open by regular dredging to allow big ships to pass. We were intending to enter the delta through a northern distributary known as the Cano Macareo. As this is not used by commercial shipping, there are no buoys. There are there no charts either. The Cano Macareo joins the main river some 120 miles upstream.

Before reaching the Cano Macareo, we sailed south through the Gulf of Paria and out through the Serpent's Mouth. It was a passage of about 100 miles, so we left early in the morning to ensure that we could enter the river during daylight the following day. The wind was light at the start but we made reasonable progress.

Barry and Julia had settled aboard well, and I took the opportunity to speak with Julia about abandoning her boat 400 miles from Dominica. She was somewhat reticent but I got the impression that the whole passage had been unpleasant for her. The main problem was that her self-steering gear broke down. Not being able to repair it, she had no alternative but to helm the boat herself. The combination of staring at 270 degrees on the compass all day, violent rain squalls, and slow progress was too much for her in the end. The desolate, lonely expanse of the ocean can engender an aching melancholia in a person's heart. Day after day there is nothing but sea, and it seems to go on for ever and ever. The horizon is unbroken, as is time itself. The boat is fixed permanently, and with perfect geometric precision, in the centre of the encircling sea. The horizon marks the limits of the world – a world that is indifferent to the sadness of the heart. When she saw another sailboat and called it up on the radio, it approached her at sea and she was able to talk to the people aboard. She told them about the problems she was having with her self-steering gear. They gave her what comfort they could and sailed on. Once more she was alone but the encounter only served to heighten her sense of isolation. A few days later, she saw a cargo ship. By the time she radioed her distress call, she was on the verge of exhaustion and despair. They lifted her off and took care of her. Her boat was abandoned to drift on its own. Julia's personal possessions – her clothes, her letters, her photographs and her make-up – were left aboard.

I also learned that her boat had turned up, on its own, in Martinique, just to the south of Dominica. The prevailing easterly winds and west-setting current had carried it the remaining 400 miles. I think this made it harder to accept, and she would probably have preferred the boat to have sunk. I didn't say it but we all knew that if she had lowered the sails, locked herself down below and stayed in her bunk, the boat would have taken her there. It would have meant enduring another 15 long, melancholy days but she would have made it.

Barry had a keen sense of humour and we were getting on well. I was the only smoker aboard and the ash-tray, which was usually overfull, made a mess every time it got knocked over. I heard Barry mutter something as it tipped on to the cabin floor while he was working on the charts. He stormed out to the cockpit with a very serious-looking expression on his face, saying, 'That's it, John, I've had enough of these bloody ash-trays. You're the skipper and you're going to have to have a word with him about this.'

'Barry, I've already talked to him about it, and he keeps promising that he's going to give up.'

'That's not the point, John. There's still a mess, and he has to do something about it. If you don't talk to him, I will.'

'Look, Barry, I took him aside this morning in the privacy of the head. I pointed straight at him in the mirror and told him it had to stop. He gave me his word, his solemn word, that the ash-trays would be kept clean. He even said he would try to cut down. Now what more can I do with him?'

'You shouldn't allow people on your boat to smoke in the first place.'

'I think you're right, Barry. I'll have another word with him later when I get him on his own.'

It took us longer to get to the south of the Gulf of Paria than we anticipated. It was dawn next day before we were approaching the Serpent's Mouth. The shoreline on either side was clearly visible, and the wind, which was dead in front of us, funnelled through. Sailing was out of the question and we had to motor. As the wind picked up our speed dropped off to barely a knot. *Borne Free*, out in front, was no longer in sight. *Chancy* and *Warrior Queen* were close together. All three boats kept in radio contact as the miles ticked off slowly.

By late afternoon *Borne Free* called up to say that they were at the mouth of the Cano Macareo and were going in. There were long periods of radio silence, in between which Bob came on air to give us a report. They had very little water, only eight feet in places. You learn to read a lot into the tone of a person's voice on the radio, and it was clear that everyone aboard *Borne Free* was worried. After another long silence, Bob came up again to tell us that they had made it. They were in the river, at anchor in 30 feet of water.

We throttled up the engine to try to get there before nightfall but it was already dusk when we saw the headland of *Punta El Tigre*. There is a bay about 15 miles wide where the Cano Macareo flows out to sea. We had an old British Admiralty chart which indicated that the depth in most of this bay is less than six feet. There appeared to be slightly deeper water close to the headland at the far end of the bay. This was where we were heading for. Night was closing in fast as we tried to make *Punta El Tigre*. It was upon us before we got there. We asked *Borne Free* to shine a searchlight to indicate her position. It stood out clearly against the vague backdrop of the jungle. She was about two miles away. We started to go in. At first we had 50 feet but the depth began to drop rapidly, and we were soon down to 20 feet. *Chancy* drew a foot more than *Warrior Queen*. She was right behind us. We kept her posted about the depth as we moved forward – 15 feet, 15 feet, 12 feet, 8 feet, 6 feet, 5 feet, bang!

'*Chancy, Chancy, Chancy*, this is *Warrior Queen*, we're aground.'

'*Warrior Queen, Chancy* here, we are too.'

There was still some mainsail up, and this, more than the engine, helped us get off. It leaned the boat over to one side, lifting the keel off the bottom. We now had six feet again and inched forward. *Chancy* looked as though she was still stuck.

'*Warrior Queen, Warrior Queen, Chancy* here, how much water have you got – right now?' I told Gordon we only had six feet. He was now free and backing off as best he could. The two boats began to drift apart. We had no more than six feet of water no matter which way we went, but *Chancy* had found a pool with 15 feet where she put her anchor down. There was no telling which way was best to go. Julia was on the echosounder, calling out the depth – six feet, five feet, bang! The whole boat shuddered as the keel thudded against the bottom. The mast shook violently. A sailboat with a heavy keel is not designed to take the ground. When afloat, the boat is weightless in the water. But when it hits bottom hard, the full impact of the mass of the boat on the seabed is transmitted through every fitting and fixture aboard. The wheel spun out of my hands as the rudder dug into the silt. With the keel on the bottom, each wave bumped her up and down. There was nothing we could do but wait until the wind in the sail leaned her over and hope that we would be blown off towards deeper water. *Chancy* was now 200 yards away. Every time we tried to approach her, the depth dropped off and we hit ground again.

Most rivers have a sand or mud bar at their mouth. The flow of freshwater is checked by the sea, causing the silt which has been held in suspension to be deposited. This river brought down billions of tons of silt. It seemed as though all of this had been deposited right beneath us. Every time we thudded on to the bottom, as a wave dropped us down an extra foot or two, the boat and everyone aboard took more punishment – six feet, five feet, bang! After the bang, the boat wallowed in the shallow water. Breaking seas crashed against the exposed hull. The wind and the waves gradually pushed her off until she was floating again, but not for long – six feet, five feet, bang! There was no end to it. I didn't know how much more the boat could take before the keel was snapped off or driven through the hull. Bill wanted me to make way towards *Borne Free*. Barry was advising me to go in the opposite direction. It made no difference which way we went. The bar was all around us. There wasn't enough water anywhere. Our lives were probably not in danger because, even though it was very rough, *Chancy* was nearby and she had a high-powered semi-rigid inflatable that could be launched in an instant. If the boat did break up, I was sure they could get us. I called her up on the radio and told Gordon to be ready.

Bob on *Borne Free* was sitting in the cockpit listening to the radio traffic and watching us through the binoculars. He came on the radio to say that he would stand by all night. Six feet, five feet, bang! Gordon came on air, suggesting I try to work my way over to the pool he was in.

'Gordon, I can't go anywhere. There doesn't seem to be enough water for me no matter which way I turn.' Bill and Barry were showing real signs of concern, uttering loud profanities each time we hit bottom. Julia was down below in the cabin watching the echo-sounder and kept her head throughout.

We had been in shallow water for nearly four hours, hitting bottom at least 15 times. I couldn't think of anything to do. I asked Barry to take the wheel before going below in despair for a beer and a cigarette. I felt like a condemned man exercising his last request. Barry asked me which way he should go. I said he could go where he wanted to. Julia, who had been down below the whole time, looked at me as I rolled the cigarette. It was a very sympathetic look. It said to me that she thought the boat was lost. The can of beer bounced off the table when we hit bottom again, and all the pots and pans banged into each other in the lockers. My mind seemed completely blank. I sipped the beer and pulled on the cigarette. The situation looked hopeless. I was beginning to think that this might be the end of the line for the boat. Resignation was setting in.

The mind of someone in a real crisis works in strange ways. When I went back out to the cockpit, I knew exactly what to do without even thinking about it. I told Barry to stay on the wheel while I worked my way forward to the bow, taking care to hold on in case I was thrown overboard when she banged on the bottom. At the top of my lungs I called out the instructions. 'A touch to starboard, Barry. Hold it there. A wee bit to port. That's good, keep her going. Hard over to starboard, quick, quick. Dead ahead. Give her some reverse now, give her more.'

Bill was still suggesting that we make our way to *Borne Free*. I said we weren't going anywhere other than where there was deep water. I now knew where that water was. The seas were breaking all about us but the moon had come out, and in every place where the depth was six feet or less, the seas were breaking more heavily than in other places. It was a wild night and the sea was boiling everywhere but the surface of the water changed as the depth fell off. With one hand on the forestay and a foot on the pulpit, I leaned forward, straining my eyes and concentrating on the surface wave patterns. The jungle now stood out against the night sky more clearly. There wasn't a solitary light in view. The moonlight caught the crests of the breaking seas while I stood at the plunging bow, knowing that the keel had only a foot or two of water beneath it. There were no more bangs or thuds as we zig-zagged through the foam. Julia called out the depth at the top of her voice so that I could hear it – seven feet, seven feet, eight feet, NINE FEET. Up until then, nine feet would have scared the shit out of me, but nine feet now seemed like an ocean beneath us. We worked our way slowly towards *Chancy*, without having less than seven feet, and anchored in the pool she was in. With the anchor down, we lowered the sail, watching *Chancy* closely to make sure we weren't dragging. The hook dug in deep.

The wind was blowing hard, and with the deluge of water pouring out of the river colliding with the open sea the boat was riding on the anchor chain like a rocking-horse. The bow was going right under before rearing up again. These violent snatches could snap the chain. If that happened we would be back in shallow water in seconds. To absorb the shock we tried to fit a snubbing rope to the chain. The chain snarled as it banged on the deck. Barry and I rode the rocking-horse, struggling to attach the rope. One false move and someone could easily lose a hand or fingers. After we had attached the rope, Barry looked at the bow of the boat plunging under and the water coming up past his ankles and said he had never seen anything like it. 'Neither have I, Barry, neither have I,' was all I could say in reply.

I called Gordon up to tell him we were beside him. He had been watching us all the time and already knew. He had also been doing some serious thinking and had been logging his echo-sounder ever since his anchor was down. The depth was changing. There was more tide here than there was in Trinidad – where there was hardly any. As soon as we were on high water, he was hauling his anchor up and going in. I asked him to radio me to let me know when he was ready to go.

It was shortly after dawn when Gordon came on the radio. Steve was already getting *Chancy*'s anchor up. Everyone aboard *Warrior Queen* rose quickly. I stood by the wheel, Bill and Barry started hauling up the chain, and Julia took her place on the echo-sounder. *Chancy* was in front, and after the drama of a few hours earlier I was happy to sit behind and let her go first. Gordon figured that there was about four feet of tide. *Borne Free* was lying in the river, her tall mast dwarfed by the trees of the rainforest. We motored straight in. The seas were not breaking as heavily as they had been in the shallow patches the night before. We never had less than eight feet all the way.

Everyone sighed an audible sigh of relief as the depth picked up once we cleared the bar. We now had more than 30 feet. Barry turned to me and said, 'You did really well last night, I thought she was a gonner.' I had mixed feelings, because we should never have attempted it in the dark in the first place. We should have anchored at the first sign of shallow water and watched the depth to establish high water before going in. But I was pleased that Barry had said what he did.

Bill prepared coffee and pancakes in next to no time. Everyone was ravenous. We sat in the cockpit, wolfing them down with lashings of maple syrup. The blue saltwater of the sea had given way to the muddy brown freshwater of the river. We were in the Cano Macareo. I turned to Barry and said, 'I'll have another word with yer man about the smoking later today.'

'You do that, John. You do that, because I can't stand much more of it.'

'Leave it to me, Barry, leave it to me.'

30. *The Edge of the World*

THE CANO MACAREO WAS WIDE AND DEEP, AND THE RAIN-forest on either side looked impenetrable and forbidding. The first settlement that we passed was on the northern bank, more than a mile away. Binoculars revealed straw-roofed, open-walled dwellings standing on stilts in the water. A few canoes were visible but we were too far away to make out any more details. The tide had turned and the current was running fast out to sea. We pressed on. Everyone was wide-eyed with wonder at the primitiveness of the jungle, and there was no end of communication over the radios on the three boats as someone saw something and pointed it out to the others.

Bill spotted a swirling red cloud about half a mile behind us – thousands of airborne scarlet ibises, which roost in colonies of up to 30,000 pairs. Egrets stood on one leg at the water's edge. Butterflies with six-inch wingspans fluttered across the river. Julia was the first to be bitten by a blackfly. She was at the wheel when she felt something pinch her ankle. The fly was sitting perfectly still, and there was a small trickle of blood running down her leg. Giant bees menaced the boat from time to time, and one got into the confines of the main cabin and had everyone diving for cover. Freshwater dolphins, with long snouts for poking fish out of the mud, surfaced close by the boat. They lacked the grace and beauty of their saltwater cousins and made you feel uneasy because they prompted the question what else is there in this murky water? The noise from a multitude of wild birds perched high in the trees was ever present, and they scrutinised us as we sailed by. Gordon called up to ask if anyone needed water, and I saw Steve and Christine take to the dinghy to get freshwater from a small waterfall that cascaded into the main river.

We continued on upstream. After rounding a wide bend in the river we saw a settlement ahead. The people in the settlement were taking to their canoes and paddling out into the middle of the river. We were about to encounter the natives. The canoes were made from tree trunks that had been burned and dug out. They sat low in the water, with no more than four or five inches of freeboard. They were expertly handled by the Indians aboard, who used one-piece paddles made from the same wood as the canoes. Three of them headed for the *Warrior Queen* and came alongside as we stopped the boat. Everyone in the canoes was standing up, holding on to the guard-rails. Unlike the people we met in La Güiria, the inhabitants of the river were of pure Indian blood. The children were completely naked but most of the adults wore brightly coloured, hand-made clothes. A few of the men had T-shirts and several of the young women were bare breasted. The women wore heavy necklaces made from 20 or 30 low-value local coins. There didn't seem to be any middle-aged people: everyone looked young or old – middle-age, it seems, is a luxury unique to the developed world. Their teeth and gums were in a very bad state, and none of them spoke a word of Spanish. They spoke their own language – the language of the Waroa Indians.

The Waroa Indians had descended from the original migrants who crossed the Bering Straits when a land bridge joined Siberia to Alaska during the ice age of Pleistocene times. Human settlement worked its way south, down through North America and on through Central America. When it reached the equatorial rainforests of South America it concentrated along the banks of the great rivers. The Orinoco Indians then crossed the sea to Trinidad and swept north along the Caribbean chain of uninhabited islands. When the Spanish arrived in the Caribbean, followed by the French and British, they found the Carib Indians, who were the direct descendents of the Waroa. The Caribs resisted the invasion of the white man bravely, but in vain. They had no answer to gunpowder, muskets and steel. They refused to live the life the plantation owners decreed and were driven into the sea. Virtually none of them survived, and the colonisers resorted to shipping in slaves from West Africa to work the land.

The Indians in the canoes alongside fingered the materials of the boat and stroked the finely made multibraid Terylene ropes. The ropes that they secured their canoes with were hand-spun from what appeared to be grass. We had talked about how we would relate to the Waroa, deciding that we wouldn't give them anything unless there was mutual trade. We weren't going to drive a hard bargain but we didn't want to encourage begging. With no cash economy, the Indians derived their entire livelihood from the river. There was no communication link with the outside world, and the nearest small town was more than ten days away by canoe. They had eggs and caught fish, iguana and alligators to eat. We would try to trade for any of these things.

That was the theory, but it's hard to trade with children. Bill and Julia had brought small things to give to the kids. Julia leaned over the rail of the boat, offering a chocolate to a small girl. The little girl looked at Julia's blue eyes and blonde hair in wonderment, before accepting the chocolate. She just held it in her hand, not knowing what it was. Everyone in the canoe looked at the brightly coloured silver wrapping paper in awe, and it was clear that no one knew what to do with it. Julia took another chocolate, unwrapped it and put it in her own mouth. The child followed her example and unwrapped the sweet, keeping the paper, but was reluctant to eat it in one go. She took a tiny nibble from the corner to reassure herself. It tasted good, and she popped the rest into her mouth. Chocolates were dispensed to all the children and adults. Bill then opened his box of plastic cars and gave these to the children. They went down very badly. No one had ever seen a car — these little bits of plastic were just little bits of plastic.

I signalled to a man in one canoe that I wanted to come aboard, and he helped me in. The children were fascinated by the spectacle of me sitting in the canoe as I pointed to *Chancy* about 100 yards upstream. The paddles dug deep into the water, and the canoe glided towards *Chancy*. When it came up to the stern, I called out to Gordon, 'Do you fancy a game of chess?'

'Holy mackerel,' was all he could say as I climbed aboard. *Chancy* also had a visiting party, and Steve and Christine had dispensed bags of flour and tinned food. No one did any trade.

We moved on upstream, waving goodbye to the Indians, who paddled back to their settlement. Everyone was animated, and we talked at length about what the Indians must have made of us. We knew we were intruders in their land. There was something unavoidably voyeuristic about the way we gawped at them and their exotic lifestyle, and if it hadn't been for the fact that I nearly lost my boat getting into this river I would have found it impossible to accept. Our boats were like spaceships to them, and we were aliens from another world – a world that had pushed them to the very edge of this jungle delta, where they continued their traditional way of life. But with each passing year, their numbers got fewer and the temptation to leave the river for the slums of the cities got stronger. Encounters with men of fabulous riches from the other world fed this temptation, and our presence here could do nothing but harm.

I had lunch on *Chancy* and Gordon beat me at chess again. Sitting in the cockpit of Gordon's boat, it was strange to see other people sailing my boat with me not on it, but I found it very relaxing. I knew I could trust everyone aboard, and navigating the river without charts wasn't too difficult because we had plenty of water. Where the river was straight, we stayed in midstream. On the bends, we swung out wide to find deep water. In the excitement of getting into the canoe, I had forgotten my cigarettes and was now busting for one. I called *Warrior Queen* up and we decided to pass them across. While motoring forward, Gordon brought *Chancy* alongside, and with about ten feet between us, Barry put a packet of cigarettes in a straw hat and attached this to the end of a boathook. When we came past, I slipped the straw hat off, took the cigarettes out, put the straw hat on my head, and lit up.

Gordon and I played one last game of chess. I had so far refused the rum that he was drinking. Reckless attacks were getting me nowhere, so I tried to play cagey and build a solid defence. Gordon pushed his queen forward. It looked as though I could, with a simple series of tactical exchanges, take it for a rook. What devilish scheme did the master have up his sleeve? I studied the board for a long time, while Gordon kept trying to distract me with conversation. I could see no scheme, but was almost too frightened to touch the pieces. When I summoned up the courage to play the first move in the exchange, Gordon smiled wryly. What did the smile mean? This was torture. He nodded his head – more torture. Then a quiet chuckle – I could barely stand it. Then he spoke – 'It looks as though you've got this queen.' I breathed deeply with relief. He pressed me to take some rum but I declined – this game was going to be mine. He refused to concede and fought back well. But I now had an overwhelming material advantage and held on to it. When he finally knocked his king over, I punched the air in celebration. 'A gentleman doesn't gloat,' Gordon said irritably.

But I couldn't stop laughing and replied, 'I'm not a gentleman, Gordon, now I'll have that rum please.' Fortified with the victory and the rum, I prepared to board my boat by standing on the bowsprit of *Chancy*. I was humming to myself the triumphalist *Ride of the Valkyries* by Wagner as Gordon brought the boats together in midstream. When there was less than a foot between the two boats, I stepped on to the stern of the *Warrior Queen*.

By late afternoon it was time to anchor, and I spotted a bend where the main river branched. The small branch was very narrow but it looked deep, and I thought it was worth trying to get in. *Borne Free* wasn't interested and *Chancy* thought it too risky. They both anchored in the main river. There was barely enough room to turn round in but we had 20 feet of water and anchored bow and stern in the middle. The jungle was all around us, and you could almost reach out and touch the trees on either side. We had brought a large roll of fine curtain-net material which we rigged up as a canopy to keep the mosquitoes out at night. The rest of the group came over in their dinghys and came aboard for a drink. It was the perfect anchorage, and I could tell that they were all kicking themselves for not bringing their boats in.

We sat eating dinner in the cockpit at dusk while a host of flying creatures, attracted by the candlelight, banged against the net. A full moon was rising when the night chorus of hoots, squawks, barks and grunts got underway. The moon rose high above the canopy of the rain-forest; the silhouette of a bat flashed across its face. A thin, wispy cloud drifted through the night sky, and the narrow river shimmered like mercury with the reflected moonlight. After dinner, I decided to go for a row in the rubber dingy on my own. As I pulled away upstream, the yacht got smaller and smaller, eventually disappearing from sight when I turned a bend. I heard splashes in the water but couldn't see anything. I stopped for a cigarette. Little bright-green lights from fireflies buzzed around the red light at the end of the cigarette, and I tried to lasso one with a smoke-ring. The slow-moving current carried the dinghy towards the bank but I made sure not to get too close. Gradually, I became aware of the appalling smell of rotting flesh – probably the remains of some half-eaten animal. I could see a few feet into the jungle. Thick, contorted tree trunks came right down to the river's edge, standing like silent sentries at the gates of a forbidden world. Mangroves spread their spider-leg roots and planted them in the water beside the sentries. It was a dark, mysterious, primeval realm: a land of trembling earth; a timeless forest of brooding intensity and savage struggle; a cradle of life steeped in pre-history and blood; a pitiless domain where only one law mattered – the law of the survival of the fittest. It was a place of lush, frightening beauty, and I was just another vulnerable creature in the midst of its awesome fecundity. I knew it was teeming with life – snakes, alligators, jaguars and big, black, hairy spiders. I finished the cigarette quickly and rowed back to the boat energetically. On turning the bend, I saw the lights from *Warrior Queen* and felt very relieved. It wasn't long before I heard Barry and Julia talking, and I felt even better. When I climbed aboard and under the net, I felt very happy.

With four aboard, there wasn't much work to do. One day you did all the cooking and the next you did all the washing-up. After that, you had two days when you were waited on hand and foot, before starting all over again. Everyone did their best to prepare good food, and the evening meal was the day's culinary highlight. We soon developed a routine as we continued up the river. We woke early, usually before dawn, and sat in the cockpit with a cup of coffee, watching the miasma that hung over the river like a blanket lift slowly as the sun came up. The birdlife was at its best at dawn, and parrots were abundant as they left their roosting places for the night and flew overhead. There was plenty of wildfowl, and if we had brought a shotgun with us, we could have had fresh duck for dinner every day. A couple of us went off for a bit of dawn bird and monkey-watching, while the others prepared breakfast. The anchor was hauled up, and we were underway by about 7.0 a.m. We took turns of an hour each on the helm and usually anchored in the late afternoon.

If there was a settlement near our anchorage, we went ashore for a visit. We were always well received, and the entire community lined up at the water's edge to welcome us. In one of these settlements there were small children bathing in the water. About 40 yards away, a man was catching piranha fish. Less than two minutes after adding a little bait to a hook, he had a six-inch orange-and-black fish flapping on the bank. This was one fish that deserved everything it got. It had about eight rows of razor sharp teeth that went all the way down its throat. We traded tinned food and flour for fish and eggs, and gave the children magazines. The pictures in the magazines fascinated everyone, and it was an incongruous sight to see a little old lady sitting in a hammock in the jungle reading *Yachting World*. I would have given the world to have had a Polaroid camera so that I could have given these people pictures of themselves – something that they had never seen.

Gordon had a parachute on board, which he had been given by a friend in Bermuda. It was another one of those 'un-negotiated fringe benefits', this time from the army. It was a huge thing designed for dropping military supplies. He had thought of trying to turn it into a lightweight spinnaker sail but hadn't got round to it. After a visit to one settlement that had given us a particularly warm welcome, Gordon raced back to his boat and dug out the parachute. He gave it to the local head-man, and the whole settlement was thrilled. This was one piece of military equipment that was going to be put to good use.

Bedtime followed shortly after dinner. Most nights we were all fast asleep by 9.0 p.m., but some nights we stayed up late and had a joint supper, usually aboard *Chancy*. Everyone brought a dish and some drink, and we finished off with a sing-song in the cockpit. Gordon played his guitar, while Bob and I, as the only two smokers, sat together on the aft deck, flicking butts into the river. I sang a few Irish rebel songs, now that I was a long way from Ireland, and Bob had a go at 'On Top of Old Smokey'. He couldn't sing to save his life but it was good to listen to him speak the words in his deep, deep voice. Hamish and I had been getting on well, and he had spent a day aboard my boat while Bill took his place on *Borne Free*. I was hoping he would join me for part of the homeward trip. We talked about this in between the songs. Gordon had a few favourite numbers, and his best one was 'Christian Island'. As he played the introductory chords, Bob whispered to me, 'I love this one.' Gordon closed his eyes, bowed his head, and poured his heart and soul into it.

I'm sailing down the summer wind,
I've got whiskers on my chin,
and I like the mood I'm in.
As I while away the time of day,
in the lee of Christian Island.

Tall and strong she slips along,
and I sing for her a song.
She's a good old boat and she'll stay afloat,
through the toughest gale and keep smiling.
But for one more day she would like to stay,
in the lee of Christian Island.

Sitting there at anchor in the tropical, wild river, the words moved me as much as any love song, and I realised how good I felt, deep down, about my own boat. All I needed now was Laura. Steve had Christine with him, and Barry had Julia. Oh, that I could have had Laura with me for just one of these rapturous days.

Before going to bed later that night, we heard the noise for the first time – a deep, guttural sound from somewhere in the jungle. Everyone went quiet. Having only heard it once, we weren't sure what it was. It came again – slow, deep and full of vibrating saliva and menace.

'What the hell is that?'

'It sounds like a dinosaur.'

'It must be a jaguar.'

'No jaguar could make that noise.'

'What on earth is it then?'

It made our flesh creep with fear and tingle with excitement at the same time. We could tell roughly where it was coming from but no one wanted to go and have a look in the dark.

At dawn next morning, the sound came again. We decided to go and have a look, taking the machete with us. There was a small bank of sand near where the noise was coming from. We sat in the dinghy about 50 yards from this bank for a long time, debating whether we should land. The noise had now stopped. We rowed forward slowly. A fresh-water dolphin was swimming around and kept surfacing near the dinghy as a bit of a sideshow.

'It can't be anything worse than a jaguar.'

'Suppose it's injured and comes tearing out of the jungle at us.'

'Maybe it's guarding its young.'

'I knew we should have brought a gun.'

We edged the dinghy up on the sand, making loud noises to scare anything off. Whatever it was, it was gone. Our confidence returned as we hacked away at the undergrowth. We never did find out what made the noise but we heard it in other places over the next few days, usually at dusk and dawn.

As we neared the end of the Cano Macareo, we started to run

aground. It was no problem because the bottom was mud and the other two boats would come to the aid of the one aground. Sometimes we motored off; other times we dragged off with an anchor. When we were really stuck fast, we took a long line from the top of the mast and used it to lean the boat over on its side. Occasionally, we took a wrong turn and had to retrace our steps, but most of the time it was obvious where the main river was. Each day the river changed, and the straw roofs of the primitive settlements at the mouth of the delta gradually gave way to corrugated iron. The first signs of agriculture appeared as we headed upstream, and the clearances got bigger and bigger. The dugout canoes got fewer and fewer, and in their place were manufactured boats with outboard motors. With less than 20 miles to go to the main river, we even saw a big open boat with a canopy and about 30 children aboard in school uniforms. This was the school bus. The wildlife thinned out as civilisation blossomed.

At the end of the Cano Macareo, we could see the wide expanse of the Rio Orinoco and were greeted with the unlikely spectacle of a supertanker making its way upstream. We picked up the channel buoys in the main river and headed out into it. There was a small town not far upriver where we could stock up with food and drink. The jungle was left behind.

31. *Poverty and Wealth*

BARRANCAS, WHERE WE ANCHORED BESIDE SOME NAVY patrol vessels, was about six miles upstream. There was considerable interest in our arrival, and several police officers were already waiting on the quayside when we rowed ashore. They inspected our *zarpas* and passports and seemed disappointed that everything was in order. It was a small town but felt like a metropolis after our time in the Cano Macareo. It was also a very sad place.

There was a shanty town not far from where we landed. This was the home of the Indians who had left the river for the lure of city life. They had a small piece of wasteland to themselves, where they lived in abject poverty and squalor. The children were unwashed, malnourished and lethargic. There weren't any houses as such. The best anyone had was a few rickety poles with a bit of rusty corrugated iron on top. Dirty hammocks were slung between the poles, and the adults sat listlessly in these or rocked slowly from side to side. We aroused little curiosity from the Indians, who seemed to have retreated into their own world of despair. The women showed more resilience than the men and did their best to look after the family. There were open fires with big black pots that contained a boiling liquid which was some kind of thin stew.

A few of them stretched out their hands to beg, and to ease my conscience I pressed a few coins into their palms. The whole place was littered with debris, and I felt guilt and shame and helplessness as I wandered through. Lying at anchor and within sight were three luxury yachts from another world. We had medicines for every ailment, fresh-water and plenty of food. These poor people had nothing: no education, no healthcare, no homes, no freshwater, no sanitation, no hope. They had made the decision to leave the river and their traditional way of life in search of something better and had ended up in hell. They couldn't even speak the language of the society they were in. If one of them had sprung upon me with a knife and cut my throat, I think I could have forgiven him. They were regarded with a mixture of contempt, indifference and fear by the townspeople, who would have liked them all to go elsewhere. There was nowhere for them to go. The journey that was begun by their ancestors more than 20,000 years ago, and had taken them across two continents of virgin wilderness, had ended in a rubbish tip.

The town was a busy place. There were shops that sold video cameras and hi-fi systems. Next to these were shops that sold sacks of flour and basic provisions. After stocking up with fresh provisions we found a small restaurant where we all had dinner later that night. Most of the Indians were asleep in their hammocks when we made our way back down to the quayside. I could see a mother and child asleep in one of them, and they looked happy and contented. In sleep, as in death, we are all equal.

Now that we were in the Rio Orinoco we had navigational informa-tion, but it wasn't needed as the main river was well buoyed. It did show, however, that there was a large city about 50 miles upstream called Porto Ordaz, which we decided to head for. We left at dawn next day to try to get there before nightfall, and with the wind behind us we were able to sail most of the way.

We made much better progress than expected, and the landscape changed dramatically as we worked our way upstream. The low-lying jungle had all but disappeared and mountain ranges came into view. By

Sailing the Caribbean

Warrior Queen *lying at anchor off La Tortuga*

The chess master and the pupil

Hamish the Parrot, just fed

Hamish the Parrot, Hamish the Kiwi and the author

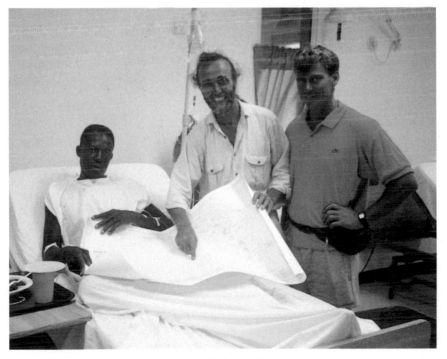

Hamish Scott, Martin Simon and the author

Delivered from death

late afternoon we could see the high-rise commercial buildings of Porto Ordaz. A guidebook indicated that there was a powerboat club up the River Caroni beyond the main port. We entered this river, only to find it strewn with large rocks sticking up out of the water. There were no channel markers. Running aground on mud is one thing, but crashing into a submerged rock is something entirely different, and we anchored straight away. A launch from the port authority came alongside and offered to pilot us upriver. The pilot boarded *Borne Free*, taking the wheel; *Chancy* and *Warrior Queen* fell in behind. The route he took was quite unbelievable as he headed straight for one rock and made a sharp turn just before reaching it, only to head straight for the shore. The depth fell off to as little as six feet at times but nobody hit anything.

The powerboat club was very swanky. It had two swimming-pools, three restaurants, four bars and six tennis courts. It also had acres of land and was surrounded by a high perimeter fence, which was patrolled by armed guards with shotguns and rifles. Our arrival was completely unexpected, and we had real novelty value. As soon as we anchored, the manager of the club came aboard to welcome us. He told us we could be honorary members and use all the facilities. It was midweek, and he asked us if we wished to have the best restaurant opened this evening especially for us. Meanwhile, the National Guard were getting ready to search the boats. My boat was last, and it was already dark when the young lieutenant and his sidekick came aboard carrying submachine-guns and sidearms. He searched every corner of the boat and accidentally poked me in the ribs with the machine-gun as the two of us clambered about in the confines of the aft cabin.

Once he was satisfied that there were no guns, explosives or drugs aboard, the clearance papers were signed and he accepted a drink from us. He spoke a little English, considered it an honour to have been assigned to the task of searching the ships, gave us the telephone number of the barracks where he was stationed, and advised us to contact him if we had any trouble.

Later that night, we had four waiters in dinner-jackets serving us, as well as a separate wine waiter. The food was top class and beautifully presented. Bob, who every now and then got his words mixed up, called the head waiter over and said, 'The chef must be complicated, make sure to do that.' It had been only a couple of nights ago, when we were all sitting aboard *Chancy* discussing the nature of beauty, that Bob had come out with his best one yet, when he declaimed with an oratorical sweep of his hand, 'Beauty is behind the boulder.'

The manager issued us with free membership cards and gave us advice about things to do and see. The main attraction was Angel Falls, the highest waterfall in the world, which was further upstream. The only way to get there was by plane, but there were plenty of flights from town. In fact, Porto Ordaz is the place tourists from all over Venezuela fly into before transferring to an old Dakota for the last leg of the journey. Hamish, who was a keen flyer and had owned a share in a small plane in New Zealand before taking off on his travels, was definitely for it, as were most of the others. Because of the expense, I decided to give it a miss and would try to make the trip when Laura flew out to join me in Caracas.

We had arrived at the club during a busy week. A big society wedding was being held in a few days' time and the national powerboat-racing championships were scheduled to take place at the weekend. We decided to hang around for the races, knowing that we would have the best seat in the house. Barry and Julia went off to a hotel for a few days to get a bit of privacy but usually came to the club in the afternoons, and most of the others took time out to fly to Angel Falls. They came back full of excitement and recommendations.

I hung around the club. In between sitting by the swimming-pools and playing chess with Gordon, I tried to buy a Polaroid camera in town but couldn't find one anywhere. The membership of the club was exclusive, and I didn't see any Indians. Everyone was keen to meet the yachtsmen who had come upriver, and Barry and Julia were befriended by a local couple who took great interest in us all. They organised a dinner party, to which everyone was invited and about half of us went.

On Saturday, the powerboat races got underway. Lorries rolled up with trailers, on which were perched gleaming, streamlined boats like darts. Each boat had two massive outboard engines on the stern. The drivers looked as though they ought to have been in a Formula 1 car. The event was sponsored by a brewery that made and marketed the local Polar beer, and a giant replica of a bottle of Polar was plonked in the middle of the river. The first race was mildly entertaining as the powerboats screeched round the beer bottle, but after one circuit we had seen it all. It was more interesting to watch the people being seen watching the races. Access to the event was for ticket-holders only, and the armed guards kept a close watch on the perimeter fence and a discreet distance from the television cameras. The wealthy and beautiful people of Venezuela had their day out.

Later in the afternoon, in a break between the races, I rowed over to *Chancy*. Two of the women who were at the dinner party the night before had come down to visit the yachts. Gordon was very excited. He took me to one side and explained why. He had just had a conversation with one of the women. Her name was Josepha, and she was part Indian. She didn't speak any English and was the housekeeper and friend of the other woman, who was very aristocratic-looking and spoke perfect English. The translated conversation that had just taken place went like this:

'Do you like Venezuelan women?'

'Yeah.'

'Would you marry a Venezuelan woman?'

'Sure.'

'Would you marry me?'

'Why not.'

Gordon had never been proposed to as quickly before. He was taking it seriously. Everyone was invited to dinner later that night, and they arranged to collect us by car. The apartment, in a well-heeled part of town, was spacious and tastefully furnished, but there were steel security shutters at the entrance. Josepha was dressed to kill, and she and Gordon eyed each other up all through dinner while her friend translated. Next night, they arranged a more intimate date. Bob and Gordon were planning to take the two women out on the town. They both went shopping and bought new clothes. Afterwards Gordon sat on the foredeck of his boat while Bill cut his hair. When they were ready to go on their date, they came down to the *Warrior Queen* for an inspection. They both straightened their collars before asking how they looked. 'Don't worry, you look fine,' I told them, and they skipped off to get their taxi. Gordon was 60, but you would have thought he had never been on a date before.

I got the full story next morning: a description of what the women were wearing; the restaurant where they had dinner; the club they went to afterwards; the way in which Josepha pulled Gordon up close as they danced to the Latin rhythms; how they had considered booking into a hotel for the night; and the ride home in the taxi. Gordon was smitten but we were leaving next morning to head downriver and back to Trinidad, so the best he could do was promise Josepha that he would fly her out for a holiday aboard his boat. She didn't have a passport and had never travelled outside Venezuela, but at 50 she had found her 'Honey Kapeetan' and would soon be sailing the seas with him.

We left at dawn next day and piloted ourselves out of the River Caroni. On the way downstream we stopped at Barrancas for a few hours to provision up, and I gave a few more coins to some of the Indians before leaving and heading on to the Cano Macareo. The jungle returned and the Indians paddled out in their dug-out canoes once more. When we passed settlements that we had visited on the way up, the entire village lined the riverbank and waved at us, beckoning us to stop. On the way upstream, an Indian had given me an armadillo shell, which I now used as a fruit bowl, but I wanted another souvenir and knew how to get it. On our last day in the Cano Macareo, we anchored beside one of the settlements near the mouth of the river. Before leaving my boat, I put my hand in an old tin can and took out the contents, which I put in my back pocket. I went ashore in a dug-out canoe. I was going to trade. Trade is supposed to be to the mutual advantage of both parties, though it rarely is, but I was convinced that this time it would be. I had something that was of no use to me but would be prized by the Waroa Indians. They had something that was of little use to them but would be a real treasure to me. Whether I should take this treasure from its native land raised a few ethical questions, but I was only going to take one and I would be doing what sailors had done since they first sailed to tropical lands.

I walked around the dwellings. They were built entirely by hand and made from materials gathered from the river and forest. On an open fire, the remains of a half-eaten small alligator gave off a pungent smell. A few mangy dogs snapped at each other's and my heels. Hamish had joined me. I told him what I was after, and we started to look for it. He came back from a foray round some of the dwellings on the edge of the settlement, telling me he had found one. We went over to have a look. The old woman who owned it was sitting in her hammock. She was wearing some ragged, hand-made clothes and a necklace. She was suspicious of us. I signalled to her that I wanted to touch it. She reluctantly agreed. I reached out and stroked the beak of a tiny chick. It had no feathers apart from a few little green ones on the ends of its wings and looked like a miniature oven-ready chicken. It was a baby Amazon parrot, no more than a few weeks old. I signalled to her that I would like to have it, but she shook her head and looked angry. My hand went in my back pocket. I produced three coins: a Portuguese 100-Escudo with a gold-coloured centre and a silver edge, a French ten-Franc piece that was heavy and bronze coloured, and a two-bob bit from Ireland. These would make the finest necklace in the Cano Macareo. Her face lit up. She took the coins from me with one hand and passed me the chick with the other. I sat there holding the chick and stroked it. She sat there holding the coins and stroked them. It was good trade.

The Indians gathered round her to look at the coins, and the rest of our company gathered round me to look at the chick. Gordon said it was the ugliest thing he had ever seen in his life, Barry said I would never get it back into the UK, and Bill said it would never live that long. Christine asked me what I was going to call it. I asked her to suggest something. 'Call it Hamish,' she said.

Hamish had found it, and I thought why not? 'OK, I'll call it Hamish. It's a funny name for a man, but a great one for a bird.' Hamish the Kiwi smiled, reaching out to stroke its beak. Hamish the Parrot made a soft little squeaking noise, opening its mouth to be fed.

32. *Growing Up Strong*

WHEN WE BOARDED OUR BOATS THE RADIO TRAFFIC WAS all about Hamish. Bob called up to tell me that he had a plastic syringe in his medical kit that I could use to feed the bird. Gordon chipped in that he had cod-liver-oil capsules. He attributed his own good health to these and suggested I should give one a day to the parrot. Hamish the Kiwi had seen the Indians feeding young birds and came over to show me how they did it. We mixed up a paste of bread, water and powdered milk, broke a capsule of cod-liver oil into it and sucked it up with the plastic syringe. Hamish the Kiwi pinched the back of the beak of Hamish the Parrot, which stimulated a frantic feeding action. The head was thrown back and the beak opened wide. The tiny little creature went into a frenzy, pushing its head up and down. I was standing by with the vicious-looking syringe and squirted the paste down its throat.

It had an unbelievable appetite – I kept having to refill the syringe. Its crop bulged with the food until you were beginning to think it was about to burst. Then the feeding frenzy stopped, and it became very still.

'Do you think we've given him too much, Hamish?'

'I don't think you can give any young animal too much food.'

'Just look at that swelling, it doesn't look right to me.'

'He'll be alright.'

The swelling took about four hours to go down while the food was digested. Hamish once more told us that he was hungry, and we went through the procedure again. At night he slept at the bottom of his basket, but with first light he was beginning to squawk and really pigged out at breakfast time.

We watched the tide at the mouth of the river all through the night. At dawn, with an hour to go to high water, we headed out across the bar. After the deep water of the shelterd jungle river, it was nerve-racking to be making our way across this bar with the wind blasting in from the east and with only eight feet beneath us. *Warrior Queen* was in front. Julia was on the echo-sounder and radio. She called out the depth every few seconds. *Chancy* and *Borne Free* stuck close behind us, listening to every word without response. Everyone held their breath and their nerve. Although the depth fell to as little as six feet, nobody hit ground. The bar that had nearly claimed my boat on the night we had first tried to cross it had been cleared. It was a barrier made by nature and was the main protection that the Waroa Indians of the Cano Macareo had from the outside world. Now that we were over it, I hoped it would silt up even more.

With the wind behind us and deep water below us, we hoisted all canvas and raced back to Trinidad. The open sea was a sharp contrast to the river. It was invigorating to be back on it. *Borne Free*, with her engine running, had taken the lead. *Chancy* was close behind us, determined to get even for the time we beat her into La Güiria. She was closing fast, before we hoisted a second headsail and left her standing. We even started to catch *Borne Free* as the boat surged forward at seven knots, straining under every inch of canvas. No one else had two headsails up, and we were giving them a lesson in how to sail. *Borne Free* was passed on the approach to the Serpent's Mouth. Hamish and Bob stood on her foredeck, taking pictures of the *Warrior Queen* as she flew past with everything up. This race was in the bag.

We ploughed ahead, leaving everyone behind. After making a wide sweep to skirt round a big oilfield with over 100 drilling stations, we celebrated with a few rums. *Chancy* and *Borne Free* were well behind, but when I looked at them with the binoculars, I knew the victory celebrations were premature. They were cutting right through the oilfield, sailing on a broad reach, the fastest point of sail. We had come so far west that to make Port of Spain we would have to beat back into the wind. *Borne Free* got there first. *Chancy* was a close second. We limped in after dark. When we anchored close by, they were all sitting in the cockpit of *Chancy*, hooting and hollering. To lose a race, when you have no chance of winning it is one thing, but to lose when there shouldn't even be a competition is something else and very hard to take.

It was one month, to the day, since we had left, and it felt like being back home. Barry and Julia transferred to their own boat. Bill, who was due to go back to Boston in a few days, checked into the Holiday Inn hotel next day to ease himself back into civilisation. We messed around for a full day with the port authorities, signing people off the crew list. Bill had a little cocktail party in his room for the four of us and proposed two toasts – one to the *Warrior Queen*, which I responded to vigorously, and one for the skipper, which embarrassed me. We settled up our accounts for the provisions and went our separate ways. Everyone knew that we were unlikely to meet up again. Bill had had the time of his life.

Next day Hamish came aboard. Laura had booked her flight to Caracas and was due to arrive in about a fortnight. There would be no problem getting to Caracas with the prevailing north-easterly winds, but it was going to be hard to head back to the Windward Islands from there. I was now beginning to think seriously about the homeward passage. Hamish was only staying with me for three or four weeks before flying on to New Zealand. He had agreed to take an enforced shore leave for a week while Laura and I had some time on our own in Venezuela. Hamish and I would then try to make Antigua for race week at the end of April. In Antigua, I was hoping to be joined by a friend of a friend from Germany who wanted to make the crossing to the Azores. I would then probably do the final leg of the homeward passage to Ireland on my own.

The parrot was changing every day. At first all he could do was squat in the bottom of his basket, making little squeaking noises. Within a week, he was climbing up the side and squawking loudly. Feathers were sprouting from him in every direction, and Hamish and I sat for hours studying these to try to establish what he might look like when he was fully fledged. He already had little flashes of iridescent blue and flaming orange on the end of his wing feathers and was beginning to grow a crown of bright yellow. He got very obstreperous before being fed, and the sound of the food being mixed up in his cup drove him crazy. Hamish was taking to his namesake in a big way and sat with a sketch pad drawing pictures of him, which he then cut out and kept in his diary. We had started to try to get the little bird to make noises, and I wolf-whistled at him every time I saw him.

Hamish and I sailed next morning. Gordon on *Chancy* came on deck, tooting his hooter as we pulled out. We tooted ours in response. Hamish was a near-perfect shipmate. He was a first-rate engineer and a good sailor. Always cheerful, he knew when to talk and when to be quiet. His only shortcoming was that he didn't know how to cook. I didn't mind this – I did all the cooking and he did all the washing-up. We had a very relaxed, easy-going regime as we sailed along the north coast of Venezuela to the island of Margarita.

On the way there, we got to know each other well, as you do when aboard a boat with someone for even a very short time. After finishing college, Hamish set up a small manufacturing company with a friend. The two of them designed and built specialised timber-cutting machinery. He had a girlfriend back home in New Zealand but before getting married and settling down, he took off on his travels, while his partner ran the business. He celebrated his 30th birthday on the river and was now out of money and heading home.

We talked about our passages across the Atlantic. His trip was made with two others. It started out fine but went a bit sour before the end. The owner of the boat he had come across in appeared to go a little nutty during the passage, stipulating the course to within one degree. He would get out of his bunk in the middle of the night to ensure that the other two crew were sticking to the precise course. He lost it altogether one day near the end, when he stormed out into the cockpit, declaring to Hamish that he was drinking his tea out of the wrong cup. 'That's my cup and this is my boat,' were the words that he had used, and Hamish would take these words with him to the grave. The other person aboard was a young woman from England whose boyfriend had recently been killed in a motorcycling accident. Hamish confided to me that he had lusted after her during the whole trip, and, had the circumstances been different, he would have made a pass. But with a crazy skipper and a heartbroken woman in the middle of the ocean, it didn't seem like a good idea.

Margarita is a popular place for yachtsmen and local tourists. Clearing in involved the usual performance, only this time, as well as dealing with the usual officials, the boat also had to be cleared by the port doctor. I was waiting in the port captain's office, expecting a pot-bellied old gentleman to come out to inspect the boat, when a beautiful young woman appeared instead. She got into the dinghy, which was leaking and full of water, and I rowed her out to the boat. After she came aboard, she spent all her time talking about the parrot before signing the papers. I was beginning to learn that Hamish the Parrot was a big hit with the women and the best fashion accessory a man could have.

I had noticed a bar along the beach that had two green Amazon parrots in a cage. They were both quite vicious. Even the management were frightened to touch them, but I decided to bring Hamish in to have a look at some of his relatives. When I approached the cage, the two adult birds went mad and started screeching at Hamish. He lunged at them through the wire, screeching back. I had never heard him make any noise even remotely like these screeches: they were ear-piercing in their tone and volume. I looked at the little thing whose beak was getting bigger and stronger each day, wondering whether I had done the right thing in taking him aboard.

After a few days in Margarita, we sailed on to the mainland to a place called Mochima. It is a vast natural harbour and one of Venezuela's national parks. The wind was behind us most of the way. We put up twin headsails and ran before it, covering nearly 70 miles in 10 hours. We anchored off one of the many beaches in the park. Having arrived at the start of the national Easter holiday, the beach was crammed with young holidaymakers who pitched camp right along the shoreline. Hamish rowed ashore and found a hut that sold ice-cold beer. I had decided that I would remain here until Laura arrived and travel to Caracas by bus to pick her up.

There was a small town at the head of the national park with a regular bus service. Next day we hauled up the anchor and sailed for it. Before boarding the bus for Caracas, I asked Hamish to have a go at killing some cockroaches. He was also going to try to catch a lizard and tie it up near the galley. If any of the little bastards came near the lizard – gulp!

Laura was boarding her flight in London round about the same time I was geting on the bus. I didn't know how she was going to take to Hamish the Parrot or cope with the cockroaches.

33. A City Without a Pump

CARACAS IS A BIG CITY, THE LARGEST I HAD SEEN SINCE leaving home. It is set among seven mountains about 20 miles inshore, and there doesn't seem to be any reason for it to be there. It has no river worth speaking about, and the mountainsides are so steep that you wonder how they ever built it in the first place. I arrived in the main bus station in the city centre shortly before dark and transferred to a taxi for the airport.

Laura's flight was delayed but it looked as though she would be in by midnight. I used the time to call round some of the upmarket hotels to try to get a good deal. I got a clerk on the desk at the

Caracas Hilton who spoke perfect English and negotiated a good price. Laura and I had rarely stayed in fancy hotels, so I thought this would be a special treat. This time I hadn't asked her to bring out rudders or oil-pressure gauges – she would be turning up with nothing more than her suitcase.

I paced up and down the building, looking in the windows of the souvenir shops at the hand-painted wooden parrots. The last time I met Laura was also at an airport. That was nearly four months ago. Since then I had had the most fulfilling time of my life, with the passage across the Atlantic, the Caribbean islands, the carnival in Trinidad and the trip up the Rio Orinoco. I had missed her every day but there were bound to be problems after so long a separation, with so much happening in between. I remembered the sulking on New Year's Eve and decided I would not allow this to happen again. An announcement told me that the flight had just landed, and I wracked my brains trying to think of what I would say.

Laura came out through the gate. I couldn't believe how good she looked after such a long flight. She couldn't believe how suntanned I was or how much weight I had lost. She gave me a big hug. It was my first hug in a long time, and I held on tight. Everything was going to be alright.

After we let go, she stood back, stretched out her hand to shake mine and congratulated me on the Atlantic passage. I insisted it was no big deal. I changed the subject, asking her about her flight, but she kept coming back to my solo trip. 'What was it like, John? It must have been incredible.'

'You would have loved it, Laura.'

'No fear, I'll settle for gin and tonics in the cockpit.'

'Actually, rum punch is the drink.'

'Uhmm, I think I could get into that.'

I carried her bags to the taxi rank and she asked, 'Where are we going?'

'The Caracas Hilton for a rum punch.'

On the way there, she told me that my street credibility back home among our close friends was sky high. None of them were sailors, and they had all been writing me off since I left Whitby. This was all sweet music to my ears. I wallowed in it, in between the kisses and the hugs. Laura never met me without a present. This time she had a new book for me. I had always wanted to read this book and was probably the only skipper of a small sailboat that had not done so, but for some reason I had never come across a copy of it. I had known people who had read it five or six times. It was a big thrill to hold in my hand a copy of *Sailing Alone Around the World* by Joshua Slocum.

The taxi drove straight up the plush drive to the Hilton. Our room was on the 18th floor, looking out over the skyscrapers in the city centre. Laura phoned up room service, ordering food and drink, while I checked out the room. I hadn't soaked in a bathtub or slept in a bed for over six months. I bounced up and down on the mattress and was running the water in the bath before the drinks arrived. The water came gushing out. I filled it to the brim and jumped in. There was more water in the bath than I had with me when crossing the ocean – somehow it didn't seem right. Laura wasn't disappointed with her rum punch. The bed was big and luxurious and the mattress was soft. There were no cockroaches in the bedclothes.

We arrived in Mochima by late afternoon next day. On the way there I told Laura about the two Hamishes. Her reaction to me acquiring the parrot was that it was wrong to take an animal from the wild, and she thought it unfair that the other Hamish would have to leave the boat for a few days. I accepted her views, in principle, on the parrot but reassured her about the other Hamish. When the bus pulled into the small town, the *Warrior Queen* was the only sailboat lying at anchor. Hamish rowed over in the dinghy. I introduced him to Laura, whom he had already heard a lot about, and Laura to him. 'So you're the man that has a bird named after him,' Laura said. Hamish replied, 'It will be love at first sight, believe me.'

Hamish the Parrot was sitting on a rope strung across the cockpit. I could see a change in him after a day-and a-half. Laura's strong opinions looked less secure when she stroked his beak, and he responded by puffing up the feathers on his neck. She couldn't help passing a comment, 'He is going to be very beautiful when he grows up, there's no doubt about that.'

'You should have seen him when we got him,' Hamish replied.

'I still think it's not right to take an animal from the wild.'

We no longer fed him with the syringe. He could take his own food provided his beak was stimulated. Hamish showed Laura how to do it. The little fellow's head bobbed up and down between her fingers. Laura thought it was all a bit obscene but she still liked doing it. There was no more talk of high moral principles. Laura was in love.

Hamish left next day. Laura and I sailed out to the beach near the entrance to the national park, from where we rowed ashore to swim in the warm tropical water. That night we sat in the cockpit with our rum punches, talking for hours on end. Because of the cockroaches, she was reluctant to go to bed. I had to shake all the bedding out before she would venture down below.

Next morning, we sailed from Mochima to the uninhabited island of La Tortuga about 30 miles offshore to the north-west. Laura had never sailed out of sight of land before but she enjoyed the trip and was very relaxed about it. On the way there, we caught a barracuda on the trailing line. It was the first barracuda I had caught but I recognised it by its long, thin body and vicious jaws. They are extremely dangerous fish: their whole body exudes a sense of evil menace and there are many reported instances of them attacking man. Laura screamed when I yelled at her to get out of the way in case it snapped at her. She jumped straight down the companionway steps. I asked her to pass me up the bottle of rum and the fish was dead in seconds, after the rum did its work. We had it for dinner later that night, lying at anchor in a bay on the leeward side of the island.

The sailing directions indicated that La Tortuga was uninhabited but there appeared to be a few small huts on the north-east shore. The island is about a mile wide, five miles long and no more than 20 feet above sea level at its highest point. Next morning, after a breakfast of pancakes, bacon, maple syrup and fresh coffee, we rowed ashore, pulling the dinghy up on the white, sandy beach. Laura was frolicking in the water when I heard four or five shots ring out. They seemed to come from a high-velocity rifle. I could see two men in the middle of the island. One of them was carrying a rifle over his shoulder; the other had one by his side. There was no indication that the shots had been fired at us but I stood by the dinghy for a while, keeping a discrete eye on the men with the guns. They were engaging in target practice. Every now and then they walked about 100 yards to set up tin cans. They then retreated and discharged another four or five rounds. I felt more vulnerable than I had at any time on the trip so far. We rowed back to the boat.

When a Venezuelan-registered yacht came into the bay and anchored beside us later that morning, I felt much more comfortable. We went ashore again to swim in a lagoon on the other side of the island. It was clear that the huts were used by fishermen who made the trip to the island to fish for a few days, before returning to the mainland with their catch. They had guns with them, probably for sport, but we gave them a wide berth just in case. The lagoon was beautiful to swim in, but I felt relieved when we arrived back on the boat. That afternoon, another yacht came in and I started to relax. Before turning in that evening, I made sure that the people on the other boats had gone to bed and were staying for the night. The thought of being boarded by armed men in the middle of the night, with me and Laura on our own, was very disturbing, but I knew that as long as there were other yachts, we had nothing to worry about.

After La Tortuga, we sailed back towards the mainland, hoping to make the port of Carenero further to the west. The golden rule when entering a strange, badly lit port is never go in at night. Carenero was more than a ten-hour sail away. To make it in daylight, we either had to sail through the night or depart at dawn. Laura wasn't happy with the idea of night-sailing, and I found getting out of bed early in the morning with her beside me very difficult. We got going about 10.0 a.m. and approached Carenero in the dark. On the way in, I ran aground yet again, but we managed to kedge ourselves off with the spare anchor, which I rowed out in the dinghy to set in deep water. Laura thought we were both going to die, but it was child's play compared with the entrance to the Cano Macareo. I had learned some lessons, however, and once we got off I edged out slowly into deep water, where I stayed put, anchoring for the night.

Carenero was not a friendly place. It is basically a holiday resort for the rich, and most of it has been built in the last ten years. There were four exclusive powerboat clubs like the one up the Rio Orinoco. Each club had its own hotel facilities for its members, as well as a surrounding security fence with armed guards. The powerboats were racked up like loaves of bread in massive steel grids. They were lifted out by crane when the owner turned up for a spin round the bay. I pulled up alongside one of the pontoons to secure the lines. Two armed guards arrived, signalling to me that I had to move, but I knew they weren't going to shoot me so I ignored them. The manager arrived later on, insisting we leave – members only and no temporary membership allowed. There was nowhere to tie up at any of the private clubs, so we went out into the channel and dropped the anchor.

The only way to get ashore was to row over in the dinghy and walk through the grounds of one of the clubs, out through the main gate in the perimeter fence. The first club refused us permission, and the second did likewise. The third agreed reluctantly, but we had to be issued with passes to get through the main gate. They told us, in no uncertain terms, that we couldn't use any of the facilities of the club. The carpark in the club was full of fancy cars, but on walking through the gate, into the streets of the small town, what we found were beat-up jalopies, dilapidated houses and rough bars. The club was for the rich, and they wanted to keep it that way. I had felt ambivalent all along about the hospitality that was extended to us at the powerboat club in Porto Ordaz, and I now knew why. Venezuela is a deeply divided society with extremes of wealth and poverty. The rich do everything in their power to make sure it stays that way. Public spaces are for the rabble and are rundown and neglected, while private spaces have resources lavished on them and end up as cocoons, defended by armed guards, for the privileged existence of the rich. To gain access to these spaces you need money or status, and in Carenero, unlike Porto Ordaz, a visiting yachtsman has no status.

Hamish had already arrived. He was staying in a small guesthouse in Higuerote, the main town of the area, about eight miles away. He had left messages at the gates of all the powerboat clubs and we quickly met up with him. Laura only had ten days, six of which we had already used. We were thinking of leaving the boat and travelling to Caracas to try to squeeze in a trip to Angel Falls. It looked as though Carenero would be my last port of call in Venezuela before sailing home.

While making the passage from La Tortuga, I noticed that I had to keep topping up the engine with water and suspected a leak in the freshwater cooling system. Hamish was happy to stay in the small guesthouse until Laura and I left the boat, but he came down to where she was lying at anchor and we worked on the engine. The water pump was knackered. Hamish advised me to get a new one.

Laura and I stayed in Carenero for two more days, enjoying the markets and street life in the town of Higuerote nearby. The food market was alive with activity, and the best sight to be had were the massive, blood-red carcases of the big tuna fishes, some of which weighed more than 200 lb. There was a funfair in town for the Easter holiday. I tried to bully Laura into having a go on all the rides but she decided against most of them. The bars in the town were wild-west saloons, complete with swinging doors. When most people approached the doors, you could see their feet below and their head and shoulders over the top. The doors swung open, the person came up to the bar, leaned against it and ordered a drink. Laura is a bit on the small side. All you could see from the inside, when she approached the door from the outside, was her feet at the bottom.

Caracas was only three hours away by bus. We left Hamish to look after Hamish. Laura gave them both a little kiss before saying goodbye. It was quickly apparent when we arrived at the local airport that a trip to Angel Falls wasn't practical in the time remaining. Instead we found a small hotel along the seafront in the seaport for our last two days. That night we had dinner in a restaurant overlooking the sea, which was open and unprotected. Laura kept looking at the sea and the waves crashing against the stone walls. She then turned to me and said, 'It's very rough, isn't it?'

'It's not as bad as it looks, Laura.' I replied, trying to reassure both of us. I knew it was over 4,000 miles from here to the end of my journey.

On Laura's last day we checked out of the hotel and travelled to the airport. Sitting in the lounge waiting for the flight to be called, she tried to get me to promise her that I would not make any more passages on my own. I knew it was likely that I would have to sail solo from the Azores to Ireland, so I refused. We had not had any disputes since she arrived, but the withdrawal and self-protection strategies were being put into operation and things were getting tense. Before cracking, I went to the toilet, where I had a stern word with myself in the mirror. On returning, I found Laura sitting looking glum in a corner. Her flight was due to be called any minute. I took her hand and, overcoming all my ingrained male emotional reticence, told her I loved her and that I was coming home soon. The flight was called, and I hugged her tight before she went through passport control.

'See you in Ireland,' I shouted, as she looked over her shoulder and waved goodbye. I felt good about the way everything had worked out and knew that she would be waiting for me when I returned home. The thing that I feared most, which was losing her, would not happen. She had helped me all the way. If it wasn't for her, I would have had to abandon the voyage in the Canary Islands. Even though she didn't get much out of it – just a few weeks' holiday – she didn't begrudge me anything. The whole voyage was somewhat self-indulgent. It certainly had no purpose. But I think she understood that the trip was hardship and rapture in equal abundant measure and respected me for putting up with one to get the other. No doubt she was a little worried about losing me, either as a result of some act of God, or by me running away with a native girl. But I knew I was very lucky to have her, and it would have taken the Queen of Sheba to get me to leave her. All I wanted now was to get home safely.

Laura's plane left just after nightfall. I couldn't help thinking how strange it was for us to be saying goodbye like this. She would be home in about 12 hours, but it would take me another three months. Neither of us knew it at the time, but hundreds of miles away a small open boat was being pushed off a sandy beach by two men. It was a routine trip and they didn't expect anything to go wrong. The plane that was taking Laura home might even fly over this small boat in an hour or so, round about the time all the passengers would be having their first drink.

Now that Laura was gone, I checked into a cheap doss-house in central Caracas and spent the next two days wandering round industrial estates on the outskirts of the city looking for a water pump. No one had the right part but I found one place that had an alternative pump that might work. It went in my rucksack before I boarded the bus back to Carenero. Hamish was worried that I had been gone so long and had been thinking of reporting me missing to the police. He was glad to see me. When I showed him the pump, he shook his head. This pump was causing a lot of problems. I had arranged for a friend to lift the engine out of the boat for a major overhaul before departing from Whitby. He stripped it down, replacing every component that was likely to give me trouble, apart from the water pump. We talked about this at the time, and I could remember him turning the pulley with his hand to assess the wear. 'You have to stop somewhere, John. I can renew it if you want, but it's all money and it seems fine to me.'

I hesitated for a moment and felt the pulley myself, weighing up the pros and cons. 'OK, we'll leave it,' I said. That decision was now holding us up. Hamish and I travelled back to Caracas and spent two more days traipsing round the streets of the city with the engine manual under our arm, a clapped-out pump in our hand, and a parrot on our shoulder.

We couldn't find the right part anywhere. I was now running well behind schedule and had to be in Antigua soon to meet up with my new crewmate for the homeward trip to the Azores. We would make do without a new one. The pump and the decision made a year earlier not to renew it had delayed us for five days. Thank God that it did.

34. *Martin Simon*

WE SAILED FROM CARENERO ON SATURDAY, 24 APRIL 1993 AT 4.33 p.m. I was on my way home. For the last eight months the compass had always been showing south and west, but from now on it would show north and east. We motored out of the anchorage, before swinging her on to a north-easterly course. I turned to Hamish, smiled and said, 'This is it, Hamish — the turning point. It's a really big moment for me.'

'I'm sure it is, John — but you do have Laura to go home to,' Hamish replied. The bow of the boat was pointing directly to where she was, thousands of miles away — over the horizon of the empty Caribbean Sea and beyond across the Atlantic Ocean, she was waiting for me. Panama was west, and if my original plans had worked out, I would have been halfway across the Pacific by now. But then I would have missed the carnival in Trinidad and the trip up the river. I felt I had done as well as could be expected, given all the mechanical problems at the outset, and was happy to be going home. There had been enough high drama for a lifetime, and I was hoping that the homeward passage would be easy and uneventful – little did I realise what lay in store.

The first leg of the journey was to Antigua – about 650 miles across the open Caribbean. Antigua race week, which had already started, was due to finish next Friday. There was an outside chance we could be there before it was all over. It was, by all accounts, a big splurge – if it hadn't been for the pump we could have got there in plenty of time. The main problem with the passage was the wind direction. It was likely that it would be against us all the way. When I talked to friends in Trinidad about making this trip, they all thought I had no chance and would be lucky to make a northerly course and hit the Mona Passage between Hispaniola and Puerto Rico. But Hamish was prepared to give it a go. If we continually tacked this way and that, taking advantage of each wind shift, we might just do it.

The coastline of Venezuela was already distant by nightfall; by midnight the lights had sunk below the horizon. There was no shipping – we were well clear of commercial shipping lanes. No other sailboats would be about – anyone sailing west to Panama would clear into Venezuela at the island of Margarita before sailing along the coast. The course was altered about six times on the first night, but we were not able to make what was needed and were already much further to the west than we wanted to be. On the second day, the wind dropped a bit, so I started the engine and we motored due east to try to make good the loss. We both kept a close eye on the water pump but decided after a few hours to close the engine down and sail, even though we couldn't make the course. The wind usually drops off before it begins to blow hard, and by late afternoon of the second day it was blasting in from the east. We sailed close-hauled on the wind, struggling to make a north-easterly course. As the wind picked up even more, we were forced to reduce canvas and bear away to the north. The seas were building all the time. Our second night at sea was a tough one. Waves came over the bow, flooding the cockpit. With the wind a good force seven, we were knocked about a bit. I had never seen the Caribbean so rough and thought it strange that there was no rain. I was thankful for the fact. It hadn't rained for a long time.

On the third day the wind eased somewhat and we managed to sail closer to it, altering course from north to north-east. Two aboard is sometimes more tiring than one, because you feel compelled to keep a 24-hour watch, only getting snatches of three hours' sleep at a time. When you are on your own, it's impossible to stay awake all the time, so once you know you are in open, clear water, you can have a good sleep. I was tired from the lack of sleep and hard sailing. On the third night I explained to Hamish that we could both go to sleep if we wanted to. He wasn't happy about the idea of the boat being left unattended but I assured him that she could sail herself better than we could and that tiredness was a real danger at sea. We were more than 200 miles from the nearest land. There was no possibility of a collision. At midnight on the third night, when it was my turn to relieve Hamish, I told him I was going to bed and that he should do likewise. Before turning in, I had a little nightcap of rum. I poked Hamish in the shoulder in a friendly way, saying, 'Don't worry. There's nothing out here, we are all alone.'

The boat sailed on its own through the night – no helmsman was at the wheel, no navigator plotted a course, no lookout scanned the horizon. Guided by the wind, it weaved its way across the dark, empty sea. Tired from hard work and fresh air, I slept the sleep that only sailors and babies are privileged to – a deep, dreamless, contented sleep. Hamish also slept.

It was a new dawn when I heard banging on the hatch of the aft cabin. Hamish was shouting. I was disorientated and asked him bad-temperedly what he wanted – he knew I didn't like getting out of my bunk without being given a cup of tea first. He rattled the hatch and snapped, 'You'd better get up, John, quick. There's a boat here. It's in trouble.' I didn't know what he was talking about. Half-thinking that there must be a large fishing or cargo boat a mile or two off, I pulled on a pair of shorts, rubbed the sleep from my eyes, slid the hatch back and stuck my head out. When I looked over the port side, I couldn't believe what I saw. There was a small, open boat less than 20 yards away. It was rolling and pitching. There was a man in the boat. He was trying to stand up, holding on to the side with one hand and waving with the other. His eyes were white and wide open. They looked straight into mine. I had never seen eyes like his before. I was transfixed. They were the eyes of a man haunted by a spectre and they spoke a thousand words – words of pain and suffering and fear and hope. They held on to me, imploring me to help him.

A boat like this had no business being so far from land, and the sight of it made me realise just how much a small boat is tossed about by the waves. Hamish and I knew that the situation was as serious as it can get. We quickly started the engine and began to lower the sails. We muttered all kinds of grim things to each other as the work was being done. At one point Hamish turned to me, saying under his breath, as if he was reluctant to express the words, 'I hope there are no dead bodies on board.' I didn't reply.

Hamish made his way to the bow to talk to the man. The engine was thump-thumping, and I couldn't hear what the man said above the din but Hamish relayed his words to me. 'He buried his partner at sea two days ago. He's been adrift for 11 days without food or water.'

I felt the muscles in my face tense as a sense of disbelief and personal inadequacy overwhelmed me. Then I heard myself call out to him. It was almost as if someone else was speaking. I couldn't believe I was saying the words. They came from somewhere deep down and were beyond my control. It was a bit like the primordial scream I screamed in the Bay of Biscay, but this time the words were directed to another human being instead of the elements. At the top of my voice, I called out, 'May God be with you.'

By the time we had lowered all sails, we were already a couple of hundred yards away from the open boat. Hamish returned to the cockpit. We started to motor back. With the sails down, my boat was wallowing from side to side and the engine seemed deafening in the silence of the dawn. The small boat almost disappeared from view in the rolling swell, and the man in it kept looking at us all the time. Hamish asked whether he should get his camera – I said it was OK but urged him to be quick about it. He was rummaging around his things, unable to find it. I told him to forget about it and to write down the time and position instead. He found a pencil but nothing to write on. I shouted at him to write it in the back of the book lying on the chart table. It was Tuesday, 27 April, and in the inside cover of Slocum's *Sailing Alone Around the World*, he wrote:

6.0 a.m.
13° 54′. 1 N
64° 44′. 7 W

I asked Hamish to take the wheel, before going aft to prepare a line. All the time, the man's eyes were fixed on me like hooks. I wanted to reassure him that whatever happened we wouldn't leave him. I called out, 'Don't worry, don't worry, we're not going to leave you, we're not going to leave you, we'll get you aboard, I promise you, we'll get you aboard.' I threw him the line. It missed. He then threw me his line, which I caught. Now that we had a line on him, I was going to try to pull him up close. It was only as he came close for the first time that I realised the danger involved. With the heavy sea running, from the winds of the previous few days, my stern was pitching up and down in the swell. His pointed bow was pitching even more. The danger was confirmed when the stern took a hit, catapulting the navigation light 20 feet in the air. His bow smashed down on the teak toerail, shattering it. Then it caught under the swimming ladder, buckling it out of shape. If a limb got in the way it would be snapped like matchwood.

The man was now close enough to talk to me. His first words, as we stood less than four feet apart in a heavy dawn sea, were the epitome of politeness – a politeness that I found almost impossible to believe in the circumstances but which was to last until we parted company. He simply said, 'I don't want to damage your boat.'

I thought of a reply, which had something to do with not worrying about the bloody boat, but didn't bother saying it. I eased the line a bit for him to back off, before hauling him up close again when the sea state permitted. I had no idea what to do but felt an urgent need to keep him close to us. As he came close for the second time, he said he could jump and had already positioned himself on the bow of his boat. Hamish called out, 'He's going to be very weak.'

I hauled him up as close as I dared and told him to wait until I gave him the signal to jump. He never stopped looking straight at me. When there was a momentary lull in the swell, I pulled him right up tight and yelled, 'JUMP.' He leaned forward with his arms outstretched and made it halfway over the back-rail. I caught hold of the upper part of his body. His arms went over my shoulders. I could feel his bones close to the surface of his jet-black skin. We seemed to be frozen in this position, but somehow his legs came over the rail. I fell backwards on the deck. He came down on top of me.

We helped him into the cockpit and sat him down. Hamish had now found his camera, which was sitting on the seat beside the chart table all the time. It was a cheap, disposable affair with two or three pictures left in it. He took one photograph of the man aboard the *Warrior Queen* before we helped him down below, where we sat him in the most comfortable place. His eyes were still wide open – two piercing white balls in a black, sunken face – but now it was with utter disbelief and an unspoken, heart-rending gratitude. He had been delivered from death, and his eyes told us that he knew it. They drilled into Hamish and me. I passed him a bottle of mineral water and poured myself a large rum. He thanked me for the water and asked, 'Do you have any ice?'

For the second or third time in less than half an hour, I couldn't believe my ears. I told him that the *Warrior Queen* was a simple cruising boat and that we didn't have any ice, but we had plenty more water and loads of food. Hamish and I watched him drink the water. The parrot had climbed along the side of the cabin cushions and was now sitting on his shoulder. 'It's very friendly,' he said, with an expression that was deadly sombre.

'We all are,' I replied, pouring myself another large rum. I offered Hamish one but it was 6.30 a.m. and he said it was a bit too early in the day for him.

There we sat, the four of us. A black man from God knows where, but without doubt the luckiest man in the world at that moment; Hamish, my crewmate and a fine one, too; Hamish the Parrot, perched on the black man's shoulder – its head cocked to one side looking straight at him; and myself demolishing a bottle of rum. He began to tell us his story. We listened silently.

His name was Martin Simon. He came from the island of Grenada. He was 29 years old. The outboard engine on his open boat had broken down a mile or so off the coast of Grenada, and the west-setting Antilles current had swept the boat out to sea. When the engine broke down it was just after nightfall, and he and his partner were heading back to the capital of St Georges after having dropped some people off at a small island at the north end of Grenada. They put the anchor down but it didn't touch bottom. They thought about trying to swim for shore but decided against it and remained in the boat. At dawn next day Grenada was gone. They found themselves drifting in a lonely sea with no food and not a drop of water. He had drunk some seawater but not as much as his partner did. His partner had died some days earlier, and he kept the body for two days before burying it at sea. He realised how lucky he was but was very distressed about the death of his friend.

We knew he would tell us more in time, but after eating a little bread he wanted to rest. Hamish and I left him to sleep and went out to the cockpit to talk. It was my first chance to think about what had happened in the last hour, and I wanted to know how Hamish had found him. I had difficulty taking in all that had occurred but what Hamish was about to tell me would be even harder to accept. When Hamish woke me, unknown to me at the time, he, like me, had been asleep below decks just a few minutes before banging on my cabin hatch. In his sleep he heard a man's voice. He thought he was dreaming and went back to sleep. He heard another noise in his sleep – this time he thought it was a seabird. Then he heard a noise for a third time, and he decided to come on deck to have a look. When he came out to the cockpit, he saw the boat upwind of us. The man in it was shouting and whistling and waving.

Had it been night, we would not even have seen him, though we might have heard him. Had he been downwind, his voice would not have carried. Had we been 10 or 20 yards further from him, he would have been out of hailing range. Had the engine been running, it would have drowned out his voice. Had I been on my own, I would have slept through the whole thing and sailed straight past him. Had he been asleep or unconscious, the two boats would have passed within 50 feet of each other, and nobody would have known anything about it. Had any of these things happened, the man's heart and spirit and body would have broken and he would certainly have died that day.

The thought that we could so easily have missed him made me feel ill. The idea of a man on the verge of death seeing a boat sail by within hailing range and not coming to his aid was too much to contemplate. As was the thought of him lying in the bottom of the boat asleep or delirious with thirst, while another boat glided past with two men tucked up in their bunks – waking up later in the day none the wiser. I had been trained as a professional mathematician, and my specialism is probability theory. I knew that the chances of us even coming within five miles of each other were minimal. We were already way behind schedule, and it was only because the water pump delayed us that we were there when we were. Apart from that, it was a crazy passage to try to make in the first place. We had been altering course 10 or 12 times a day since leaving. Even ignoring all these factors, the likelihood that the two boats should come within feet of each other in an area as big as France and Spain put together was beyond comprehension.

Hamish and I sat and talked about these things but the conversation wasn't very coherent. There was lots of, 'I can't believe it' and, 'I can't either.' Hamish then rested his head in his hands. He looked down, as if he was staring into some deep pool of emotion, and said very quietly and with true humility, 'It's a good feeling to save a man's life.'

I thought for a long time before replying and tried to say, 'It's a rare privilege,' but I wasn't able to get the last word out.

I was deeply moved by Martin. Everything about him conveyed strength and stoicism – there wasn't a trace of self-pity or self-impor-tance. In his circumstances any man could be forgiven any amount of these vanities but he displayed none of them. I resolved to do all I could to help him. Now that he was safely aboard, the next priority was to take care of his boat. It was only attached by a thin line. Hamish went over the side to swim to it in order to secure a strong rope. He was a little worried about sharks, but I did my best to reassure him before he took the plunge. He was aboard in less than a minute and attached a heavy line. When he swam back and I helped him up the buckled swimming ladder, he told me that there was a terrible smell aboard.

The boat that we were towing was a heavy, fibreglass, general-purpose open boat – the kind that you see all over the Caribbean and the type used by the boatboys who come out to meet you at sea to offer to escort you into an anchorage. We were worried that it would come racing down the side of a wave, crashing into the stern of the *Warrior Queen*. I was next over the side and was climbing aboard in even less time than it took Hamish. I felt very uncomfortable in this boat, knowing that a man had recently died a terrible death in it. It was like being in an open grave. I didn't linger. Hamish threw me the end of my longest and heaviest rope, which I tied to the stern and trailed out the back. This acted like a shock absorber and helped prevent it careering into the stern of our own boat. It still didn't tow right because the prop from the outboard was in the water, offset to one side. Hamish went over the side again and managed to lift the outboard engine up to get the prop out of the water. We now had it under control – she stayed a long way back and towed straight.

The best place to head for was Grenada. We swung the boat on to the new course but the wind was against us and the current that had set him and his friend 210 miles out was now keeping us from getting there. After a few hours of going nowhere, I explained to Martin that we couldn't make Grenada but would try to sail to Antigua. That was still 255 miles away in a straight line, but more like 350 by the time we had put in a few tacks. One way or the other, it was going to take three or four days. The fact that his boat was 25 feet long and mine was only 35 feet slowed us down even more.

When Martin woke from another sleep later that morning he asked me if he could bathe. The engine had been used earlier so there would be plenty of hot water. We helped him in to the head, where I showed him how to use the shower. I got him a fresh towel, gave him a clean white shirt, a pair of trousers and underpants, and told him to use as much water as he wanted. When he came out half an hour later he was wearing my clothes and looked a bit better. I asked if he minded me examining him, to try to establish his condition, and he agreed. There were skin ulcers all over his body, and his feet and hands were swollen. I asked him if he was in pain. He acknowledged that all his joints were sore but made no fuss about it. He went back to sleep with a bottle of water by his side.

I had never believed in being sentimental about boats – with all the mechanical problems, my own had nearly broken my heart at the start of the trip. It was nothing special, just a mass-production plastic boat designed for family sailing, mostly in coastal waters. I knew nothing of her history and had seen many fancier yachts since leaving home. She had many faults and design drawbacks, as well as a few good points – she did have a long, heavy keel, which made her a fine sea boat, and she sailed well. It was the boat that found Martin. While Hamish and I slept, she sailed on her own through the night and came straight to him. Now she had, as Hamish said, a spirit. I began to think of her as something almost animate as I stroked her coaming, while leaning over the side, gently patting her bottom, saying aloud, 'You're a good girl and a beautiful one.'

On his first night aboard my boat, Martin was troubled by bad nightmares. He kept thinking that the gurgling noises from the seacocks were made by his friend trying to talk up through the pipes. That night, at about 3.0 a.m., I was sitting at the chart table playing chess with my computerised board. I found it hard to concentrate on the game, and the pieces were sliding about the board a little. The only light burning was the small chart-reading lamp, which cast shadows all over the confines of the cabin. The parrot was out for the count, perched on one leg with its head tucked over its shoulder. Hamish was even deeper in sleep, tucked up in the forepeak. Not more than three feet away from me, this other man from another country, another culture and another race was sleeping fitfully – on the bunk that my brother had collapsed on to after our party in Scotland; which Keenan had snored in when he joined me in Ireland; which I had made up into a little cot when I crossed the Atlantic; and which I had recently made up into a double berth when Laura visited in Venezuela. This little space, which was more intimate to me than any bed, now had someone I never expected sleeping in it.

His presence was all-pervasive; I couldn't take my mind off him. The yacht was sailing through the night – alone again on an empty sea, save for the boat of death towed astern. I could hear Hamish's snores from the forepeak, and every now and then Martin made disturbed sounds as if he was gasping for breath. The water lapped against the side of the hull, and the bow made regular soft pounding noises as it cut through the seas. The ropes squeaked in the sheaths, and I could feel the gentle vibrations of the propeller feathering in the water beneath the boat. Out of the corner of my eye, I saw Martin toss and turn. I knew that by every rule in the book of chance, he should be a dead man. These thoughts flooded my mind, and I found it hard to believe that this emaciated man was lying next to me. All Hamish and I had done was pick him up at sea – anyone would have done that – but somehow there seemed to be more to it than this. Up until now I had been playing a game – the game of the sailor in his yacht. It's a good game to play and it has high stakes but ultimately it is only a game and it was as meaningless as the chess pieces in front of me. I wasn't earning my living from the sea, and I didn't need to be there. But now, for the first time, the entire voyage, and even my life itself, seemed to have what it never had before – a vague sort of purpose.

Martin awoke from his restless sleep to go outside to relieve himself. I sat where I was but kept a close eye on him – I didn't want him falling overboard. When he came back down below and was unable to sleep, he asked me to teach him how to play chess. We had a few games. It was nice for me to win for a change. After the chess, he got his wallet out and showed me pictures of his beautiful baby daughters, which he had looked at every hour while he was adrift. He wasn't married and the kids all had different mothers, but he loved them dearly and the thought of seeing them again had kept him going. At one point, his eye passed over the bookcase and fell upon a classic sea tale – *Survive the Savage Sea* – and he said that maybe one day he would write a book.

As the days and nights passed, Martin's condition improved and he told us more details of his ordeal. At first, he was disoriented in relation to time and couldn't remember the precise sequence of events. It emerged that he had been adrift for nine days – not 11 – and that his partner, a man called Rodney Cord but known as Rastaman, had died after six days and was buried at sea the day before we picked Martin up. While his friend was alive, they talked about what they would do when they reached land (they would never have reached land alive) or were rescued. They both agreed that they would get a bucket of ice, fill it with water and drink the lot. That's why Martin asked for ice when I gave him the first bottle of water. His friend died in his arms. The last thing he asked for was a strong mint. After his friend died, he still found the body company. During the night of the force 7, when we had been knocked about and I was thankful that there was no rain, Martin had been alone aboard his boat with the body of his dead friend beside him and was being swamped with large waves – the sheer horror of that was impossible to imagine. He thought the boat was lost and had decided to use his outboard fuel tank as a buoyancy aid should it sink. Somehow he managed to keep the boat afloat to survive that night. He wanted to keep the body of his friend, so that he could return it to his relatives, but decided that it was unwise to do so after two days. It only rained once while he was adrift and only for a short while. He had no way of catching rainwater, but he was able to lick up the droplets from the inside of his boat. The night after he buried the body, he imagined hearing his friend call out to him all through the dark hours and was 'surrounded by evil spirits'. Then a sailboat with two sleeping sailors and a comatose parrot aboard came over the horizon with the rising sun and was, as he told me, guided straight to him by an Angel of Mercy in answer to the prayers which he had said all night long.

Throughout the time he was aboard the boat, he never complained once despite his swollen feet and skin ulcers. When he was ready for solid food, I prepared some lasagne. I took great care over its preparation and set the dining table in the cabin with Laura's dinner set of parrot plates. Hamish the Parrot sat on my shoulder the whole time I worked at the galley and stayed there over dinner. Martin seemed to enjoy it and ate it very slowly. Italian food is not widely available in the Caribbean, and he had never had the dish before. When he finished he said, 'You are a good cook, John. I want you to give me the recipe for this.' Hamish and I drank beer with dinner, but all Martin would have to drink was water. 'You need water, man, you need water. You can't live without it,' he said. Everyone knows that water is essential for life, but as he spoke these words, while looking at the glass of water in his hand, Hamish and I knew we were hearing a fundamental truth.

The thing that troubled him most was the death of his friend. I knew he was thinking about this all the time. He sometimes had a distant expression on his face and would sit on his own for hours without saying anything. At other times, he talked about his friend and the suffering he endured and how he died peacefully in the end. His decision to bury his friend's body at sea had been the hardest of his life, and he needed reassurance that he had done the right thing. There was no doubt that he had. I told him that if his friend's body had been aboard when we picked him up, I would have buried the body at sea, even against his will. This reassured him.

· We eventually picked up the outline of the coast of Antigua at dawn on the last day of race week and spotted the first shipping we had seen since leaving Venezuela. While sailing between the islands of Nevis and Montserrat, an open boat, similar to the one we were towing, approached us to find out what was going on. I was asleep in the aft cabin at the time but I was wakened by the sound of their voices and came on deck to have a look. Martin and Hamish were explaining to them what had happened. I could see that they were surprised to encounter a yacht that had been towing a boat like theirs for 300 miles.

They gave us all a clenched-fist distant handshake – more like a salute – and I remembered the men who had saved my boat when it nearly went ashore on the island of Canouan. We were all brothers at sea. My debt had been repaid in full.

Antigua was coming up fast. On the way in, two miles from English Harbour, the ever-vigilant Hamish looked over the stern and saw that the line on Martin's boat had parted. His boat was gone. Amid loud cries of swearwords, we scanned the horizon and could just spot it. A quick turn round and we were alongside it in less than half an hour. We were not going to tow it all these miles only to lose it in broad daylight in the last two.

I boarded Martin's boat at sea for the last time and secured the lines. When it was safely under tow, I hitched a short ride on the high, pointed bow. It was a glorious sunny day, with only a few puffy, white clouds hanging in the sky over the islands. We were now in relatively shallow water. The deep blue of the open Caribbean had changed into mint green, and the sunlight from a thousand aqueous fleeting mirrors danced over the small ripples of the sea. In front of me I could see Martin and Hamish in the cockpit of the *Warrior Queen* doing a little sail-trimming. To the west I could see over 100 sailboats round Johnson Point on the last leg of the big race. I glanced over my shoulder to look at Martin's boat. I could see the half-dismantled engine that they had tried desperately to fix, rusted tools scattered all over the deck, and two pairs of shoes.

35. *Antigua*

WE NUDGED INTO THE CROWDED HARBOUR AT 2.0 P.M. ON Friday, 30 April. It looked as though the winners of the big race, flushed with excitement and good cheer, had already arrived. There was very little room, and it was difficult to manoeuvre the yacht with Martin's boat on tow. We found a spot near the main channel and were about to put the anchor down when a woman on the boat nearest to us came on deck to tell us we couldn't anchor in this place. 'You shouldn't come here during race week,' she said, as if we were trying to pitch a tent in her front garden.

I found another place. Just as I was about to let go the cable, a man aboard the boat next to us called out to say that we couldn't anchor in this spot either. By the look of things, he had probably been moored where he was for about four months and resented being crowded. I explained that we had a sick man aboard whose boat we had towed for over three days. He replied, 'I don't care what you've been doing, buddy, you can't anchor there. Now fuck off.' If there had been a gun aboard, I would have been tempted to get it and shoot him, but I had no interest in arguing with him right now. We found another spot well out to the seaward end of the harbour.

Shortly after the anchor was set, when we were getting ready to go ashore, Hamish decided to make a bid for freedom. He was growing up fast, and we knew it wouldn't be long before he could fly. Without warning, he launched himself from the cabin cushions, flying straight out of the companionway. Over the back-rail he went, up in the air, higher and higher. He was squawking with excitement, flying big circles around the masthead. Hamish and I were both calling out, 'Hamish, Hamish, come back,' and Martin was whistling. We must have appeared very strange, what with the open boat on tow, a black man aboard, all of us shouting and whistling, and an escaped parrot squawking its head off. After about four circuits of the boat, he flew off and landed in the cockpit of another yacht nearby. Hamish rowed over to get him. He came back without protest. From now on he had to be tethered, so I tied a string to his leg before perching him above the spice-rack.

As my radio wasn't working, we all needed to go ashore to report the incident. After towing Martin's boat with my little dinghy, we made our way to the immigration office. I had been accustomed to dealing with these people since leaving home and didn't expect it to be easy, but was not prepared for what was about to happen. The immigration office was jam-packed. There was a fat slob of a corporal, with a scowl on his face, in charge. He clearly enjoyed the power of his office and made no effort to be civil to anyone. Martin, Hamish and I stood in line. When our turn came, I explained what had happened. The fat slob said nothing at first. He then looked straight past me, saying to Martin, 'Why did you not die if your friend died?' I had never heard such heartless or cruel words. All I wanted to do was hit him but I knew that would get us nowhere. Once again, I explained the situation, and we were told to wait. I asked permission to use the phone but was refused. Inside the office there was an atmosphere of bad-tempered impatience, as people jostled us out of the way to try to get to the counter with their clearance papers.

Things didn't look good. I thought we should make some phone-calls right away to try to get Martin on to his family at home in Grenada. We stepped outside to the phonebox. The entire dockyard was coming apart at the seams, and there were long queues for everything. Hamish and I stood in line once more while Martin went and sat down nearby. I eventually reached the head of the queue, and after messing about with coins, cards and operators I got someone who could put Martin through to Grenada. When I called him over to make his call, an irate man who was in line behind me tapped me on the shoulder, saying, 'Excuse me, but it's my turn next, I have a very important call to make and I was here before he was.' I couldn't take much more of this but I managed to summon up the last of my patience and explained that I had been standing in line for Martin.

Martin spoke to a friend at home, who agreed to break the news to his family. They had all but given up hope. Shortly after, police officers from St Johns, the capital of Antigua, arrived. We were told that we would have to go to the police station to make a statement. We got in the police minibus to be driven across the island. On the way there, we drove through Nelson's dockyard in English Harbour and on past Falmouth Harbour. There were yachts everywhere – I had never seen so many big boats. Row upon row of high-speed racing machines with crews of 10 or 12 or more. There was very little conversation during the journey, which lasted about 30 minutes, but I told Martin not to worry.

The police station was built around a courtyard. When the bus pulled in, it was clear that Martin was going to be treated like a criminal. The offices for the CID staff were on the first floor, which was approached by way of an external metal staircase. As we ascended the stairs, several officers fired off questions from all directions.

'What's your name?'

'Where do you come from?'

'What were you doing?'

'How did the other man die?'

'Why you bury the body?'

With each step I took up the stairs, I got more angry; by the time I reached the top my blood was at boiling point. In a loud voice, I declared myself the captain of a British-registered sailing vessel, pointed out that the man had done nothing wrong and needed all the help and assistance he could be given. The initial impact of this was quite dramatic. The abrupt questions stopped as quickly as they had started. We were then shown into a run-down, poorly furnished office – the chair I sat on collapsed under me when one of the legs gave way. The inspector in charge waived the house rules, allowing me to smoke – much to the chagrin of the junior officers. Each time a new officer came into the room, I was told to stop smoking but I just carried on and told him to see the inspector.

Eventually, though, the effect wore off. Six hours later we were still in the police station. I had been questioned at length by a gun-toting detective sergeant. His questions demonstrated that he had no conception of what had happened. He couldn't understand that when an open boat is drifting hundreds of miles out to sea people die, through no fault of their own or anybody else. Martin's first words to Hamish, when Hamish went to the bow of the boat to call out to him, had been about the death of his friend, and I kept repeating this to the detective but it had no effect. There was a phone on his desk, and I kept asking him to ring the coastguard authorities in Grenada who would confirm everything. His only response to this was to say over and over again, 'When you are at sea and in your own boat, you are the captain and in charge, but you are no longer at sea. I am now in charge and I will do things my way.'

After I had given a long statement to this detective, Hamish gave an identical statement to the same person. Martin was next in line. It was 9.0 p.m. and he had had nothing to eat or drink since breakfast. Leaning against the wall in his swollen, bare feet, he displayed the same stoicism I had seen at sea. Despite the fans running, mosquitoes were swarming all over the place. I maintained that Martin was in no fit state to give a statement to anybody, pointing out that what he needed was food and medical attention.

Then the bombshell was dropped. The inspector informed me that, although he was going to keep our passports, Hamish and I would be allowed to go back to the boat for the night. He then went on to tell me that they would have to hold Martin. I asked where they were going to hold him, only to be told, 'That's not your business.' It was clear they were going to put him in a cell – a mosquito-infested, urine-soaked hole in the ground at the bottom of the police station, which I had seen on the way in. I tried to explain, very calmly, that Martin needed a hotel or, better still, a hospital and that they did not have the facilities to look after him. I got nowhere. My calmness quickly evaporated.

Everybody's patience was wearing thin, and they made it clear that they were quite prepared to lock me up. I insisted that Martin was my responsibility, trying all the time to think of some aspect of maritime law to bamboozle them with, but it didn't work. Hamish kept his cool throughout, never once getting involved in any of the arguments. I was beside myself with panic and could not accept what was about to happen. For some reason, they had backed off from taking a statement from Martin for the time being, and as we were all just hanging around I said I had to go outside to make a call home. When I got to the phone I called the British High Commission – no answer! I called the local hospital and got a receptionist who wouldn't put me through to a doctor. Returning to the police station, I could only mutter to myself, 'I don't know what to do.' On the way up the metal staircase to the main office, I decided that if they were going to lock Martin up, then I would stay with him. We would leave Hamish on the outside to get help the next day. I began to feel good because I realised that the only sure way of getting locked up was to hit one of them, and I started to think about which one would give me the most satisfaction to hit. It was too late to have a go at the fat slob in the immigration office but the gun-toting detective sergeant would be a good second prize.

The release of tension associated with the prospect of getting even cleared my head. There was one last card to play – Martin needed to go to hospital for a check-up. Once more I did my captain's imperson-ation, insisting that Mr Simon be taken to a hospital immediately. At first they refused, but when I pointed to his swollen feet, skin ulcers and general condition, they had no choice. We were in a police car heading for the hospital.

When Martin's name was called I went with him to see the doctor. I asked him to leave all the talking to me. I explained to the doctor who I was, what had happened, and the terrible predicament that Martin was now in. It was my third or fourth speech of the day and the best one yet. It ended with the words, 'Please admit this man tonight.' It worked! The doctor, who had listened to me carefully, could already see that Martin was in a bad way, even without a detailed examination. The detective sergeant entered the room during the talk. Although he tried to interject he was silenced by the doctor with one finger of a raised hand. When I had finished, the doctor nodded at me, and I knew he was going to take care of Martin – I felt like giving him a big kiss. Martin was safe and in good hands. This was confirmed immediately when the doctor refused to allow the detective to handcuff Martin to the hospital bed.

The inspector was surprised when we returned without Martin, and the detective was clearly embarrassed at having lost his prisoner. After insisting on a lift back to the boat, the detective was told to drive us there in his car. He tried to make conversation, but Hamish and I ignored him.

When we arrived in English Harbour, the three of us pushed our way through the crowds, down to the small jetty to look at the boat we had towed in. It was a sad sight, sitting there perfectly still, with rusty tools and the personal belongings of two men strewn about. The detective made a cursory inspection of it before leaving. Hamish and I tidied up the gear as best we could. As this was the last night of race week, the big party was in full swing. Hamish and I were tired, sober and hungry. All around us were people seemingly without a care in the world. If circumstances had been different, I would have been one of them, but to me at the time they all appeared strange and out of place. Everyone, like me, was foreign, white and rich. Martin was local, black and poor, and I thought what are all these people doing in this country?

The women were suntanned, overdressed and mostly young – some of them had flown out to Antigua for race week and others crewed on the big yachts. The men were drunk and were either very young or middle aged. Most of them seemed to be quite well off. The majority of people were either English or American. A lot of them had clearly known each other for a long time and came year after year. There were exclusive cliques that buzzed around older men, who were probably the rich owners of the big racing yachts. Everyone who served the food and drink was black; everyone who ate and drank it was white. Hamish and I had very few EC dollars but enough to get a small bite to eat and one beer between the two of us. As we finished off the beer, there was a woman nearby, lying on a table on her back. She was wearing shorts. Her knees were up in the air and her legs were apart. Two men were slobbering all over her, one of whom had his head between her legs. The woman was virtually unconscious. When she struggled to her feet, supported with her arms over the shoulders of the two men, she leaned forward, vomiting in front of Hamish and me. Then she cried. I didn't like the place.

We rowed out to the boat to feed the parrot, which was starving. He was glad to see us and gave us a great welcome.

The next day the police, as arranged, were waiting for us at the dock. They wanted to get going straight away, but I kept them waiting for as long as I could. I made an excuse that I had to make a telephone call and went for a walk instead. Hamish and I had talked about what we should give Martin as a souvenir and had decided upon a chart of the entire Caribbean. We found one in a local chandlery and marked the spot where we picked him up. Both of us signed it, and we wrote the name *Warrior Queen* along the top.

We were taken to police headquarters to be interviewed by a senior officer, who thought I had brought the chart for him. We went along with this misconception and rolled the chart out on his desk. When he saw just where Martin had been – basically in the middle of nowhere – his suspicions fell away. While we were in his office, a call from the Grenadian coastguard came through, and all the pieces started to fall into place. He left the office to take the call in another room, leaving us sitting in front of his desk, which was stacked high with piles of folders marked Homicide, Rape and Arson. We flicked through these folders. They made very grim reading.

The senior officer returned, happy with our account of events now that they had been corroborated by the coastguard. It turned out that there had been a major search while Martin and his friend were adrift – aircraft had been used to try to find the boat, but the search was abandoned after three days. We talked at length with the officer, who put a police car at our disposal for the rest of the day.

First stop – the hospital. Martin was lying in bed wearing a white cape. He had a drip in each arm. His breakfast, which looked good and which I wouldn't have minded sharing with him, was sitting half-eaten on the table beside his bed. He put his knife and fork down when we came in. The doctor who had been on duty the night before had gone home but his replacement came down to meet us. We unrolled the chart on the bed while everyone gathered round to look at it – the doctor, the nurses and the policeman. There was an expanse of blue in the middle of the chart and a small 'X' at the spot where we picked Martin up. Everyone looked at the size of Antigua on the chart, which wasn't much bigger than a thumbnail, and at the expanse of blue. The policeman whistled, the nurses shook their heads, and the doctor said, 'My goodness.' One of the nurses asked what Martin had said and done when we first found him. 'He was singing and dancing and asked whether we had any women aboard,' I replied, and everyone burst into laughter. Hamish had got another disposable camera, so we asked the doctor to take a picture of the three of us with the chart. We told Martin that we would come and visit him again the next day before leaving in our chauffeur-driven police car.

As luck would have it, this was the opening day of a test match between the West Indies and Pakistan. Next stop – the cricket ground. We managed to get some cheap tickets at one of the gates and took our place on the crowded terraces. Cricket is a national passion in the West Indies. It was good to soak up the atmosphere, sitting in the warm sun, watching the deliveries and the batsmen strike the ball. The crowd erupted when Hooper scored a century for the West Indies, while

Hamish and I drank lots of local beer. Throughout the play there was loud reggae music, and as Bob Marley said: 'It's a new day' and 'Everything's gonna be alright'.

I had been on the phone to Laura to tell her what had happened. She informed me that the friend of a friend from Germany was keen to fly out to join me. I sent him a fax with details of when and where we should meet. He must have thought I was a lunatic, because the address was:

Admiralty Inn
Nelson's Dockyard
English Harbour
Antigua

I also told him he would be able to recognise me because I would have a parrot on my shoulder. Hamish was accepting his confinement reasonably well, but one day, while sitting on my shoulder, he bit my ear. I yelled at him. He looked stunned. Then I stroked the back of his head for about ten minutes, talking to him very soothingly, making soft cooing noises. After mellowing out, he took the end of my earlobe in his beak and held it very gently, as if to say sorry. There was no more biting.

As the other Hamish was due to leave in a few days, we both visited Martin for the last time in hospital. He always seemed to be asleep when we came in but he was recovering his strength, the swelling in his feet was going down and the skin ulcers were clearing up. It was a little awkward saying goodbye in the hospital. No one knew what to say. Martin was due to fly home to Grenada soon, but we all agreed that some day we should get together again – none of us really thought it would happen. I was glad that I had Hamish with me when we said goodbye and left.

Laura had been urging me to try to talk Hamish into sailing back with me to Ireland, but I knew he needed to get home to New Zealand soon and barely had enough money for his flight. She even offered to pay for his flight home from Ireland but I wasn't prepared to put this to him. I walked with him to the bus in the dockyard at 7.0 a.m. on the morning he was due to leave. Before he got on the bus, I wanted to embrace him, but I had never found it easy to express emotion physically to another man, so I took his hand instead and held on to it for a long time. As the bus pulled away, Hamish leaned out of the window and called out, 'Take care of that bird.'

'Which one?'

'Both of them!'

I yelled after him that I would. Hamish was gone but I knew I had found two friends for life. They both had the same daft name – one was a Kiwi and the other was a parrot.

On the day before my new crewmate from Germany was due to turn up, I was sitting in a small bar having a beer when I saw the customs officer from English Harbour. Unlike the immigration official, he was a real gentleman. It turned out that he was also a friend of Martin's brother. He told me that Martin had been flown home. I had already noticed that the boat which we towed in had gone from the small jetty, so I asked him if he knew what had happened to it. He was surprised that I didn't know. 'It's quite unbelievable what happened,' he said. I asked him to explain.

The police had decided to bring the boat round to St Johns, so they sent the small coastguard vessel to tow it. On the way back there, the coastguard vessel ran out of fuel, leaving both boats adrift at sea. They radioed the main coastguard vessel, which turned up and tried to put a line on the small vessel. The line was attached, but in the process, the loose end became entangled in the prop of the big ship. Three boats disabled and drifting! They called the port authorities, who sent the dredger from St Johns. It took all three in tow. When they arrived in port a diver was sent down to untangle the fouled rope. The diver drowned! He left a widow and two fatherless children behind.

The account shocked and disturbed me deeply. I was not able to talk to anyone or eat for the rest of the day. I kept thinking to myself that I shouldn't have brought the boat in – if I had sunk it at sea, a man who was now dead would be alive. The boat itself had tried to break free on the approach to Antigua, as if it didn't want to be towed ashore, but we had turned round to get it – ten more minutes and it would have been gone forever. No one in St Johns wanted to have anything to do with the boat – everyone thought it was jinxed. It was a horrible thought, but it was as if the sea was going to extract two lives in tribute, and one man's life had been traded for another. I somehow had played a pivotal role in this unfolding of fate, and I couldn't help feeling responsible for the death of the diver. Nor could I help thinking that there were forces at play here undreamed of in my philosophy. Maybe the jinx would be passed on to my own boat? Was it wise to sail home? I tried to be rational about it all but I couldn't shake the dreadful and stupid thoughts from my mind.

I went aboard my boat late that night and sat in silence for a few hours, trying to discern I know not what. But the longer I sat and the quieter it became, the more certain I was that my own boat was not jinxed. Next day my crewmate arrived from Germany. I didn't tell him about what had happened to the open boat and the diver. He turned out to be a first-rate sailor and a fine man. It was time to go home.

36. *Arrival and Departure*

EIGHT MONTHS LATER, I AM ON THE PLANE TRAVELLING out to the West Indies for Christmas. It stops at Tobago before flying on to Grenada. As it takes off for the last small hop the sun is going down, and I can see a bay I anchored in nearly a year ago. From the air, the coral reefs stand out so clearly that it's almost like looking at a chart. Grenada comes into view just before dusk. By the time we touch down it's already dark. The doors of the plane open, and Laura and I walk the short distance across the tarmac to the terminal building. The night air is warm and the tradewinds are blowing fresh.

I had not asked Martin to meet me at the airport. In the terminal building, I keep a sharp lookout, just in case he turns up. Laura asks me, 'Do you think you'll recognise him?'

'Maybe all white men look the same to black men and he won't recognise me.'

'I didn't mean that.'

'Are you sure?'

She gives me a withering look of rebuke and we collect our bags. We are on an all-in package holiday, and a minibus is waiting to take us to the hotel. The hotel is a modest affair, away from the beach, and we check in at the small reception office. The woman behind the desk tells me that a Mr Simon called round earlier in the day. He left a message saying that he would phone later. Laura and I are both a little tired after the travelling and have dinner in the hotel – fresh tuna fish with rice and salad.

By 9.0 p.m. local time, Martin has not phoned, and we decide to turn in. I leave instructions with the receptionist that if he phones later she should ask him to get in touch in the morning. From the balcony of the self-catering apartment there is a view of the sea and the wide bay of St Georges. Laura has gone to bed. I lean on the railings, smoking a last cigarette. With the warm, tropical night air it almost feels like being in the cockpit of the boat again. I look out across the bay and further to the west. All that sea – so much of it; with its own rules and struggles; its changing moods and deep mysteries; its powerful currents and unforgiving ways. It was probably a night like this when the engine on Martin's boat cut out.

Next morning, while having breakfast at the hotel, the woman from reception comes to our table, saying that there is someone to see me. I go with her to the desk. Martin is standing there. We look straight into each other's eyes. I see him again as I first did when he looked at me across the waves that morning we picked him up at sea. It is a frozen moment that takes us both back in time, but it lasts for no more than a split second. He has put back all the weight he had lost, and he isn't as black as I remembered him being. We both smile at one another. He reaches out and puts his arm around my shoulder.

I invite him up to the restaurant for breakfast. Laura is sitting on the edge of her chair. She has heard a lot about him and is slightly nervous but quickly relaxes once we all start talking. After breakfast, I ask Martin about what happened when he arrived home from Antigua, and it's clear he was treated very badly. The Grenadian police arrested him as soon as he got off the plane. As he tells me the details, I can hardly contain my anger. They held him for 36 hours, interrogating him non-stop. He was accused of murdering his friend, and at one point they put it to him that he had eaten the dead body. He had borne his terrible ordeal at sea with unbelievable resilience and courage and should have been coming home to a hero's welcome. He had been alone at sea without water, adrift in an open boat in the tropics. The body of his friend was at his side, and he himself was ready to die – yet when he came home they put him in jail and accused him of murder. I cannot imagine a greater injustice.

To make matters worse, the family of the dead man rejected Martin and held him responsible for the death. Martin is happy to tell me all these things, because of what we went through in the police station in Antigua and also because Hamish and I had never doubted him. I would never know what the experience must have been like for him during the nine days in which he was adrift but I did know that Martin was a brave man and a good one. I also knew that the man who died would turn in his watery grave if he knew that Martin was being made to suffer more and was being falsely accused.

After I sailed home, some friends had asked me how I was sure that there hadn't been foul play. Even if there had been, it wouldn't have made any difference, but I knew that there wasn't, and everything I read

261

about people adrift at sea confirmed this. One of the most famous cases in English Law is about the wreck of the *Mignonette*. Four men took to an open boat after their ship went down in a storm in the South Atlantic in 1884. Although they had a little food and water, after 17 days the captain killed the cabin boy by stabbing him in the throat. The three survivors ate the dead boy's heart and liver and drank his blood. They then fed on the rest of his body. The decision to kill the boy was made after days of deliberation and only because the captain had the half-hearted support of one of the other two survivors. When the boat was picked up four days later by the *Montezuma* the first thing its crew noticed was the remains of the dead boy's body. None of the survivors had even thought of concealing it. There were no human remains on Martin's boat!

When the survivors were prosecuted and found guilty of murder, there was a national outcry. It was widely held that, despite what they had done, no one had any right to judge them. Queen Victoria commuted the death sentences to six months' imprisonment. Other tales are different. When the mutineers on the *Bounty* set the loyal crew adrift in an open boat, Captain Bligh navigated it across more than 3,000 miles of sea. At one point Bligh had to threaten one of his men with a cudgel when this man suggested killing a weak crew member and eating his flesh, declaring to him as he held the cudgel over his head, 'If we are going to die, then we will all die together as civilised men.'

I tell Martin these stories – I have no intention of patronising him. The first one raises a look of sickened horror on his face, but the second one soothes it away. I offer to go and talk to the police and the family of the dead man to reassure them that what happened was simply a tragedy of the sea, but he doesn't think it a good idea. The police hadn't pressed any charges, and the pain caused by the rejection of the dead man's family is so hard to bear that he doesn't want to re-open the wounds.

He also has another wound but this one is physical. Martin earned his living from the sea. A couple of months after returning to Grenada, he had speared a barracuda while fishing with another man about 30 feet down the side of a coral reef. He was putting it in his underwater bag when the fish, which he thought was dead, turned on him, almost severing his foot. He surfaced quickly, and his friend raced the boat ashore. They jumped in a taxi and headed straight for the hospital. He was hospitalised for two months and had two six-hour operations to stitch all the tendons together. His foot was saved but it was a close call. I ask him to show me the wound. He takes his shoe off and rolls up the leg of his trousers. I always seem to be looking at Martin's feet – the first time I had looked at them they were swollen like loaves of bread. This time there is a big hole where the upper part of his left foot joins the lower part of his leg – it looks as if it has been filled with putty.

Laura and I have two weeks in Grenada, and we discuss our plans with Martin. He is having difficulty walking as a result of the barracuda attack but is happy to fall in with whatever we suggest. His standard response is, 'That's no problem.'

We agree it would be a good idea to hire a car for a few days to drive round the island. Martin wants to come with us and bring his girl-friend. I tell him, 'That's no problem.' He also wants us to come to church with him the Sunday after Christmas. His experience while he was adrift and the circumstances in which Hamish and I picked him up made a deep impression on him, and he had since rediscovered his childhood faith in the Baptist Church. It was there that he met his girl-friend, and he fell in love with her when she visited him in hospital every day while he was recovering from the barracuda attack.

The three of us catch the bus into St Georges. Martin gives us a tour of the streets and the market. He is very well known and introduces me to some of his friends, one of whom takes my hand and says, 'Thanks for saving my brother.'

I am taken aback and ask, 'Are you Martin's brother?'

The man looks at me as if I am a bit simple and says, 'I'm not his real brother but every man is my brother.'

'Well, I suppose that makes Martin my brother too.'

'It sure does.'

When I first anchored in St Georges, almost a year ago, I had rowed over to a little floating bar attached to the quayside, called Delicious Landing. I now want to have another drink here. While we are sitting talking, Martin is looking out over the small bay. After about five minutes he draws my attention to a boat nearby. It is in the middle of the harbour, and there is one man aboard. He is pulling the cord on his outboard motor. 'I'm watching this boat very closely, John. Everybody is just passing by. He can't get his engine working. See how easy it can happen.' The boat is beginning to drift, very slowly, out of the harbour, and we keep a close eye on it. After a further ten minutes another boat pulls up alongside and takes it in tow.

Laura and I travel back towards the hotel by water-taxi – another open boat with an outboard engine. I have a good look around – no oars and not a drop of water. If it was night-time and we were a mile offshore and the engine broke down, we would all be swept out to sea. One by one we would die of thirst. If Laura went before me, I would have no choice but to put her body over the side – the body that I loved as life itself, committed to the deep by my own hand. The water-taxi takes us to Grande Anse beach just south of St Georges. It is a magnificent stretch of golden sand running for several miles. We have a swim in the warm water, before walking the rest of the way to the hotel. I am expecting to hear from Gordon on *Chancy* and hoping he will bring his boat up from Trinidad, where it had been left for six months while he went home to Canada, but there is no message for me.

That evening we arrange to meet Martin and his girlfriend, Karen. He is very proud of her and has every right to be. Laura and Karen hit it off immediately, and we all have dinner in a Chinese restaurant. Karen and Martin are planning to get married but she doesn't want him to have anything more to do with the sea. It's difficult to see how he can earn a living any other way, and, despite everything, he still loves the sea. Even after his days adrift in the open boat and the death of his friend and the barracuda attack, the sea holds on to him. Laura and Karen can't understand this, but I can. Martin had been trying to get some work with one of the big yacht-charter companies. Quite often someone would charter a yacht from an island further north and sail it south to Grenada, where it would be left to be returned by a local crew. The work is difficult to get and unreliable, but he is hoping to make inroads and has a chance of a delivery in a week or so.

On Christmas Eve, I invite Karen and Martin to our apartment for dinner. The oven is difficult to regulate and I end up burning the lasagne. Even Martin, for all his politeness, has to admit that it isn't as good as the first one I made him. We sit on the balcony, drinking white wine. He has told Karen all about his time adrift but he still finds a need to talk about it, and this is even more urgent now that I am here. When he was on my boat, I hadn't asked him much about what had happened, but I now ask him what he felt like when he first saw us. He shakes his head and laughs a little laugh of disbelief before telling the story.

During the night before we picked him up, he had had a dream in which a yacht had passed. They took him aboard, gave him some food and water, and then put him back in his boat to carry on drifting. He asked them to tell other people that he was out there. They agreed and sailed on. He awoke from this dream just before dawn and forced himself to sit up to look about. He had already resigned himself to the fact that he was going to die in the boat. This day, he thought, would be the last day of his life. In the gloom of the dawn, he saw a tiny fleck of white on the horizon. He thought at first it was a wave breaking in the distance and refused to allow any false hopes to build. The white persisted in the same place and got bigger. He began to think that he was hallucinating. But the white mark on the horizon became more distinct. He now knew it was a sail but told himself that it would probably pass by a long way off. The sail got bigger still. It wasn't long before he could see the hull of the boat and knew it was heading in his general direction. His hopes began to rise but he was still trying to deal with the unbearable thought that he might be missed and refused to allow these hopes to dominate. The boat kept coming – closer and closer. It was heading straight for him. The hope that he had held on to for nine days, and had almost lost, now took hold of him. By the time the boat was bearing down on him, he could see that there was no one on deck. He knew this was his only chance. When the boat was less than 50 yards away, he summoned up the last of his strength and struggled to his feet and began to shout. There was still no one on deck. As it sailed by, he whistled and whistled and whistled. There was no possibility of swimming for it. With his last whistle, he saw a man come on deck. The man stretched his arms above his head and yawned. The man then turned his head and looked at him. He then disappeared down below. Next thing, he saw my head coming up from the aft cabin. By now the boat had passed. He didn't know if we were going to stop. But when the headsail started to come down and the bow swung round, he knew he would live.

Laura can't take it all in.

I had long been troubled by the way Martin had looked at me that morning we picked him up, and I now know that in his near-delirious state, and with the dream of having been almost saved still fresh in his mind, he was thinking that we would sail past. All he had to hold on to us with were his eyes, and I now understand why he had never taken them off me. After telling us the story, he shakes his head in disbelief and manages to smile a little. I refill the wine glasses, and he tells us some more.

He didn't think it right that anyone should be buried at sea and had agonised for a long time before putting his friend's body over the side. In the heat of the tropical sun, the body putrefied quickly. After two days it was in a dreadful state, with pus coming out of every orifice. His friend had died with his eyes open, and he found the dead body company and talked to it a lot. Before letting it go over the side, he tied a buoy to it so that someone might pick it up at sea. The rope and the buoy and the body got stuck under the boat. He had to go over the side himself and swim underneath to set it free. Through the glass in his face-mask he saw his friend looking at him with his open eyes. The arms of the dead man floated in the water, reaching out to him as he struggled to untangle the rope. He was desperately lonely after he buried his friend's body, and it was at this point that he resigned himself to dying in the boat.

When they had been adrift for three days, they saw the spotter plane that was out looking for them. They stood up, waving their shirts and shouting. The plane banked and flew off in the other direction. This dealt a massive blow to their morale. It was at this point that the other man started to go downhill and drink seawater. They had some rotten shellfish, which the other man ate, making him ill. The dehydration caused by the illness, and accentuated by the seawater, finished him off. Martin found the hunger from lack of food easy to cope with but the thirst had been unbearable, and he was not able to describe it. Even if he could have described it, I wouldn't have been able to understand. The nights were long and hard and cold, and the scorching sun blazed down on him during the day and never let up.

'Do you remember how black I was, John?'

'What do you mean, how black you *were*, you *are* black.'

'No. I was really black – from the sun.'

He is right: he was the blackest man I had ever seen when we picked him up, and now he is just a good shade of dark brown.

He remembers details of the time aboard my boat that I had since forgotten. I had always liked singing aboard, but I couldn't recall having done so while Martin was with us. He says, 'I remember hearing you singing one night out in the cockpit.' He turns to Karen and says, 'John's a very good singer.' Laura nods in agreement. I can see that they might want a song any moment. I ask him if he remembers what the song was. He says he had never heard it before and I was singing it very quietly but it had something to do with anchoring in the promised land. 'Do you know the one, John?' I know it alright, and I sing the chorus line again on the balcony of the apartment, as I had on so many nights at sea.

It takes a long pull to get there
It takes a long pull to get there
It takes a long pull to get there
But, we'll anchor in the promised land
In the promised land
Land

We talk about the plans I have for my boat, and Martin is disappointed to hear that I am going to sell her. He has an even deeper emotional attachment to the *Warrior Queen* than I have and won't hear a bad word said about her. 'She is a real queen and she fights the seas like a real warrior. That's a good name for your boat, John, – the *Warrior Queen* – a good name for your boat,' he says. At midnight on Christmas Eve, I top up our glasses and we drink a toast to Hamish. It was Hamish that had heard Martin call out and whistle – without Hamish aboard that night, Martin would now be dead. He asks me what happened to the other Hamish, and I am able to tell him that I managed to get the parrot imported into the UK and that he is now fully grown. Laura is besotted with him, and he has transformed our relationship. It is the perfect *ménage à trois* – Laura loves Hamish but Hamish doesn't love her, Hamish loves me but I don't love him, and I love Laura but she doesn't love me – everyone has someone to love and is loved by someone in turn. Before Martin leaves, in the early hours of Christmas morning, I give him the few little presents that I had bought in the gift shop at Gatwick Airport.

The Sunday after Christmas we are on our way to church. Apart from the funerals of Laura's parents, I haven't been to church in 20 years but I am happy to go this time. A minibus collects us from our hotel and stops off along the way to pick up more people going to church. Everyone is wearing their Sunday best and is carrying a Bible. As each new person gets on the bus there is a chorus of, 'Season's greetings, greetings of the season, season's greetings.' The church is plain and simple. Everyone shakes hands before the start of the service. Laura and I sit with Martin and Karen, and we all stand to sing the first hymn. As well as singing, everyone claps their hands. Martin can't sing a note or keep time with the hand-clapping. He has no sense of rhythm. The pastor starts his sermon by talking about the sea. It is, he says, a source of bounty and a source of life but it can also be a place of death. I am beginning to suspect what's coming, and he asks me to stand while he talks about brotherhood and the common blood we all share. These are sentiments I fully agree with but it doesn't make standing there any easier, and I am glad when he tells me to sit down. The service ends with two or three more hymns. The pastor plays the piano, while an old man with white hair and a pencil-thin moustache strums an electric guitar.

We hire a car next day, which is a public holiday, and the four of us take off for a tour of the island. We visit remote beaches, lush plantations and an old rum distillery. Some of the white rums are 150-degree proof. One good swig of these is enough to put you to sleep for the afternoon. On the way back to St Georges we get held up in a small traffic jam. Crowds of people are milling about and everyone is dressed in their finest. It's a funeral – and a very big one. Karen mentions that it must be someone very important, and Martin whispers something to her which I don't hear. After the funeral cortège passes, we drive on and stop at a waterfall, where Martin and I strip off to go in for a swim. I ask him to show Laura all the other scars he has from earlier mishaps. There is one right across his chest that he got while messing about in a game of tag with knives as a kid and another on his head when he hit a rock while diving. On the way back to the car, Laura asks whether I had heard what Martin had said to Karen when we passed the funeral, and I tell her I hadn't. He had said, 'Every man's death is important.'

Martin visits the hotel almost every day. When I open the door to him there is always a split second of frozen eye contact which takes me back to our first encounter. He gets a delivery trip returning a boat to St Lucia, and Gordon turns up on *Chancy* for the last week, as does Bob on *On The Way*. It's good to see them all again, and we spend a few days sailing and having barbecues on the beach. We leave the hotel for three days – they must have thought we had done a runner. I had been practising very hard at chess ever since I returned to work and had got a new chess program that taught me some good openings. I was sure I could hold my own against Gordon. It was a waste of time. He beats me with the same ease as before. Martin comes down and spends a day on Gordon's boat after returning from his delivery trip, and later that evening we go off to play pool in a bar. Martin had said he was good at this but I want to show him how kids from Belfast play the game. He assures me that I have no chance – I warn him not to put his earnings from the delivery trip on it. It's a close-run thing but I have the edge in every game.

On the day we are due to leave, Martin and I arrange to meet on Grande Anse beach. I had written a short story for the yachting press about picking him up at sea and had sent him a copy. He had enjoyed reading it, and he now wants me to write a book. We're sitting there playing with our toes in the warm sand, tossing the occasional pebble into the sea. I explain that it would entail a lot of work and I'm not sure if I can do it. Even if I did write it, getting a publisher would be a long shot. He looks at me very intently and says, 'Mister John, you can write that book, and I want you to do it.'

I tell him, 'Don't hold your breath, Mr Simon.'

He comes with us to the airport. We check in and go up to the rooftop bar. I ask him what he wants to drink. He has a glass of white wine. We sit on the bar stools, fingering the stems of the glasses while waiting for the flight to be called. In between sips, he tells me that he worked on laying the tarmac for the runway and had detonated dynamite. We talk about his plans for the future, and he tells me that there is a big company from the Middle East in Grenada at the moment recruiting labour. The work is in Kuwait, and if he gets hired he will be away from Karen for about six months. The job is laying new pipelines in the minefields left over from the Gulf War.

When the last call is made, we walk down to the security barrier. Martin and I embrace. I feel his muscles under his shirt and remember how skinny he was when I first held on to him over the back-rail of the boat. After letting go, and before going through to the waiting lounge, I turn round and glance over my shoulder. We look straight into each other's eyes. I go into the lounge and sit down. Laura is beside me. I start to cry. The people who had been on the outward flight are now going home. They are all looking at me, trying to pretend not to. I don't care. Laura puts her hand gently on my shoulder and asks, in a soft voice, if I am alright. I say I am fine but I just can't help it. I am thinking of all sorts of things: the childhood dreams and the long years of waiting; John from Whitby and Tim and Kenny and Bob and Alex throwing up over the side; the gales in the North Sea and the Irish Sea and the terrible storm in the Bay of Biscay; the breakages and the problems; Veronica with her bottle of vodka in her handbag and Tony sitting all alone in the candlelight on *Potlatch* and Peter who loved the Lord and women; the empty expanse and solitude of the deep ocean, and the wind – always the wind; the rum and the ganja and the swaying palms; the Dragon's Mouth and the Serpent's Mouth and the keel of the boat banging on the bottom; the poor little children in the shanty town in Barrancas and their brave mothers struggling against all the odds to give them a life – God Almighty, the world is a cruel place; Josepha's look of love and longing and Gordon's smile of anticipated pleasure; the room in the hotel in Caracas with its big double bed, and the damn water pump; the night before we picked Martin up at sea when the boat sailed on its own through the dark hours while he was praying his heart out and the Angel of Death was upon him, and what the water must have tasted like when he put the bottle to his lips and took his first sip – sweet, that's what it would have been, water so sweet that it must have made honey seem sour; Hamish somewhere in the southern hemisphere; and the *Warrior Queen* in a cradle in Scotland. I don't know what any of it means, but I can't stop crying.